Team Management

Creating Systems and Skills for a Team-Based Organization

Written By
Jennifer M. Howard & Lawrence M. Miller

With much help from the consultants, staff, and clients of
Miller/Howard Consulting Group

Published by Miller Howard Consulting Group, A Towers Perrin Company
One Atlanta Plaza
950 East Paces Ferry Road
Atlanta, Georgia 30326-1119
(404) 365-1600
www.millerhoward.com

ISBN: 0-9629679-3-9

Revision 2.4

Acknowledgement

The co-authors of this book, Jennifer Howard and Larry Miller want to acknowledge that this book is a result of the efforts of a much larger team, both inside and outside our firm. Individuals contributed in many ways, a creative idea, a constructive suggestion, or in Krissi Rouquie's case, many hours of typing and retyping edits. This edition was written to incorporate the suggestions and lessons learned since our last edition was published two years ago. You will find more information on developing teamwork between groups, more white collar examples, and implementation tips at the end of each chapter.

Our thanks go out to the members of our consulting staff who apply these concepts every day; Tom Akins, John Burden, Camon Criswell, Duane Cross, Jack Hinzman, Will Jones, Annemarie Kern, Pierce Murphy, Carol Phillips, Ron Robinson, Susan Shaw, Helene Uhlfelder, and Al Wilgus.

We also thank our clients who have participated with us in developing team systems in their organizations for over sixteen years. They are our best resource for learning and improving our processes. A special thanks goes to several people who made special contributions to this edition, they are Mark Miller of Chick-fil-A, Inc., Neil Samuels of Amoco Production Company, and Wendy Wersel of Northern States Power.

Table of Contents

Preface

Introduction

This manual is to help explain how the organization is a dynamic system that is ever-changing, much like a family. In families, as the children grow-up, marriages mature, and individuals develop through education and different life experiences, the relationships and support needs change. Similar dynamics occur in the whole organizations and in individual teams of the organization.

In order for an organization to thrive it must be able to respond to changing customers' demands, to the changing demographics of its workforce, and to utilize the competencies and technology being developed every year.

The tools, techniques, and philosophies described in this manual are not unique. All of them can be found in other quality books and through other quality experts. What has achieved dramatic results for many organizations is <u>execution</u>. All the knowledge and technology in the world won't help unless you can execute and effective <u>execution</u> is <u>through your people</u>. Regardless of your field, *people are the source of your competitive advantage.*

The key to successful execution is understanding the systems that affect the people in your organization and capturing the best of your people's capabilities. Why do we believe teams to be a critical element in execution? Teams contribute the following benefits:

1. In large organizations, teams are more flexible and are able to respond to changing demands.

2. Well-functioning teams built around key processes perform better than loosely banded groups or individuals focused on individual tasks.

3. The behavioral changes required of a continuously improving culture are better supported by teams. Just as in change strategies practiced by groups such as Weight Watchers or Alcoholics Anonymous, the commitment of the team and the accountability felt by team members greatly increases the chances of maintaining behavior change.

4. The complexity of our world today and the ever increasing demand to continue learning new skills greatly support the need for team-based organizations. No individual can be competent in everything. We need teammates.

5. Working on teams makes people feel more connected to a greater good. It brings challenge, diversity, new insights, and fun to daily work!

6. Teams provide a forum for people with diverse ways of thinking, diverse views on how work can be accomplished, and diverse experiences to share their views and opinions in a constructive manner.

The Third Era: Managing in the Nineties

This workbook represents more than merely another opportunity to learn useful skills. It chronicles a historic transition from one era to another. Worldwide assumptions about the role of managers and employees, about rank and hierarchy, and about what is important in an organization are entering a new phase. *This workbook presents the third major era of human organization for production, the team-based organization.*

This revolution is determining the result of competition between global corporations and nations, as well as the progress of small corporations and individuals. A failure to understand and participate in this transition will doom any organization to the "horse-and-buggy age." The new assumptions about organizations apply equally to service and manufacturing. Some dramatic results have been observed within engineering, marketing, and information processing organizations.

The **first era of production was the craft shop and family farm**. A small group of people, intimately related, worked closely together with complete control over their own work. A furniture craftsman took complete responsibility for an entire piece of furniture. From cutting the boards to final finishing, the craftsman paid careful attention to the details of his work and took pride and ownership in his product. The benefits derived by the craftsman were directly related to his skill and the success of his business. If the furniture craftsman produced poor quality furniture, his children would go without shoes; yet if he performed well, he would prosper.

There were advantages to craft production. The organization met both economic and psychological needs. The craft shop was an extension of the family. It "felt" like the family as people worked closely together in a highly interdependent manner with long-term relationships and stability that caused them to invest in and help each other. They took great pride in the quality of their work. Because they took responsibility for a whole piece of furniture, musical instrument, or carriage, they understood how the pieces fit together and worked to improve how the piece was constructed.

However, during the era of craft production the majority of people were poor. They were poor because the means of production were not efficient. One worker produced only a few pieces of furniture. One farmer produced only enough for his family and perhaps one or two others. The wealth of a people is ultimately determined by one factor: their ability to produce quality goods in an efficient manner. Today one American farmer produces enough food for fifty to 100 families. One furniture worker produces enough furniture for more than 100 families. This kind of mass production is the result of a new system of work.

The **second era of production, mass production**, began with Henry Ford's factory. Henry Ford was driven by a passion to make the automobile available to the common man. He knew this could not be done with the traditional system of production; thus began the evolution to mass production.

Henry Ford's factory simplified work so that workers who spoke as many as fifty different languages could work together to produce a consistent product. Ford developed the interchangeability of parts: one tire had to fit every car. One piston would fit in any engine. In contrast, in the craft shop each part was fit individually. The most numerous workers were "fitters" who adjusted parts until they fit. Ford's factory produced each part to identical specifications, eliminating the need for fitters. Ford also created the moving assembly line, reducing the motion of workers and creating a consistent pace of production.

Ford's factory and the transference of his methods to accounting departments, housing, railroads, and even to fast food restaurants increased the wealth of the nation by improving the productivity of employees. Today the average person can own a car, television, and several suits of clothes. This fact would not be true were it not for the development of mass production techniques.

However there were problems in the organization of mass production. Specialization and simplification reduced the importance of the individual. Not only were parts interchangeable, but employees became interchangeable and, therefore, easily replaceable. They were seen by management as simply another piece of equipment in the production process. They lost dignity and the ability to control or improve their work, and they lost the feeling of family, a small group of people working together for a common cause. Rebellion against this system was inevitable. It took the form of alienation from the work itself, alienation from management, increasingly poor workmanship, and eventually the creation of unions.

The illness produced by the system of mass production affected not only factory workers but also professionals and management. As work became highly fragmented, engineers specialized in research and development, product design, and the manufacturing process. Within each area there were increasing numbers and layers of specialists, each with their own society, their own journals, their own language, and their own walls of defense and protection against the "others." Within finance and accounting, information management, human resources, and virtually every other professional group, the same process of fragmentation was at work.

Unfortunately to get a new car or other product designed, into production, marketed, and into the showrooms required the integration of all of these functions. The more specialized they became, the more difficult this integration became. Each was concerned with his own narrow responsibility and not with the whole. This slowed the rate of change, learning, and development, making the organization uncompetitive. No person was to blame. It was the system that was broken!

We are now entering the **third era of production and system of organization, the team-based organization**. It is based on an understanding of the essential nature of the team and a focus on quality. It is based on a recognition of the benefits and deficiencies of each of the two previous systems.

In this third era the organization that can compete most effectively will be the one that is fast and flexible. It will be the organization that responds quickly to customer demands and utilizes the skills and processes to maintain low inventory, fast product changes, data-based decision-making, and employee involvement. The culture of this organization will respect the diversity of the individual while valuing the products of teamwork.

If there was a single critical point in the development of the new system, it was in 1950 when Eiji Toyoda, the president of Toyota, and his production chief, Taiichi Ohno, were faced with a crisis. Unions in Japan were more rebellious than in the United States. Toyota had just suffered a strike so severe that the president resigned in dishonor. Resources were fewer, and markets were smaller. Toyota could not afford the huge investment in the machinery of mass production found in U.S. factories.

Taiichi Ohno made many trips to the United States to study Ford's factories. He concluded that the U.S. system could not work in Japan. He had to develop a system that was more flexible in which one piece of equipment could produce small lots, quickly change over to another product, and produce another small lot. He focused on the stamping press that formed car body parts. At Ford there were die change specialists, die change engineers, and industrial engineers who managed the work of changing from one production run to another. This procedure was possible because of the extremely long runs of a single part. At Ford, die change was infrequent. In Ohno's factory change would have to be every few hours. If he relied on the same methods, his employees and equipment would be idle more than they would be productive.

Ohno experimented with different approaches. He found that dies could be changed quickly if the workers themselves changed the die, working together as a team. If they had knowledge of the die change process, understood the needs at the next stage of production, and understood the materials and supply with which they had to work, they could manage their own work more efficiently. He also found that the employees could track down the cause of problems and change the process to eliminate them. He worked with the teams to eliminate waste in time, motions, and materials. The best results came when they worked as a team, taking responsibility for improving their own work process!

This system was adopted on the assembly line where each team worked closely with the team proceeding it, following their operation, eliminating the need for in-process inventory which existed because of the lack of flexibility in mass production and the inability of workers to adjust their process. The system was also adopted in product development where engineers from different functions were on one team with a team leader who was capable of assuring that the petty rivalries and prejudices of different functions did not stand in the way of the most important work.

Today the Toyota Production System has become the world model of quality and efficiency. Its success has nothing to do with the superiority or inferiority of the Japanese people. It has nothing to do with wage rates. It has to do with the advantages of a different system. Henry Ford's revolution of mass production increased the availability of goods to all and became the model for the rest of the world in almost all industries. The superiority of Total Quality Man-

agement in a team-based organization is being discovered in virtually every industry in many countries.

At Metropolitan Life, Xerox, Milliken, Texaco, Kodak, and hundreds of other companies, the new system of teams taking responsibility for managing their own work, quickly responding to their customers, studying, and improving their process is repeatedly achieving superior productivity and quality. This new system requires new skills and new assumptions about decision-making and responsibility. This team management system requires very different behavior on the part of managers and employees.

Teams Are Natural Learning Centers

Common sense supports that people are more likely to achieve personal satisfaction and be motivated when working in a socially cohesive group. This, in turn, leads to greater learning and higher quality output.

The family is the first building block of society. It is the first organization to which we all belong. Our years of greatest learning occur when we are most dependent on the support of our parents. As we mature, we play with other children. The sharing, problem solving, and cooperation of play are the natural learning environment for future tasks. As teenagers we participate in teams, social clubs, groups, or even gangs, and we practice working together for mutual benefit, support, and feelings of success. And then we come to work and are told, "Just do your own work!" This is the prescription for psychological alienation causing the worker to say, "Don't ask me. I just work here."

To achieve high quality, an organization must achieve optimum output from its people. It must create a system in which people learn, are motivated, care about their work, and seek continuous improvement. High performance is the purpose of teams.

Isolation inhibits learning and reduces energy. Interaction with team members is a source of learning and stimulation. Teamwork creates human energy. Working alone when the results of work are based on the efforts of many people results in frustration. Teamwork among those same people results in satisfaction. Creating teamwork with its resulting increased energy and satisfaction is one primary goal of this workbook.

There are a number of critical components to team implementation:

1. Establishing A Team System

2. Developing Teams

3. Defining Customer Requirements

4. Developing Scorecards

5. Managing Key Processes

6. Managing Human Performance

7. Having Effective Meetings

8. Making Decisions in Teams

9. Solving Problems in Teams

10. Renewal: The Continuous Improvement of Team Systems

Each chapter of the manual describes the components in developing a team-based organization. Additional chapters (11 and 12) address application of quality principles to one's personal life and offer case studies describing the team implementation process.

The Team Process: A Chapter Overview

1. Establishing a Team System

The organization should be structured into natural unit teams. These are teams of people who work together with a common customer, common process, or common objectives. These teams are permanent (as long as needed) and non-voluntary. These teams will develop their purpose and principles as they begin to improve their work.

2. Developing Teams

There are different types of teams and teams with different functions, however teams have much in common as they evolve. Understanding the stages teams go through and assisting them through early developmental rough spots is critical to a successful work output.

3. Defining Customer Requirements

The team must know where their work goes and why it is important. The recipient of the team's work is their "customer." Teams will talk to customers and define their requirements. Teams also have suppliers. They will work to develop partnerships with customers and suppliers.

4. Developing Scorecards

Teams are motivated when they see measures of their performance. Graphs, charts, and scorecards let them know how they are improving and controlling their work.

5. Managing Key Processes

Teams are empowered to take action. They are the management group for their work process. They can act to improve that process and see the effect of their improvement.

6. Managing Human Performance

Celebrating major successes or small improvements is key to keeping teams highly motivated and creating an environment of innovation and creativity.

7. Having Effective Meetings

Teams routinely need time together to share ideas, solve problems, and review performance. Making effective use of their time together is critical to creating high quality work product.

8. Making Decisions in Teams

Not all decisions will be made by an entire team. Team leaders and members need a clear understanding of what style best fits different situations.

9. Solving Problems in Teams

Most problems in today's environment are too complex for any individual to solve alone. Therefore teams need to know how to apply empirical tools and work together to solve them collectively.

10. Renewal: The Continuous Improvement of Team Systems

In team-based organizations the role of the manager changes significantly. Moving from controller and inspector to mentor, educator, coordinator, and boundary manager presents some special challenges to many individuals. Continuous improvement is a way of life. As teams learn they will discover disparities in their existing system and their vision of the future. This will create a healthy struggle between what is and what could be!

11. Case Studies

It is helpful to see how the team process has been successfully implemented in other companies. Each company is unique but lessons can be learned from the experience of others.

12. A Personal Note

Many of the skills and tools of this book have application on an individual level with families and relationships outside of the workplace. This chapter is offered as food for thought for these other applications.

13. Assessment Instruments

To help you evaluate progress and define improvements in your team's performance.

Chapter One

Establishing A Team System

Creating a team-based organization needs to be understood as a business strategy. In order to deal with an increasingly complex marketplace, demanding customer requirements, and a diverse workforce teamwork is no longer a luxury, it is a necessity to successfully compete.

Objectives

1. To define a team-based organization.

2. To define the process of creating a team-based organization.

3. To identify benefits of teams.

4. To define the purpose of teams.

5. To define the principles of a team-based organization.

6. To identify different types of teams.

7. To identify the role of senior management in changing the culture of an organization.

8. To describe the critical success ingredients to create a team-based organization.

What is a Team-Based Organization (and what it is not)?

Structuring an organization into teams should be seen as a business strategy. It is designed to improve the bottom line of the organization's performance. Teams are not an end in themselves but a means to involve people into managing their piece of the business more effectively.

Participating in a team is not voluntary any more than producing a high quality product should be a choice. Senior management needs to see this as a vision of the future that will focus one hundred percent of the organization on serving their customers in the most cost-effective way possible.

Teams should be empowered to make decisions concerning their portion of the business rather than merely just making recommendations to higher levels of authority. While team structures may change and people will serve on several teams, teams should be seen as a permanent fixture in the organization, not a temporary answer to a business crisis or quality problem.

The most important thing to understand about a team-based organization is that changing the structure requires changing support systems such as information dissemination, appraisals, promotions, and even compensation. For teams to truly improve the business requires a great deal of change on both the manager's and the employee's part. This workbook is designed to help teach team leaders and members some of those critical skills.

WHAT IS A TEAM-BASED ORGANIZATION?

➢ Teams are seen as a business strategy.

➢ One hundred percent of the organization participates on a team.

➢ Teams are formed to manage performance.

➢ Teams are a permanent part of the organization.

➢ Participation on teams is mandatory.

➢ Teams make decisions.

➢ Organizational systems are aligned with empowered teams.

➢ Managerial behavior is consistent with empowered teams.

Understanding the Process

In creating a team-based organization, there are some critical "stakeholders" to consider. These constituents all have a stake in the process and a critical role in the success of the process. They are the leadership team who steers the process, the "performance teams" who are managing their piece of the business, the team consultants or coaches who assist the teams in their assimilation of the new skills; and the customers and suppliers both to the organization and to the individual teams.

As the process diagram shows, each of these stakeholders have a critical role to play.

The leadership team should:

1. Define the mission (What is our purpose?) and the business principles (What do we believe in?) they want to drive through the organization.

2. Define their vision of the organization in the future. This vision answers the questions, "What it will be like to work here?" (internal) and,

"What performance results do we expect to be achieving?" (external). These outcomes should be the focus of the change effort they are leading. Every decision they then make should be evaluated under the lens of this future vision. This vision will help demonstrate the constancy and commitment.

3. Plan the change process. The senior team should be heavily involved in planning the improvement effort with their change agents. If the senior team does not understand all the implications of the change effort, it often leaves the consultants or coaches without the leverage to push the process forward. It also leaves the executives unable to model the changes they expect of others.

4. Learn and practice. The senior team should undergo all the same training and implementation steps expected of the rest of the organization. This enables them both to practice their skills within their own team as well as to "testify" to the impact it has had on them personally.

5. Role model. One of the keys to effective leadership is to "practice what you preach." Every individual in the organization will be watching the senior team to see if their behavior changes

LEADERSHIP TEAM	DEFINE BUSINESS PRINCIPLES & MISSION	DEFINE DESIRED OUTCOMES: VISION & PERFORMANCE	PLAN PROCESS	LEARN & PRACTICE	ROLE MODEL TEAM PROCESS	PROVIDE ACCOUNTABILITY	REINFORCE IMPROVEMENT	EVALUATE
PERFORMANCE TEAMS	DEFINE TEAM'S PRINCIPLES	DEFINE ROLES & EXPECTATIONS IN TEAM	DEFINE CUSTOMER REQUIREMENTS	DEVELOP SCORECARD	MANAGE WORK PROCESS	DIAGNOSE & SOLVE PROBLEMS	REINFORCE IMPROVEMENT	EVALUATE
CHANGE AGENTS	DEVELOP PROJECT PLAN	EDUCATE	CONTRACT WITH CLIENT	FACILITATE PRACTICE	PROVIDE FEEDBACK	DIAGNOSE & SOLVE PROBLEMS	REINFORCE IMPROVEMENT	EVALUATE
CUSTOMERS & SUPPLIERS	DEFINE ROLE RE:TEAM	PROVIDE INPUT	PROVIDE FEEDBACK	EVALUATE				

during the implementation process. Questions will always surface such as, "Do they make team decisions? What does their scorecard look like?"

6. Reinforce improvement. The only way organizations survive the agonies of rearranging themselves is through experiencing success along the way. The senior team needs to play an active role in giving recognition to those who are even attempting to change. It's a mistake to wait for the "big hits."

7. Evaluate results. Just as in the Shewhart cycle of Plan-Do-Check-Act, the senior team needs to constantly evaluate the results of their efforts to plan the next move. This cycle is the spirit of continuous improvement. Don't look for a "finish line"; think of this cycle as a life-style change to make the organization continuously healthier and more competitive.

As the organization evolves, each performance team will also undergo changes. It is important, however, not to look at the steps in a linear fashion. Each team will be at a different level of maturity. Their work and service to the customer may be at very different stages of urgency. *It is important to let business needs drive your decision about where to begin the journey, rather than follow the steps as they are described.* For example if your team is having a serious and urgent customer service problem, fix it! Don't stop to have the team define their principles while you have an irate customer waiting! At some point in the process each team should:

1. Define your team's principles around your organization's vision and how you want to work as a team.

2. Clarify roles and responsibilities of the team leader and the team members. How directive the leader or how empowered the team members need to be depends on how effectively they are currently working together.

3. Define your team's key customers. Interview them to determine their requirements around quality, cost, timeliness, accessibility, etc. Let your suppliers know your requirements of them.

4. Develop a balanced scorecard reflecting your team's performance in both key business indices as well as customer satisfaction measures.

5. Analyze its current work processes and analyze them for improvement opportunities in output, cycle time, and quality.

6. Prioritize and work on its most critical problems. As problems surface as a result of scorecard or process analysis, the team should change.

7. Give recognition to the team and to those who contribute to the team's improvement progress. Each team leader and team member should make this his or her personal responsibility.

8. Evaluate periodically to determine if the intervention strategies are having the desired result and to design the next improvement step.

The success of the process is highly leveraged by the change agents. Whether using external or internal consultants, this person or group of people are the "messengers of the world." They need to be well-respected by the organization, effective communicators, passionate about the change effort, and competent at using the quality tools described in this manual.

The change agent's role includes:

1. Developing a project plan with input from their senior sponsors.

2. Training and educating their team leaders and members in the quality process.

3. "Contracting" with each team leader and team as to their role and relationship as well as their expectations of the team.

4. Facilitating practice so that each team leader becomes competent at teaching the team to use these skills.

5. Providing feedback to the team leaders and teams regarding their progress.

6. Diagnosing and helping teams solve particular implementation problems. The change agents often help facilitate solutions between teams or with systemic problems within the organization.

7. Reinforcing behavior change is a big role for coaches as they tend to be the people who observe on a day-to-day basis.

8. Evaluation is a constant process to determine appropriate next steps towards continuous improvement.

Customers and suppliers affect all the inputs and outputs of the team. They either control what comes into the team (suppliers) or accept or reject what the team produces (customers). Obviously a close relationship with both stakeholders is critical to the team's success. Both customers and suppliers should

1. Have a clearly-defined relationship with the team. Some even choose to participate in the team's meetings on a regular basis.

2. Provide input to the team's work process.

3. Provide feedback to the team.

4. Participate in evaluating the results of the team's improvement efforts.

Creating Teams: Why Bother?

Hundreds of organizations are now implementing a management process based on teamwork. Some of the benefits that they are experiencing are as follows:

Motivation and a Sense of Belonging

Why do we enjoy playing on teams? Why do children naturally get excited about being on a baseball or basketball team? Teams celebrate success together, suffer their losses together, and form bonds of friendship around the activity of the team. Teams have fun because they have common goals, keep score, and gain the satisfaction of succeeding together. It is natural for teams to try to perform to the best of their ability. Teams also become important social groups that provide a sense of belonging and recognition of individual contributions which enhance self-esteem.

Improved Communication

The team process involves everyone in the organization. Both employees and managers serve on teams. Teams are forums for communication. Communication is more efficient because the group discusses, asks questions, and clarifies decisions together. A question that is on the minds of many is often asked by one person. Efficiency and morale are improved when members of a team have the same information and feel that information is being shared freely.

Lasting Behavior Change

Many training programs produce a temporary boost in performance. People get excited and behave differently for a short while; then things often return to the old, normal way. This happens because a new, better system of management that involves everyone has not been created. Having all managers participating on teams provides ac-

tive support and modeling of teamwork. Total involvement sends the message that the team process is worthwhile for everyone and allows the process to evolve into the normal way of life.

Shared Learning From a Diverse Workforce

There is a special sense of group power and "esprit de corps" in meeting a goal or winning as part of a team. Teams provide the employee with an opportunity to contribute particular strengths to the larger group and to learn from the strengths of others. Each of us is "wired" differently. We think differently, analyze the world differently, and present our thoughts and ideas in various ways. Teams are a vehicle for capturing the richness afforded us through our diversity. Individuals also learn to value the different competencies and ideas of others within the team.

Performance Results

Performance with the team process will improve. In fact the most critical components of competitive advantage in today's organization are the result of how groups of people perform together. Improving process performance is the most important reason for teamwork. Listed below are four performance areas which can be improved by this process.

1. Quality

The primary focus of teams is defining their customers and improving service to customers. Quality is anticipating, conforming to, or exceeding the customer's requirements. Quality may be on-time delivery, reliability, performance within specifications, courtesy, responsiveness or other factors that are viewed as desirable in the eyes of the customer. If your internal customers are your employees, quality may be defined by providing clear direction or timely decision-making.

2. Creativity

To compete in business, an organization must continuously find ways to do things better. Success does not come from standing still. Finding better ways is the result of human creativity. Groups of people exchanging ideas openly, listening to each other, and working towards a common goal stimulate each other to come up with new ideas.

3. Cycle Time

A work process is measured from the input into the organization to the output to the customer. For example a bakery receives flour, sugar, milk, and other raw material as input. The input is transformed by mixing it and baking it. It is then delivered to the customer. This work is a process with a normal cycle. That normal cycle may be twenty hours or forty-eight hours. Other cycle time examples are as follows: the time it takes mail to be delivered after it is placed in a mail box, the time it takes to write a computer program, the time to design and manufacture a computer chip, or the time it takes to get decisions made. The longer the cycle time, the less responsive to customer needs and the higher the cost.

4. Cost

It is fairly obvious that the lower the costs in the process of achieving service to the customer, the greater the advantage. Hundreds of companies go out of business every year because their costs are too high. When costs are low, job security is increased. Funds can then be spent on research and development, marketing, and creating new products and services which expand the business.

Every team in the organization should be tracking performance measures that affect these areas. This is what will lead to more satisfied customers and a more profitable company.

Benefits of Teams

✓ **Performance Results** (Cost, Quality, & Cycle Time)

✓ **Motivation**

✓ **Improved Communication**

✓ **Lasting Behavior Change**

✓ **Shared Learning**

✓ **Increased Creativity**

Exercise:

Identify specific ways that your organization could help to improve quality performance in each of the following areas:

Quality: Quality is anticipating, conforming to, or exceeding the customer's requirements.

_____

_____

_____

_____

_____

Creativity: Creativity is continually finding ways to do things better and finding better things to do.

_____

_____

_____

_____

_____

Cycle Time: Cycle time is the time it takes to transform an input to an output.

_____

_____

_____

_____

_____

Cost: Cost is resources consumed during the transformation process.

_____

_____

_____

_____

_____

Creating a Quality Culture Through Teams

You cannot achieve total quality just by understanding specific techniques such as statistical process control, brainstorming, or any other mechanics of how teams function. Managing quality through teams is not like a new type of equipment. While there are tools and methods that must be learned, there is more. Quality is a set of ideas, feelings, and values that cause people to behave differently every hour of every day. The team process represents a new culture, and cultures are created from the beliefs, values, and visions of leaders and members of an organization.

The history of the world illustrates that cultures enter periods of transformation when they clash with another culture or when they must compete. When East met West during the European Crusades, a transformation began which became the Renaissance in Western Europe. This cultural transformation led to new ideas as well as new organizational structures.

Today we are in the midst of a renaissance in the life of western organizations. This renaissance is the result of competition and a clash with an eastern culture, but this time it is the result of commercial rather than military competition. Competition with Japanese and European companies is producing a global transformation in the culture of organizations. There is a paradigm shift taking place, a shift in the basic thoughts that drive management practices. And again this transformation is in part the result of challenge from other cultures.

In history it has often been true that the response to challenge proves superior to the challenge itself.

Your organization's competitive edge will be through its response to this challenge. The response is in execution of change. Everyone is learning the same tools and techniques. Those who come out ahead will be those who implement these techniques most effectively.

From Involvement To Empowerment

When American companies became aware of the importance of quality, many began to develop quality circles. They heard that Japanese companies used quality circles, and they found these problem-solving groups to be a relatively easy method to adopt. Today, however, we understand that to achieve total quality, we must do much more. We must have everyone involved and everyone accepting responsibility for improvement. We need a different system based on new assumptions.

Typically quality circles request volunteers to participate with others to select a problem, focus on improving that problem, and work to implement a solution. Circles provided a channel for human energy to flow, energy that is an asset of the organization. However many managers and employees did not participate on quality circles. The same holds true today for many other ad hoc team models designed to problem solve or improve performance, such as process improvement teams or continuous improvement teams. They require only partial involvement of the organization and very little change in management behavior. A team-based organization is different. Everyone, including all managers, is on a team.

When quality circles were implemented, managers approved their recommendations and were often left with the burden of implementing recommendations from many different circles. Managers were often not given training and not asked to change their own behavior.

In a team-based organization, on the other hand, teams accept responsibility for managing their own performance. They ease the burden of managers. Managers and all employees must be trained. Teams may make recommendations to managers when they encounter problems outside of their realm of control; however they are em-

---

powered to make decisions to improve their own work process.

Moving Towards Self-Management

There is the question of whether any team is ever totally self-managing. Some teams are "very leader dependent" because they are not accustomed to making decisions together and are not trained in the use of quality tools or dynamics. Other teams are very "autonomous" because they work very well together without management involvement. One of management's greatest challenges is guiding a team through the stages of development towards becoming more self-managing or self-directed. Teams evolve through stages just like people. In chapter two we will further discuss the evolution of teams and the role the manager plays in that transition.

Team Formation

There are at least three types of teams that may exist within an organization. All are important and serve different purposes as the organization attempts to find its best methodology and structure to provide excellent customer service in the most cost-effective manner. It is important to build an organization that is flexible and fluid, enabling it to respond quickly to changing market conditions or customer demands rather than a permanent "ideal" structure. Each team configuration has its own various strengths and weaknesses. Some options include the following ideas:

Functional Team

A functional team is comprised of members who all have the same skills and expertise (e.g. marketing, finance, engineering, etc.). The advantage of this type of team is maintenance and enhancement of technical competency. It provides a "resource pool" to move people in and out to support various other customer needs. One disadvantage is that members can become unresponsive to customers and too focused on their particular piece of the puzzle.

Cross-Functional Team

A cross-functional team is one in which members retain their individual functional expertise but work with people from other disciplines. They serve a common customer, work on a common process, and strive for a common goal. The advantage to this structure is that the members have a better view of the "big picture" and the end product, enabling them to combine their support, input, expertise to better meet the needs of the end-user. This formation tends to break down departmental walls and eliminate the slow decision-making of functional bureaucracies. The challenges to these teams are as follows: team leadership is often less clear and requires different skills (facilitation vs. directing or eliciting input vs. controlling-inspecting); the need for input of individual team members may be unequal (there may be greater need for engineering expertise rather than human resources or vice versa); and communications between team members who don't have common technical or discipline expertise can be more difficult. An example of a cross-functional team would be a new product-development team comprised of marketing, engineering, research and development, and operations personnel.

Multi-Functional Team

In this team formation, team members share competence in some or all of the disciplines necessary to deliver the output of the team. For example, accounting, marketing, and operations members can perform each other's functions, or everyone on the team is capable of painting, welding, and installing a car door. The advantage to this team design is that it allows the team tremendous flexibility in delivering their outputs to their customer. Communication is enhanced since everyone understands each job and the difficulties involved. Members have greater job satisfaction because their work is more varied and challenging. Typically the product or service is

higher quality, and cycle time is reduced because of the competencies of the members and the lack of "wait time" often required in traditional work processes. The difficulties in attempting this team model are that not everyone is equally competent at different skills; some skill sets require a great deal of education and technical training; and it can be more difficult to stay competent in a quickly-changing specialty area if people don't practice these skills regularly. For example, a system programmer could lose his technological edge if he spent six or eight months learning to be a human resource specialist.

These team structures are not mutually exclusive. It would not be unusual for a person to serve on more than one type of team concurrently. For example an engineer may "organizationally sit" on a functional team that meets monthly or quarterly to discuss continued education and skills acquisition as well as how it is serving its operational groups (internal customers). The engineer may also, however, spend more of their time meeting in a cross-functional team comprised of internal and external customers where ninety percent of its products and services go. As its customers or products evolve, so would the team formation.

A team-based organization looks different than the traditional organization. From top to bottom it is recognized that work is best performed, decisions are best made, and problems are best solved when people work in teams.

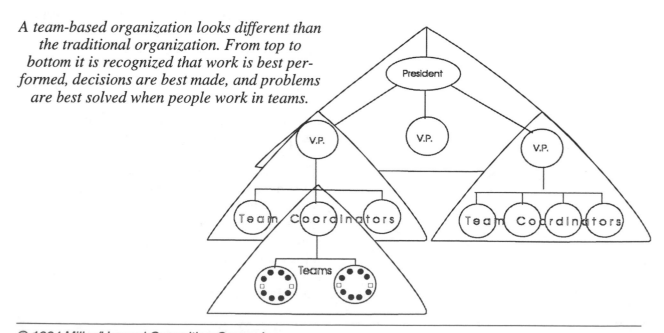

Defining Your Team

Initially in designing a team-based organization, we recommend that you start with your existing organization chart and simply define teams as "everyone who reports to the same manager or supervisor." As a team goes through the process of defining customers, suppliers, key processes, and common objectives, it sometimes becomes clear that this initial team configuration is not the most appropriate to develop into high performance teams. As this evolution takes place, the organization will need to redefine some of the teams and possibly restructure the organization more effectively to serve is customers.

What are the Functions of a Team?

Regular team meetings help companies implement quality improvement. When teams meet, they are not meeting just to decide if there is a problem; rather they are meeting to review their ongoing work performance, review their goals, and discuss how to improve their performance. The team is responsible for managing its performance, and there is always room for improvement.

The following are the primary functions of a team. Each will be covered in detail in the following chapter.

Teams define the requirements of their work to satisfy their customers.

Teams will communicate with their customers. They may go and meet with their customers, telephone them, or survey them; all team members will understand what their customers consider to be superior performance.

Teams study and improve their work process.

Most quality problems are the result of poor work systems or processes. The team is responsible for their own work process. They define the work process, analyze, and improve it.

Teams develop scorecards and set performance goals.

What team performs well without knowing its score? It is natural for teams to gain satisfaction from knowledge of their performance. This is true in athletics and in business. Once the team has listened to their customers and studied their work process, they will have little trouble identifying performance measures and setting appropriate goals.

Teams solve problems.

There is always a problem. The problem is how to improve. Improvement will continue forever as the team identifies opportunities for improvement, sets goals, and develops action plans.

TEAM FUNCTIONS

 Define and Meet Customer Requirements

 Study and Improve Work Processes

 Develop Scorecards and Set Goals

 Solve Problems

 Develop and Implement Action Plans

Teams develop and implement action plans.

Teams are responsible for their work and can make decisions to improve their process. They do not merely submit recommendations to someone else for approval. It is from the implementation of their ideas that the teams gain greater knowledge. This knowledge results in higher levels of performance and further efforts to improve.

Principles of a Team-Based Organization

For implementation to succeed, it is very important to have a clear vision of what you are trying to accomplish and what driving principles are behind that vision.

Consider the following principles of a team-based organization to develop your vision.

Total Involvement

Everyone in the organization must participate to change the culture. An organization's culture is the sum of its members' habits. This includes how decisions get made, how people dress, how people communicate, how conflict is resolved, etc. A culture cannot be changed without everyone in the organization participating in the change.

Customer Focus

Commitment to the customer is more effective in creating high quality than compliance to rules and procedures. Too often people spend their days creating reports, filling out forms, or responding to requests that have nothing to do with satisfying a customer. This is a guaranteed recipe for going out of business. Every single team member should know where his or her work goes and why it is important to the customer.

Diversity

Differences in thought and opinion add value to the end product. Compliance and conformance are not necessarily good things, but we are often taught to try to "fit in" and not cause any conflict. This assimilation process is becoming harder to do as our workforce becomes more diverse. We are also learning that it denies our team's exposure to other ways of doing things. In order to maximize creativity, solve complex problems, and get total involvement from everyone, cultural differences will need to be accepted and explored by teams.

Shared Information

More information and knowledge yield higher involvement and greater quality. A team cannot be expected to solve problems or act like business managers without all the necessary information. Withholding knowledge is like expecting a carpenter to work without his tools.

World's Greatest Experts

The people doing the work are usually the best resource for improving that work. Too often the people actually performing the jobs are told what to do by others. While there will always be work that requires specialists to advise and solve problems, often much of the solution is known by those closest to the action. Those employees who are valued and respected as experts feel encouraged to look for and implement solutions.

Scorekeeping

Performance scorecards lead to higher levels of motivation. People are motivated by feedback. Without feedback we don't know how we are performing. When we don't know how we're performing, there's no reason to improve.

Listening

Listening to others can show them the greatest form of respect. A team-based organization values the ideas of all of its employees. Listening is the most fundamental step in showing others how much you value their suggestions or ideas.

Continuous Improvement

Constantly seeking better ways to serve the customer and manage the business should become a way of life. It does not end. Remember the old adage "If you keep doing what you've always done, you'll keep getting what you've always gotten."

Belonging to a Team

People feel secure, or challenged, and grow by being a member of a group that values their input. Even for people who are "individual contributors," it is important for them to see where their work goes, how they add value to the big picture, and how their work affects other people's. We are all members of a team at some level.

Adding Value

People need to feel that their work makes a difference. If work is not adding value, it should be discontinued. There are always customer needs not getting met and new ideas not being developed. If employees aren't doing work that meets a customer's needs they should be helping someone who does.

Recognition

People perform at higher levels of excellence when given appropriate recognition. Everyone needs recognition. Whether a CEO, a file clerk, a scientist, or a factory worker, at the end of the day we want to go home feeling like "that was a job well done." Every single team member has the responsibility of providing recognition to others.

Exercise: Creating a Vision

Considering the previously-described principles or values of a team-based organization, describe what you would envision your organization (or your team) to look like five years from now.

How would work get done?

What would your relationship be with your customers and suppliers?

What would your relationship be with your fellow employees (bosses, peers, and subordinates)?

What would it feel like working in this organization?

Ten Critical Success Factors to Implementation

When creating a team-based organization, there are ten critical ingredients to a successful implementation. Be sure to address the following in your planning:

1. 100% Percent Participation

The implementation of teams is considered to be a business strategy to gain a competitive advantage. It is not voluntary. Everyone should participate on a team.

2. Line Management Driven

The process should be initiated, endorsed, and practiced by line management. Its success is dependent on managers modeling the process, holding them accountable for its implementation, and rewarding those who actually participate.

3. Results Based

The objective of the team process is to achieve business results. The tools and techniques of teamwork and problem solving are a means to improve performance, not an end in themselves. If performance results are not achieved, the process will not survive. Milestones and activities should be tracked to manage the process. An eye on ultimate business outcomes is critical to maintain focus.

4. Natural Work Teams Managing the Business

While team structure may be flexible depending on the changing needs of the business, most employees will serve on permanent teams built around key processes. These teams manage the process and make decisions regarding their performance.

5. Customer Focused

In order to break through clogged channels of bureaucratic busy work, it is imperative that every team have a clear understanding of their customers' needs and of how their work satisfies those customers.

6. Team Scorekeeping

Every team should have a balanced scorecard. It should reflect both customer satisfaction scores and business or financial indicators. This lets the team know how they are managing their piece of the business.

7. Continuous Improvement

This process is not a "flavor of the month" project but a permanent change in how people perform their work forever. Continuous improvement can encompass small incremental changes in process to major breakthroughs or the total elimination of unneeded processes.

8. Internal Coaches

In order to change cultures, habits must be changed. Changing habits means changing behaviors. Changing behaviors is brought about through coaching. Every team should have their own coach who serves as an objective observer working from the sidelines to give the team help and feedback on implementing the change.

9. Reward and Recognition.

Behavior change is difficult. In order to speed up and sustain the change, people need both recognition as well as rewards such as promotion or desirable assignments.

10. Systems Alignment.

To move towards their vision of the future, organizations need to change the current systems that support current behaviors in the organizations. This will require analysis of all practices including hiring, firing, training, appraising, and compensating plus managerial practices of problem solving, decision-making, and information sharing. Next, these systems must be revised so they are aligned with your organization's vision of the future. This often takes several years to accomplish and should incorporate the ideas of all employees.

A Note to the Senior Team

The importance of the role of the senior team in initiating a team system cannot be overstated. The organization will always be "looking up" to see signs of commitment and leadership throughout the implementation of the process. The senior management team has a major role in making this change happen.

Leadership: Creating a Vision

Whether you are a plant manager, the department head, an executive VP, or the CEO the organization you lead will be looking to you for a vision of where its going and why its changing. If your leadership team isn't comfortable describing the business results you expect and the culture you're trying to create for your organization, then keep discussing it until you feel you can describe it to others in your organization. Your employees will frequently be looking to you to create the passion to push forward with all these changes.

Integration of the Quality Process into Your Business Strategy

For the quality process to maintain its effectiveness, you must incorporate your quality principles into your business strategy. This includes the creation of teams, the necessary training for employees, and the expectation of financial results through continuous improvement efforts.

Management and Accountability

Your organization will be watching to see if all this effort to change really pays off. If you "talk teamwork" but ignore it in your appraisal and promotion decisions, your words will ring false. Even before you see measurable bottom-line results occur, take every opportunity to give recognition to those who are trying hard to practice the new methods. For those who choose not to participate, make sure they clearly understand in which direction the organization is moving. Tell them that you expect everyone to be on the train when it leaves the station!

Symbolic Action

Many times the greatest impact an executive team can have is through symbolic action. An action may take the form of eliminating special perks for executives or conducting "fireside chats" on your employees' home turf to hear their opinions or visiting team meetings in casual attire.

Constancy of Purpose

Create a clear vision of where you want to take the organization, and preach it whenever you get the chance. In fact create the chance on a regular basis to talk about your view of the new organization and its values and behaviors.

Role Model/Walking the Talk

Your team needs to participate in the same training and to practice the same techniques you are asking everyone else to practice. You should publicize what your team has done, such as customer interviews or scorecard development, and the progress your team is making. This recognition will be very encouraging to others and show that you are truly committed.

In general every team should master the key milestones of the team process outlined in chapter two. It is important to note three things as teams proceed:

A) The steps are not necessarily sequential and should not be followed lock-step without flexibility. They are used as a guideline to help teams proceed through a quality process.

B) Much of the quality effort occurs outside the team meeting. Implementing the quality process is like changing your life style; it permeates all the daily decisions you make and the way you treat the people with whom you work. Don't assume you go to a meeting once a week to "do quality" and then return to your real work. Total quality is your real work and should be reflected in how you conduct your business and interact with all the associates in your workplace.

C) Be visible. You cannot talk too much to people about your commitment to the process. Reinforce participation and ask questions; learn from the people in your organization, and they will learn from you! Look at the frequency you communicate with your organization and multiply it by ten. People need to hear from you much more than you think.

Action Assignment

1. The leadership team and the internal coaches should make an initial attempt at defining the appropriate structure of "natural unit teams" for the organization. Using the existing organizational chart, start by defining teams as all the people who report to the same manager or supervisor. While this will definitely not be the ultimate answer, it will be a place to start as the teams are trained in the tools of quality and continuous improvement.

Your organization will initially look something like this:

It may later look like this:

or like this:

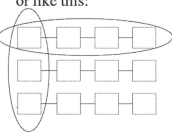

2. The leadership team should review the principles of a team-based organization and write a description of the organization they would like it to become. This will be your vision.

Your vision should include how you want to run your business, treat your customers, and treat your employees.

The leadership team's vision will be a good starting place for the teams as they define their own team's vision and values.

3. The senior team should review the ten critical success factors and discuss how each fits into their implementation plan.

Implementation Tips

1. Have a clear vision from the leadership team about "where we're going and why."

2. Be prepared for resistance. Most organizations have been through other change efforts and perceive this one as another passing fad. Show "constancy of purpose."

3. Don't try to get the team structure perfect in the beginning. Start with your current organizational structure to get people trained and thinking. They will eventually have plenty of opinions about the best team design for their work.

4. Choose good internal coaches. Well-respected, competent coaches and strong leadership are the two most critical factors to a successful implementation.

5. People will often resist "sheep dip" training and want to customize everything to the individual team, it's often important to get people through the same educational experience so they can customize the application to their specific team.

6. Consider this an iterative process. The organization will go through many phases before it "settles" into a comfortable rhythm. Look at change as inevitable.

7. Remember this is not a linear process. While there are steps of the process outlined, each team is unique, and the process needs to be tied to the **needs of the business**. If you are in a critical stage of the business, address that immediately.

8. Get the teams to develop scorecards as soon as possible. This gives them focus and identifies key result areas. The sooner measurable results are attained, the faster resistance drops!

Chapter Two

Developing Teams

The process of team development can be a rocky road. However with clear sense of purpose and underlying principles, a group of individuals can evolve into a highly productive team.

Objectives

1. To understand what constitutes an effective team.

2. To define the team's principles.

3. To identify the activities of teams to develop continuous improvement.

4. To identify stages teams and team leaders go through as they evolve.

5. To describe benefits and examples of team-building activities.

6. To give some implementation tips for this stage of the process.

Building A Team

Just putting people into work groups and calling them a team does not result in improving the output of that group. It takes more than meetings and the label *team* to have true improved performance results from a collective effort.

There are ingredients that significantly affect people working as a true team. Some groups will never achieve all of these attributes while others will seem to evolve readily. The critical ingredients to maximizing the potential of teams are as follows:

1. Having a clear sense of purpose. Why are we a team? What are we trying to produce?

2. Having clear performance goals. What is our output? Who are our customers? How will our performance be measured?

3. Understanding the value of a team that works together. How is the whole greater than the sum of the parts? What value are we adding as a team?

4. Having a sense of interdependence. What responsibilities do we have to each other that produce a higher quality product? Where can the collective wisdom of the group outperform individual outputs?

5. Holding each other accountable for the output of the team. Are we willing to hold each other accountable not only for our individual contributions but also for the output of the team?

Defining the Team's Principles

Anyone who has ever participated on a team, led a team, or educated a team, knows that every team needs a clear sense of purpose. In a team-based organization, the team's purpose is to manage its piece of the business by serving its customers in the most efficient and cost-effective manner possible. This is the purpose or "why" of the team process. There is also the "how" or the principles and values side of the team process.

To address the principles and values issue of the team, it is often helpful to look at the larger organization's mission or vision statement and discuss what implications this vision has on your individual team.

For example, a team may look at the principle of "total involvement" and decide that this means everyone on the team will assume responsibility for contributing to improving the quality of their output. They will work to get equal participation during the team meetings.

Each team should think about what is important to their vision of the future and establish a short list of driving principles that will give their team a sense of direction.

Activity: Principles for Our Team By Which to Live

1. Discuss your organization's mission/vision/values statement or review the eleven principles of a team-based organization described in chapter one.

2. Choose four or five principles that your team agrees should drive how it wants to perform its work, treat its customers and members as it evolves.

Worksheet

Choose four or five key principles, or develop your own. Define them for your team. Evaluate how well you are currently practicing this principle. What can you do to improve?

Principles of a Team-Based Organization

Total Involvement	Listening
Customer Focus	Continuous Improvement
Diversity	Teamwork
Shared Information	Adding Value
World's Greatest Experts	Recognition
Scorekeeping	

1 Almost Never **2** Rarely **3** Usually **4** Often **5** Almost Always

	Principle	Definition	Practice	Improve
1			1 2 3 4 5	
2			1 2 3 4 5	
3			1 2 3 4 5	
4			1 2 3 4 5	
5			1 2 3 4 5	

Team Activities

When building a team-based organization, there are some specific activities that teams need to accomplish in order to improve the quality of their work output and satisfy their customers. While these activities are simply tools and techniques that create the framework for a quality organization, their accomplishment does not necessarily change the culture of the organization. Both heart and mind eventually have to come together to have the true spirit of a quality organization.

However having each team accomplish the following milestones will be a major step forward in changing behavior and achieving measurable results.

Team Activities

1. **Establish consistent time and place for regular team meetings.**
2. **Develop team's purpose and principles.**
3. **Develop ground rules, and begin using action record.**
4. **Identify team's customers.**
5. **Identify team's products and services.**
6. **Identify team's roles and responsibilities.**
7. **Identify customer contact person/plan interviews.**
8. **Interview the customers.**
9. **Identify team's key processes.**
10. **Analyze team processes (mapping).**
11. **Identify the team's business measures.**
12. **Analyze the customer feedback.**
13. **Develop the team scorecard (graphs) for business measures and customer satisfaction.**
14. **Graph and track measures, and draw goal lines.**
15. **Recognize teams for success on above goals.**

Team Development: When to Let Go of the Reins

Corporations are rushing to become world class competitors. One significant contributor to developing a culture of continuous improvement is to involve every employee on teams that manage their own performance with their customers. However, for managers to let go of control and for employees to accept responsibility for their performance; a maturity rarely reached without tests or trials is required.

In many companies managers are pushing decision-making down to employee teams before the teams are prepared to accept responsibility. In other companies teams are prepared to accept responsibility before their managers are prepared to let go of the control. Both cases may result in one group's blaming the other for their hesitancy or lack of commitment. This can result in the effort being abandoned by the organization.

The tensions can be eased if both managers and employees have empathy for the natural learning each group must go through. It is important to see that both sides share responsibility for change. Managers have the responsibility to provide the necessary training, to design the support systems and structure, and to provide the necessary information, tools, and environment for teams to manage their own performance. On the other hand employees also share the responsibility of making this transition. They must be willing and prepared to seize the burden of responsibility and recognize that as team members they become "business" managers, focused on managing quality, productivity, and costs. If progress is to be smooth and tensions minimized, this development will be consistent with management's movement from a telling/controlling style of decision-making to a more advising/delegating style. These two dimensions—teams assuming responsibility for performance and managers participating more—are the primary drivers for teams becoming more self-directed and independent.

Performance Initiative

The development of teams can be measured by the degree they accept responsibility for their performance. A good indicator of responsibility is their taking the initiative to measure, improve, or control significant business performance. When teams are first formed, they may have little knowledge of performance, lack competence in technical areas, or lack the problem-solving skills required to manage their own performance. They may also simply not be in the habit of thinking about performance. If they have grown up in a traditional organization, they have become dependent on their managers worrying about performance. However for a mature team their central focus and purpose is performance.

Management Style

The behavior of managers and the nature of the systems they control is the other key dimension which explains team behavior and maturity. As teams develop, managers must make a transition from controlling and telling to teaching, delegating, and advising. When a manager hires a new employee or when employees do not have the skills or habits to assume responsibility for performance, the manager is absolutely justified, even required, to assume control. But it is the job of the manager and the management systems to develop the skills and habits of employees so that they will assume responsibility. Gradually as the teams develop the skills and habits to assume responsibility, the manager must delegate and advise the teams, only stepping in with more direction as needed.

The Team Development Path: Maturity and Decision-Making Styles

The development of teams is very similar to the development of maturity in individuals and the changes parents make in their own decision-making styles. Parents of a five-year-old child are much more likely to tell (command and control) decisions to their child because the child has not yet learned to make mature judgments. But as the child becomes a teenager and then a young adult, the parents can delegate increasingly more decisions. Or the parent can take on the role of advisor, consulting with the young adult as he or she makes her own decisions. If parents give up control and assume a delegating decision style before the child is capable of accepting responsibility, the probable result is the "spoiled brat" syndrome. On the other hand, if parents seek to overcontrol a maturing youngster who is ready to accept responsibility, they are likely to confront the "rebellious teenager."

The goal in team development is to make a smooth transition from early team learning to maturity. Deviating from the development line, wandering into either the rebellious teenager or spoiled child quadrants of the following team development path, results in dysfunction. While the development process is represented as a straight line, it is much more likely to wander on either side and then return toward the center as managers and employees learn their roles in a team-based organization. The more wandering from the direct route of "obedient child" to "mature adult," the greater the anxiety, cost in effort and time, and higher the probability of failure.

The Team Development Path
Maturity and Decision-Making Styles

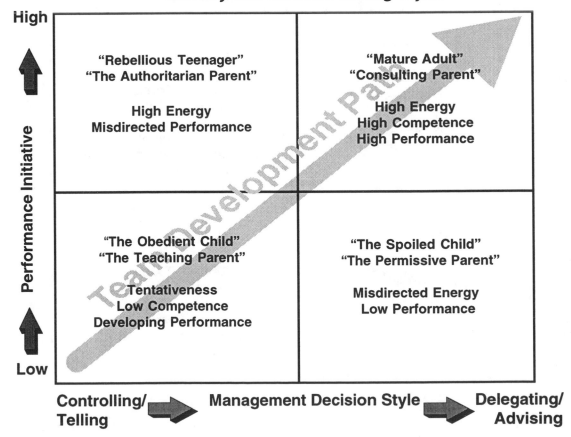

The key to successfully building an organization that optimizes the involvement of its employees through self-directed teams is to manage the development of both managers and employees.

The Team Development Path: Management Tasks and Behavior

Parent-Child Model

In parental organizations most decisions are made by a few managers who have greater competence and control than those below them. This usually occurs during the early stages of a company's development when the firm's founders possess the vision of the future and may have great technical competence.

In this organization the manager cannot rely on first-level employees to make significant decisions or accept significant responsibility. This reluctance may be well-founded if the gap in competence between managers and employees is genuine. Employees are not likely to resent this lack of trust if they understand the competency gap. For example, in professional service firm such as a law firm where a senior partner is recognized as an expert in an area of legal specialty, the junior members and law clerks will not expect to be entrusted with significant decisions. They are likely to appreciate and value the expertise of the senior partner's contribution to those decisions.

The task for this organization is the development of its members. If the organization's employees are going to accept greater responsibility, they will have to free the "expert" to continue devoting his energies to more compli-

The Team Development Path
Management Tasks and Behaviors

High

Performance Initiative

Low

Over Control

"Rebellious Teams"
"Controlling Managers"

**High Energy
Misdirected Performance**

High Performance Teams

"Mature Teams"
"Consulting Managers"

**High Energy
High Competence
High Performance**

Parental

"Obedient Employees"
"The Teaching &
Telling Manager"

**Low Competence
Low Energy**

Premature Empowerment

"Spoiled Teams"
"The Permissive Managers"

**Low Energy
Low Performance
Internal Focus**

Team Development Path

Controlling/ Telling → **Management Decision Style** → **Delegating/ Advising**

cated tasks. First, the "expert" will have to focus on the training and development of the Junior associates. As their competence develops, they will work as a team with the experienced manager, share in decision-making, and gain experience and knowledge. Gradually the manager will delegate more complex and important decisions to junior associates, while reinforcing their success and providing feedback for their improvement. It is critical that the manager avoids creating fear caused by reprimand or ridicule. Fear will inhibit the team's development and willingness to accept responsibility.

These actions are necessary to move teams to more autonomy:

Team Member Actions:

- Continue to pursue technical skills and knowledge.
- Become familiar with performance measures and begin graphing these measures.
- Learn problem solving and process improvement skills.
- Become familiar with customer needs and requirements.
- Learn the key requirements for supplier inputs.

Management Actions:

- Continue to provide training in both technical and team-process skills.
- Provide frequent coaching and feedback on technical skills.
- Provide frequent coaching and feedback on team-process skills.
- Design the systems and structure that will encourage and enable teams to manage their own performance.

Prematurely Empowered Teams

In this stage, development of the team has been deficient. Management has made the mistake of delegating too much responsibility, while providing insufficient direction, feedback, and help to the team. Management may have failed to provide adequate teaching/training during the initial stages of team development, or team members may have failed to understand that they are now responsible for improving and monitoring business performance.

Performance is likely to be poor; employees are likely to focus more on satisfying their own concerns rather than the concerns of their customers or of the larger organization. Even though they seem focused on improving the quality of work life, they rarely achieve the kind of satisfaction that comes from improving business performance or satisfying a customer.

Because managers misunderstand the concept of empowerment, they allow employees to wander in their quest for self-satisfaction. These managers mistakenly believe that their job is to allow employees to make all of their own decisions. However they failed to assure that the employees have the training, competence, and understanding required to succeed with this responsibility.

This stage cannot last too long. Managers will soon recognize that the teams are failing to manage themselves. Management's own accountability for the organization's performance cannot be ignored for long. They will soon become frustrated with the absence of performance improvement and will jerk in the reins, reasserting control. After than, the employees will blame the managers for their lack of faith in employee involvement. Thus, managers will have good justification for their skepticism of the entire theory of employee teams and empowerment.

Team Member Actions:

- You should expect and request clarifications and objectives to help develop your team.
- Define your customers and their requirements.
- Define your key performance measures, graph them, and discuss how to improve these scores in each team meeting.
- Define and focus on improving your own work processes.
- Avoid talking about the "other guys" (gossip) who are outside your immediate influence.

Management Actions:

- Provide team training on managing performance, customer focus, and process improvement.
- Personally coach your team(s) to assure that they stay focused on meeting their customer's needs.
- Ensure that they are receiving necessary information.
- Reinforce those teams that are making progress toward managing performance.

Overly-Controlled Teams

In this stage, management has been unwilling to delegate decisions regarding the management of performance. Employees have the skills and are willing to take responsibility. Managers may simply be unable to break the habits of tampering or concerning themselves with familiar tasks instead of tackling the more complex and challenging tasks of strategy, planning, analyzing future market and customer needs, and determining the fundamental capabilities of their organization.

Employees often respond to this by seeking to exert control over anything that they can in their environment. People tend to become either angry and hostile or apathetic when they feel overcontrolled. There can be a great deal of blaming, often aimed at management, for weak performance

This period will not last long if management provides the necessary training and systems to enable responsible decision-making. But more importantly management must clarify team responsibility to include significant control over managing their own performance.

Team Member Actions:

- Meet with your manager(s) to clarify your decision-making and responsibility boundaries.
- Have patience with management's efforts to delegate decisions.
- Make deliberate efforts to demonstrate to your managers that you are interested in improving business performance (quality, productivity, costs, and customer satisfaction).

Management Actions:

- Define the value-adding work that is done by your management team.
- Work with employee teams to define their performance responsibilities including their customers, suppliers, measures, and processes.
- Reinforce teams who are initiating action to improve performance.
- Begin efforts to increase the amount of your time focused on strategic issues, particularly the capability of your strategic systems to meet customer/market needs in five years.
- Modify management systems to reinforce teamwork, shared performance goals, and bonuses based on the team's shared performance.
- Develop a plan for delegating decisions to teams.

High Performance Teams

This stage is characterized by high performance and high self-management among employees. For both managers and employees to develop smoothly from immature to mature teams, the managers have to focus on strategic tasks such as anticipating customer's needs, planning how to make the business grow in five years, and defining the critical competence the team will need to meet these challenges. The direct management of day-to-day performance should be in the hands of first and second-level employees who fully understand the capability of their processes and have complete and immediate information on their performance. In addition, they should continually initiate efforts to improve their performance. If senior managers intervene in their efforts at this stage, they would be seen as *"tampering,"* unless there is a serious drop in performance.

Team Member Actions:

- Continuously seek to define customer requirements and anticipate future requirements.
- Continuously improve your processes.
- Seek improvements in technical skills and team process.
- Assure continuous feedback to suppliers to help them improve.
- Assure communication of improvements among teams.

Management Actions:

- Intermittently monitor team progress, and reinforce their success.
- Focus on strategic system capability (total manufacturing, marketing, research and development, etc.)
- Define five-year market/customer requirements and design future capabilities.
- Seek wealth-creating business opportunities.

Activity

1. Review the four quadrants of the "Team Development Path: Maturity and Decision-Making Styles" on page 41 and discuss where you think your team currently belongs.

2. Review the four quadrants of the "Team Development Path: Management Tasks and Behaviors" on page 42, and discuss your team leader's current style.

3. Develop an action plan to move the team forward on the development path to "High Performance Teams."

Team Building and Join-Up

Teams vary a great deal in their ability to function together. This is often a result of the clarity of their sense of purpose and how interdependent the members feel.

For some teams, smooth-working relationships and intimacy will occur simply because they follow the milestones of the team process. They become close by doing a better job of getting out their work product. Other teams who do not have as clear a sense of purpose and who perform their work more independently may never feel that same intimacy and may need more assistance in building closer working relationships.

For these teams we suggest more structured team-building exercises with the sole purpose of getting to know and trust each other more.

These team-building exercises can range from very dramatic weekend retreats doing a survival exercise to very simple "join-up" exercises at the beginning of each team meeting. The purpose of a join-up exercise is to speed up the group's personal knowledge of each other, to increase trust, and to help the team appreciate its own diversity and commonality.

Some examples of join-up exercises you could do at your team meeting are as follows:

- Take five minutes for each team member to tell what he or she did over the weekend.

- Have team members pair up and find three things they have in common with each other.

- Give each team member a sheet of flipchart paper and have him write down a) where he went to school, b) where he was born, c) what his birth order is, and d) what his favorite pastime is. Hang flipcharts on the wall, and discuss the differences and commonalities in the group.

- Have each team member write down his first impressions of each other and share them with the group.

- Have each member share one thing he enjoys about working with the other team members.

These are just a few examples of positive join-up exercises. There are literally hundreds of team-building books available in bookstores with exercises designed for team building. Experiment and have fun. Perhaps rotate the responsibility for facilitating a join-up exercise among members for each team meeting.

Action Assignment

1. Based on your team's self-analysis, determine one or two behaviors both the team members and team leader can work on to begin moving towards a higher performance team.

2. With your team try one or two of the "join-up" exercises found on this page (or design some of your own) at your next team meeting.

Implementation Tips

1. Realize that all teams are not created equal, and don't expect them all ever to look exactly alike.

2. Those teams with a clear business purpose and a high degree of interdependency will always look, feel, and work more like a real team than a group of people loosely held together by common interests or similar skills or shared titles.

3. Decide which milestones all teams <u>must</u> complete. Then, let each team decide which tools and skills it will use to reach its goal. For example, every team should know its customers, measure its performance, and take steps to improve its work process. The team can decide who and how they want to recognize good performance.

4. Wherever possible, start out with managers/supervisors in the role of the team leader. If they are expected to change their managerial style, they need the chance to practice it.

5. The role of the team leader is dynamic and should ebb and flow as the team matures. Rather than managers fearing that they have no job, they need to realize they now have a much more challenging one.

6. Be patient with the pace of change. Putting people together for the first time and asking them to work together towards a common goal can often feel like a blind date. They may go dancing into the night, but they're bound to step on each others' toes.

7. The remaining chapters of the book explain the skills teams need to improve business results. However, don't overlook the interpersonal skills needed to build trust and a safe environment to take risks.

Chapter Three

Defining Customer Requirements

To know and serve one's customer, internal or external, and to improve continuously, is the purpose of every team.

Objectives

1.   To identify your customers.

2.   To determine a method for gathering customer input.

3.   To translate customer feedback into a team scorecard.

4.   To identify your suppliers and a feedback system to your suppliers.

Quality Defined

The purpose of this chapter is to discuss the most basic principle of quality management: *customer focus*. A customer-focused team is a team that can answer the question, "Where does our work go, and why is it important?" The key to quality is being in touch with our customers and suppliers. We must continuously work to improve service to customers, internal and external. They are responsible for the health of our business. We must also determine our supplier needs and give them regular feedback on performance.

Frequently both employees and managers in large corporations lose sight of their customers. This is particularly true with respect to internal customers. The end result is inefficient processing of goods and services that are ultimately received by external customers. When this occurs, external customers who have a choice of companies providing similar services may take their business to another company that will satisfy their expectations.

Quality is defined not by a team's perception of quality but by the standards and expectations of its customers. All of the goods and services that a team produces are received by either an internal or external customer. A team's purpose or reason for being can be defined in terms of those customer expectations.

When employees are given responsibility for improving their work process to serve their customers more effectively, they are not just involved; they are *empowered*. Empowerment is feeling that you can make a difference and that you can exert some control over your work and your life. Empowered teams feel that they have the discretion to make decisions about serving their customers and improving their work process without going through multiple approval levels. Bureaucracies are so restricted by procedures, checks, and controls from above that those who do the actual work feel powerless. This destroys initiative, creativity, and concern for the customer.

Entrepreneurial companies are adding to the wealth of our society by creating new products, new services, and, therefore, new jobs. In these companies employees are frequently involved in decisions and feel that they are part of the risk/reward game of business. They are empowered and ready to take the initiative, be creative, and show concern for the customer. They are part of a *system* that gives them responsibility for managing their own work.

The primary source of motivation for every team comes from knowing its customers and meeting their expectations. Teams start defining quality by identifying what their customers, both internal and external, expect from them. By defining these expectations, teams form the foundation for developing measures of team performance. Team performance measures allow teams to focus their energy on work that is most likely to lead to increased customer satisfaction. It is only when team members understand customer expectations and translate those expectations into measures of team performance that the improvement process begins.

Quality performance is achieved by anticipating, meeting, or exceeding the needs and requirements of the customer.

In the past quality was most often defined as reliability or meeting specifications every time. Our understanding of quality is broader today. There is little point in reliably meeting specifications that are not those desired by the customer. The product may never fail, yet it may be out-of-date technically, perform poorly, or lack the "feel" desired by the customer. Quality is many things, and the most important things depend entirely on the context and content of the work, and the customer is the world's greatest expert on what is important!

Exercise:

List some examples of products and services that your team delivers to a customer.

_____

_____

_____

_____

_____

_____

How do you think your customer would define *quality* relative to the above-described products and services?

_____

_____

_____

_____

_____

_____

What is Quality?

Quality is...

...Anticipating, meeting, and exceeding customer requirements and desires.

...Continuous improvement in product and process.

...Cycle time improvement.

...Cost competitiveness.

...Creating real wealth.

Identifying Customers and Suppliers

Every individual in an organization should do something that creates value. Likewise each team should provide goods and services that create value for some customer. The value of those goods or services, however, is greatly minimized if it does not meet the needs of the customer for whom it was produced. It is only with an understanding of the key role a customer plays in the value of the goods or services that the highest quality product or service can be delivered.

Each organization is a series of internal supplier and customer teams. Every team is both a supplier and a customer. A team receives some input that it is responsible for transforming into an output of goods or services. The input supplied can include specification orders, information, decisions, money, or the actual product. The team that receives the input from its supplier is a customer of that supplier team.

The team receiving the input from its supplier is also a supplier to another team within the organization. This relationship exists throughout the organization. Each team that supplies goods and services to either an internal or external customer should continuously attempt to discover the expectations of its customers and strive to meet those expectations.

Identifying a team's customers can sometimes be more confusing than it first appears. It often helps to start with the external or "paying customer" and trace the final product and service back through the organization to determine the internal customer-supplier relationships. For example in a fast food restaurant start with the person who approaches the counter, and trace the customer-supplier chain back to the server, order taker, food preparer, food broker to the headquarters staff such as human resources, marketing, planning, and accounting. It helps to define your priorities to determine how your service ultimately impacts the end-user.

What Teams Do

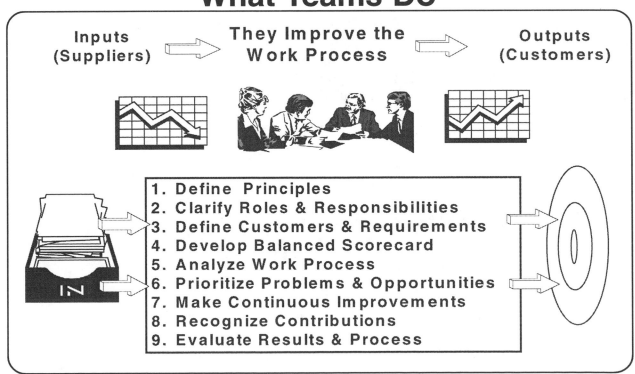

Inputs (Suppliers) → **They Improve the Work Process** → **Outputs (Customers)**

1. Define Principles
2. Clarify Roles & Responsibilities
3. Define Customers & Requirements
4. Develop Balanced Scorecard
5. Analyze Work Process
6. Prioritize Problems & Opportunities
7. Make Continuous Improvements
8. Recognize Contributions
9. Evaluate Results & Process

The manager's job is to provide advice, directions, resources, feedback, clear communication, and leadership. This enables those who are actually performing the work to provide better customer service at the lowest possible costs.

One of the keys to the success of the Japanese auto companies has been a completely different relationship between them and their suppliers. For example Honda Manufacturing in Marysville, Ohio, has dedicated suppliers within a fifty mile radius of their plant. The Stanley Electric Company supplies the headlight and taillight assemblies. They make deliveries several times a day, minimizing or eliminating inventory in both plants. Japanese companies have an average two-hour inventory where many American companies have two weeks of inventory. When a defect is discovered, Stanley will know of the defect in one hour or less and will correct the problem immediately!

These customers and suppliers work together as one, as an extended family, with trust and in a spirit of mutual benefit.

A Fable:

A sea captain stood on the bridge of his ship, the newest, largest, and fastest ship on the oceans. He soon saw a light approaching dead ahead. It seemed to be on a collision course. He grabbed the microphone of his radio and called out, "This is the captain of the ship you see approaching. We are on a collision course. I order you to turn fifteen degrees to port."

In a few moments a voice came over the radio, "Captain, I will not turn. You turn fifteen degrees to starboard."

The captain was incensed. He grabbed the microphone again and ordered, "This is the captain; we are on a collision course, and I order you to turn fifteen degrees to port."

Again a voice came back over the radio, "I will not turn. You turn fifteen degrees to starboard."

The proud and exasperated captain, seeing the lights quickly approaching, once again seized the microphone. "I am the captain of the largest, fastest, and newest ship in the world, and I am ordering you to turn at once."

Once more a voice came back over the proud captain's radio, "Captain, I will not turn; you turn fifteen degrees to starboard. And I am the keeper of the lighthouse which you are rapidly approaching."

Why is a customer like a lighthouse?

Traditional organizations look like this:

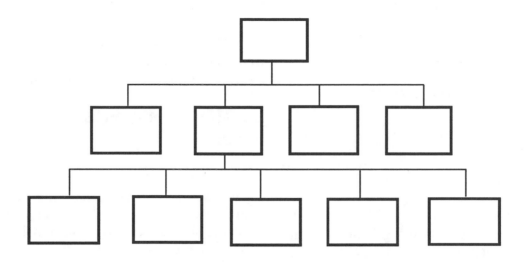

However, work flows like this:

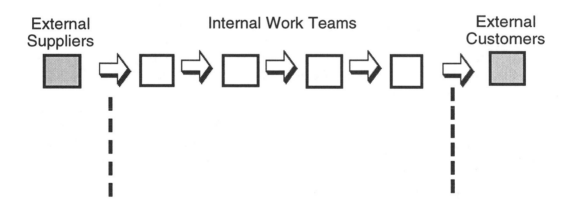

Organizations concerned about quality need to rethink how they support customer needs, not their organizational hierarchy. In fact most high performance teams tend to be self-managing. The idea of a self-managing team is often misunderstood. No team is completely self-managing. Teams will always be affected by suppliers and must perform to satisfy customers' changing demands while working under budget constraints of the organization. A high performance team is one that is working <u>primarily</u> to satisfy its customers, responding to customer feedback by improving its process and managing its suppliers. When teams become performance-focused, they often need little direction or control from above. This team further eliminates wasted, non value-adding effort.

Customer Analysis

Every team will begin the team-management process by defining their customer expectations through a customer analysis. This process involves the following seven steps:

Identify the team's customers.

The team should first identify its internal and external customers by using the brainstorming process. The focus should be on those customers your team deals with directly on a day-to-day basis.

The other, often confusing, concept is who "owns" the customer? Who should make the contact and conduct the interviews? Often managers find they have no direct contact with customers down the line. Be careful when determining whom you serve to meet customer needs. Most managers should be interviewing their subordinates as customers, not vice-versa!

Apply the 80/20 rule to identify your key customers. What 20% of your customers receive 80% of your work? Narrow your customer list to five to seven key recepients of your work output.

Identify the products and services (outputs) that your team provides to each of your customers.

After the team has identified its primary internal and external customers, it should define the products and services it provides to each of those customers.

Identify contact people in the areas the team has identified as a customer.

The most logical person is the one with whom the team has the most contact. This can be more than one person if appropriate.

Develop questions to ask each customer.

As a team, develop a series of questions that you would like to ask your customers. These should be used only as guidelines for interviews. Team members should not feel compelled to ask only the questions developed by the team, particularly if the customer wants to discuss other areas of team performance.

In talking to your customers, determine from them what your team is a) doing now that they could stop; b) not doing now that they should start doing; c) doing now that they should continue.

Some performance areas about which your team can inquire include the following ones:

Quality	Quantity
Timeliness	Accuracy
Availability	Flexibility
Courtesy	Speed to Respond
Speed to Improve	

Decide upon the method for getting customer feedback.

The team has three options for obtaining feedback from its customers:

Conduct a personal interview.

This method permits the team member to ask follow-up questions and to clarify any vague or ambiguous statements.

Conduct a telephone interview.

This is most appropriate for customers who are frequently out of the office or at another location. The customer may be sent a copy of the questions in advance to facilitate the interview.

Send a questionnaire.

A cover letter may be attached explaining the purpose of the customer analysis. The letter should also include a request that the customer return the questionnaire by a certain date. There are two disadvantages to the questionnaire. One is that some customers may not respond or may respond later than the response date you request. Another is that there is no opportunity to ask follow-up questions or to clarify vague or ambiguous statements.

Don't overcomplicate this process. Beware of pitfalls such as spending weeks designing the perfect interviewing instrument or overwhelming your organization with too many surveys. The critical issue is to get a clear understanding of what your key customers expect and how to satisfy them.

Analyze customer feedback.

After the team has interviewed its primary internal and external customers, the next step is to analyze the information in a team meeting. The customer feedback will provide the team with agenda items for some time to come. Feedback can typically be segmented into four categories.

The first category is feedback belonging to another team. In some cases the customer feedback may be directed to a more senior or junior team. If this is the case, that feedback should be passed on to the appropriate team.

Second is the quick fix problem. This is when the team receives feedback that requires immediate attention. The team could decide that the problem identified by the customer is one that can be fixed immediately because the solution is obvious to the team.

Third if it is not a "quick fix" problem, the team should apply the problem solving model or process analysis tools and develop an action plan to resolve the problem. These problems are often systemic processes that can be mapped for improvement.

Fourth, certain types of customer feedback are indicators of on-going activities or performance levels that should be monitored to ensure customer satisfaction. (Chapter four contains guidelines on creating a balanced scorecard.)

It is suggested that each team member who collected data prepare a brief summary of customer feedback. If questionnaires were sent out, they simply can be copied and given to each team member. Each team member should have an opportunity to review all of the customer feedback prior to the team meeting.

Agree on customer-based team performance measures.

During a team meeting the team should brainstorm all the possible team performance measures that were identified through the customer feedback. Consider using the worksheet on the next page. For example the team's customers may have stated that the turnaround time on completion of projects was slow. As a consequence the team could measure their turnaround time from the time of receipt of the request to the time the project is completed. Another example would be customer complaints regarding programs developed by the team. The team could measure user satisfaction with programs as a performance measure.

After your team has finished brainstorming all of the possible measures, you should agree on quality measures most critical to providing good customer service. Chapter four provides more information on setting up a scorekeeping system. The team will want to review its performance measures periodically to consider whether those selected are the best indicators of how well they are meeting customer expectations.

For management teams it is often more difficult to translate feedback into measures for their team. However it is important for these teams to address managerial behaviors through the team process. For example senior teams are often given feedback that they are inaccessible and aren't out with the troops enough to know what's truly going on. A measurement tool for this feedback might be a "visibility graph" tracking the number of visits to the field the senior team makes each month. Speed of decision-making is another common complaint. The team could track the number of days it takes them to return a decision or to return requests for capital expenditures. These are all appropriate for the team's scorecard to be reviewed regularly at team meetings.

Some important aspects of customer satisfaction at the executive level may not easily lend themselves to measurement. For example often customers, whether internal (employees) or external (paying customers), don't expect executives to have solutions to technical problems; but they do expect to see these people and to be nurtured by these people. So while some behavior may be more symbolic than substantive, it is still important for executive teams to have some measurable way of tracking customer satisfaction relevant to their team.

Exercise: Defining Customer Expectations

Begin defining customers and customer requirements. What do we now know about our customers and their requirements?

1. Who are our team's internal and external customers?

_____

_____

_____

2. What are the specific products or services that we supply to each of these customers? List each customer and the specific product or service he receives from your team.

_____

_____

_____

3. Who are the contact people?

_____

_____

_____

4. What do we now believe to be their most important requirements and expectations?

_____

_____

_____

5. How will we communicate with our customers to specify their requirements and obtain input into how we should change to serve them better?

_____

_____

_____

6. How can we anticipate our customer's future needs? Many times what we provide today will lose value if we don't anticipate future change in needs.

_____

_____

_____

_____

Guidelines for a Customer Interview

Each team member should review these guidelines before conducting an interview with any of the team's customers. These guidelines will ensure that the team obtains the most important information from the interview. Both the team and the customer will benefit if these guidelines are adhered to throughout the interview.

Clearly explain which team you are representing.

Are you representing the team you lead or the team of which you are a member? In other words explain which team's performance you are asking for feedback on during the interview.

Ask open-ended questions to draw out your customer.

One example would be, "What would you like to see our team do in order to improve our service to you?" Your goal during the interview should be to obtain as much specific feedback as possible about the team's performance with respect to that customer.

Avoid becoming defensive if your customer gives negative feedback.

Keep in mind that any feedback, either positive or negative, will help you serve your customers better. However, try to keep the customer focused on "how it should be" rather than "what is wrong."

Avoid explaining away negative feedback from your customer.

This may make the customer defensive and unwilling to continue the interview. For example, if your customer tells you about your team's late deliveries, don't start explaining about how the late deliveries from your supplier caused the problem. Instead, try rephrasing the problem. Ask if there is anything else, and move on to the next question.

General comments should be followed up by specific questions.

If the customer makes general comments such as, "Your team is doing okay," or "I don't really have any complaints," ask specific follow-up questions such as, "What could we do to improve quality?" You always need to leave the interview with a clear idea of what to do differently.

Customer Interview Guidelines

➢ Identify your team

➢ Ask open-ended questions.

➢ Avoid becoming defensive.

➢ Avoid explaining away negative feedback.

➢ Follow up on general comments.

➢ Educate your customer.

➢ Create continuous feedback system.

Educate your customer.

Sometimes you may have to educate your customers about all the products and services your team could provide. You may also have to explain the cost/benefit associated with some of their requests. They may ask for things without realizing the expense associated with them; however be sure you are listening carefully - they <u>are</u> your customers!

Explain to the customer that your team would like to receive feedback continuously on its performance.

Feedback is the only way any team can continue to serve its customers well.

Customer Interview Guideline

Product/Service	Importance to You On a 1-7 scale: 1=Low importance 7=High importance	Effectiveness of Our Delivery On a 1-7 scale: 1=Poor 7=Excellent	Specifically How Ccould We Improve?
1			
2			
3			
4			
5			

Translating Customer Feedback to Your Scorecard

On the following page you will find a chart that may help you translate your customer interviews into a scorecard.

Supplier	Our Process	Products/Services We Provide	Key Customers	Contact Person	Key Issues/Questions to Ask	How to Measure Progress
1						
2						
3						
4						
5						

Helping Suppliers Succeed

For the entire quality management chain to fulfill the objective of serving the end-use customer, it is critical that you give your suppliers high quality feedback. You want to give the feedback in the sincere spirit of helping them to succeed. You cannot succeed without them. Therefore a spirit of cooperation with your suppliers is critical to pleasing your customers!

The traditional relationship between customers and suppliers went something like this: *"I'm paying them good money to send me first quality goods. If they can't do it, then I'll find someone who can!"* This attitude assumed that a supplier could fulfill all of your requirements if they really just "wanted to." Good guys want to; bad guys don't. If they're good guys, they don't need to hear from me. If they're bad guys, forget them!

What is the difficulty with this approach?

The problem with this attitude is that most suppliers want to do a good job just like most employees. When they don't, it is usually because they lack information or understanding. The information or understanding they lack most often needs to come from their customer.

You are a supplier to some type of customer in your delivery chain. You want the best possible feedback from your customers so that you can do a good job for them. Your suppliers are no different. This is a case where the Golden Rule is very appropriate. Just as you would like to receive helpful feedback, be sure that you give helpful feedback to your suppliers.

The highest quality companies today are developing long-term relationships based on mutual trust, respect, helpfulness, and shared economic interests. These relationships include as much positive feedback as negative. Suppliers are often involved in both long-term planning and short term problem solving with their customers. Look for ways to involve your suppliers in your team meetings so that they will have a clearer idea of how they impact your work.

Exercise: Identifying Suppliers and Requirements

Your team should discuss the following questions:

1. Who are the suppliers for our primary process? Who provides the primary input?

2. Who are the suppliers of information, materials, training, assistance, etc.?

3. For each supplier who are the key contact people with whom we should communicate?

4. List each supplier, the input received, and the specific requirement for quality input. The requirements should include quantity, specifications, timeliness, flexibility, responsiveness, etc.

5. Discuss how we can improve our feedback to each of these suppliers.

Supplier Feedback Analysis

Key Suppliers	Contact Person	Products or Services Provided to Our Team	Requirements: Time, Cost, Quality, Accessibility, etc.	Feedback Mechanism
1				
2				
3				
4				
5				

Action Assignment

Meet with your team, and be sure that you have developed and committed to an action plan to improve your response to customers and your feedback to suppliers. Action plans include *who* will do *what* by *when*. Answer the following specific questions:

1. List your three to five primary customers. Has your team interviewed them to help define their requirements? If not, who will conduct interviews? By what date will they be completed? Consider assigning each customer to one or two team members as an sme (subject matter expert) function.

_____

_____

_____

_____

_____

2. Define how you will track your performance to your customers. Will all team members be able to see this feedback?

_____

_____

_____

_____

_____

3. List your three to five key suppliers. Have you defined your requirements for these suppliers? If not, develop these requirements and decide how you will provide feedback on a regular schedule. Who will do this? Consider making a team member responsible for supplier communication.

_____

_____

_____

_____

_____

Implementation Tips

1. Help teams understand the implication of being customer-focused even if they have no direct contact with an external, *paying* customer.

2. Often teams resist the concept of having an internal customer because they equate *supplier* to mean *server* or *servant*, therefore, somehow working at the whims of their internal customer. If the terminology bothers them, try using other jargon such as *partnering* or having a *user* of your service. The key here is <u>everyone</u> needs to have a "customer mentality" of collectively serving the external customer, and every team needs a very clear understanding of how their work affects people down the line.

3. Be careful not to get bogged down in trying to interview too many customers. Focus on the key few who receive most of your work.

4. Don't try to devise the world's most perfect assessment instrument to interview your customers. If you talk to them openly, they will tell you how they feel. Just be sure to leave the interview with a <u>clear understanding of their requirements</u>. Sometimes team members will return with feedback on how the team is perceived but no clear understanding of what the customer is looking for in the future.

5. Identifying customers and customer satisfaction measures for managerial teams is often a complicated task. These teams need to look *horizontally* at teams who receive their work and ask, "What unique value does our team add to the output?" Frequently what results from this type of analysis is that the management team sees the employee teams as the *customer* and the services provided are such things as coordination, timely response to requests, clear vision and goals for the team, and allocation of resources.

If you identify your boss as your primary customer, it often results in increased paperwork, slower response time, and the cementing of bureaucratic practices.

While the shareholders and the corporate headquarters are considered a type of customer or stakeholder, they would best be served by everyone's paying most attention to his impact on the external, paying customer.

6. Be very aware of cultural sensitivity when interviewing customers. In our global economy, many teams may have both foreign customers and suppliers. Being well educated about cultural mores before the interview is critical to ensuring a clear understanding of requirements and to avoid offending anyone.

Chapter Four

Developing Scorecards

Team members must have accurate facts about their performance. They must gather data, increase their knowledge of performance to help them improve, and celebrate their success.

Objectives

1. To identify types and sources of feedback that can help guide the team.

2. To help teams develop balanced scorecards.

3. To help teams develop meaningful visual displays of their performance.

Why Keep Score?

Can any team perform at its best without knowing how it's performing - without feedback, without a scorecard?

It is unlikely.

In sports athletes have a passion for numbers, an intense desire to know how well they are doing. Golfers carry scorecards in their back pockets, marking down the score at each hole and computing whether they are currently ahead or behind their previous performance on this course. It is the fun of the game.

Games are little more than work with intense scorekeeping, self-management, and immediate celebration added.

Imagine a job so mindless that all the worker is asked to do is run around in circles, sweat, ache, pant, and suffer. Any fool could do this job. In fact if one is to continue doing anything so totally lacking in creativity, novelty, or decision-making, it's best that the applicant be a fool. However we discover that doctors, machine operators, executives, teachers, and others who otherwise appear intelligent, engage in this work. In addition we find that they do it without being paid.

Of course this activity does have the benefit of keeping the body strong, but the participants actually report that they enjoy this work. What is there to enjoy? It is amazing what some people will do of their own free will.

To runners keeping score is not work; it is a game. They report that they not only enjoy but often love this activity. Why is this fact true?

Runners who continue running will keep score. They may keep a log of their efforts, a graph or chart of the number of miles per week, minutes per mile, and/or cumulative miles per week or month. Break last month's record! Set a new record for miles in a week. Set a new record for best time over a three-mile course. And all of this scorekeeping has nothing to do with beating an opponent. It has nothing to do with applause from the stands. It is entirely for the purpose of self-management and self-enjoyment.

Motivation is one benefit of a good scorekeeping system. But there are others.

Twenty years ago players and coaches around the National Football League made jokes about the Dallas Cowboys and coach Tom Landry's computer. The Cowboys were the first NFL team to use a computer to gather and analyze data. There were numerous kinds of data. Some of the data was used to predict opponents' offensive and defensive plays. Other data was on the Cowboys themselves. No one is joking anymore! Today, every team uses computers to track their athletes' performance.

The best-coached athletic teams provide the best feedback to their players. Several years ago, one of our associates consulted with the Chicago White Sox. They had begun to collect data on a computer, but they made minimal use of it. We helped them establish a feedback system for each player based on the identification of key performance variables for his position, previous performance for himself, and for other players in the league. That year the Chicago White Sox won the pennant.

The Cowboys and the White Sox analyzed the data to find opportunities for improvement. Then they coached, taught, and helped the players where it was needed. Each position involved different performance criteria. For example how many seconds the quarterback took to release the ball is a measure of performance for that position. Knowing that his average release time is greater or less than last year or another quarterback's helps. It lets him know what to work on. Similarly, on every play, the wide receiver's coach will time the twenty-yard dash

71

which the receiver runs down the sidelines, independent of whether the play involves a pass. Consistency in this performance increases the probability of catching the ball when it is thrown and increases the ability of running backs to get through the defense.

As we have described, a second use of scorekeeping is to enhance **analysis for problem solving**, **coaching**, and **improvement**.

There is a third function or effect of scorekeeping. Scorekeeping not only affects individual motivation; it also affects how groups work together and how they feel towards each other. Group scores create common purpose and social unity within the group.

For many years in the factory, incentive systems have been based on individual performance. Industrial engineers studied the potential and actual performance in individual jobs, and individual performance ratings were established for managers. This was consistent with the increasingly specialized or fragmented nature of work.

The greater the management focus on individual scores, the greater the number of problems involving poor cooperation or poor teamwork.

Several years ago Red Auerbach, the Boston Celtics' owner, one of the most successful sports franchises ever, said that he never judged a basketball player by how many points he scored. He judged him by how much he contributed to the team. Not only did the Boston Celtics win as a team; they also had some of the greatest individual players ever to play the game!

Red Auerbach recognized that basketball required intense teamwork, helping each other, and sacrificing for each other. Selfish players, concerned about how many points they personally scored, did not belong on the Celtics. Scoring was based on concerted individual performances. Passing, rebounding, and playing de-

Scorekeeping Helps

✔ **Motivation**

✔ **Analysis of Performance**

✔ **Common Purpose**

fense were equally important. By de-emphasizing individual numbers and emphasizing the team's score, Auerbach was managing the behavior and attitudes of his players. He was focusing them on that which was important.

If you ever want to turn monotonous or boring tasks into fun events, try setting up scorecards and rewards for performance. Experiment with your children on tasks they resist like cleaning their rooms or doing homework or yardwork. You may be surprised at the difference in their behavior.

Another function of scorekeeping is to direct effort and focus performance. Team scores *create common purpose and common effort.*

Using Scorecards for Performance Feedback

Providing feedback means giving information to an individual or group about their performance. A scorekeeping system is a mechanism for continuously providing feedback in a timely and meaningful manner. When the feedback is translated into an objective, measurable, and often visual form, it becomes a scorekeeping system.

Every team must know how it's performing. If a team is to manage its responsibilities like a small business, it must establish a performance measurement system to provide itself with timely and useful performance feedback.

Like any business, a team has customers, suppliers, and a process to manage. It needs tracking. Tracking performance should be developed to help employees know their score, not to impose control from above. Control from above becomes unnecessary when the team accepts responsibility for their own performance monitoring.

The team's scorekeeping system is a critical element of the PLAN-DO-CHECK-ACT (PDCA) cycle. It provides the team with the information necessary for them to plan or solve problems. It provides a check on their results of performance. And it provides the information required for further action.

Developing Performance Feedback into a Scorekeeping System

A scorekeeping system is a method of providing regular, ongoing feedback about performance to the team. Feedback is extremely effective in improving performance. A review of eighteen studies on feedback in the *National Productivity Review* (Winter 1982-83) reported that objective performance indicators increased after providing feedback in each case. These increases ranged from 6% to 125%, with a median increase of 53%.

Here are some examples of effective scorekeeping systems:

Scorekeeping in a White Collar Environment

A product accountant in the headquarters' location of a major energy corporation wanted accounting personnel to increase their on-time submission of financial data. Each month closing and balancing data were late coming to her. For headquarters this resulted in overtime and delays in forwarding closing information to the Vice President of Refining. Since she did not directly supervise the location accountants, she felt helpless and frustrated in her attempts to get their cooperation. She believed that professionals should want to do their best, which included sending her the data on time. Although they seemed friendly and competent enough on the telephone, each month was a problem. They seemed to resist cooperating fully with her. The working relationship was not strong and healthy.

The accountant's objective was to (1) improve on-time submission of monthly financial data and (2) improve the headquarters-location relationships.

The headquarters' accountant set up a chart for herself to check when the data was received.

The headquarters' office notified the location counterpart when the data was received. Care was taken to avoid comparing on-time performance of the locations. Comparing locations was thought to be antagonistic to improving the working relationship.

When the location data came in on time or early, the headquarters' accountant made a personal telephone call to reinforce verbally the location accountant. Headquarters emphasized a team effort. The message of appreciation stressed that the location professional was helping the headquarters' accountant to do her job more productively. When a location had three to four months of on-time data submission, headquarters sent the location accounting supervisor a memo highlighting the excellent cooperation of the location's accounting staff. The location staff member received a copy of the memo.

After three months of this approach, the accountant reported an eighty-five percent improvement in response time. She began sharing her scorecard with peers and noted that several began volunteering their information, thus eliminating the need for her to make phone calls.

Scorekeeping in a Manufacturing Environment

In the assembly department of a can manufacturing plant, controlling the amount of scrap produced was a key objective. Teams posted graphs on a large bulletin board showing the cost of scrap produced for each manufacturing line on a daily and weekly basis. Each graph had a colored band showing a target level of scrap costs and a line showing actual performance. Daily highlights of scrap performance for each line were written on a flipchart by the department head. The department met its scrap goal for the first time in years.

A plant that rebuilds diesel engines provided training for every employee in accounting. Every employee was on a team, and each team had a monthly profit-and-loss statement for their department. At their monthly meeting they discussed cost variances, cost increases, and cost reduction. They were also paid bonuses based on their team's financial performance. This same plant also has flashing signs that report daily production, new records set, and other "news" about performance.

Guidelines for Developing Scorecards

Whether working in a blue or white collar environment, there are a number of issues that a team should consider in designing effective scorecards:

1. Select a performance that is important. There is no point in creating a feedback system for performance that does not contribute significantly to team goals. In designing your scorecard, try to stick to five to ten key performance indicators for your team, reflecting both customer satisfaction and team efficiency.

2. Define the performance in a measurable way. For example percent of files updated on schedule, average turnaround time on data entry priority jobs, costs per unit produced, and rework are all items to be considered.

3. Define the performance in units most meaningful to the team. For example department-wide productivity may not be as meaningful to a team member as a team cost-control measure.

4. Measurement should be frequent enough so that team members can use the data to improve performance or solve problems quickly. For example quarterly feedback is not likely to influence daily outputs or behaviors.

5. Be consistent. Discuss scorecards at scheduled intervals rather than only when you happen to notice a problem. Consistent, periodic feedback is more likely to be objective and prompts both positive and negative feedback.

6. Design scorecards to track desirable behavior whenever possible. Traditionally we do not share information unless there is a problem. Therefore feedback is often negative. In sports most reports of numbers, records set, highest number of yards run, etc., are positive statements. Work is fun and motivating when the numbers are stated positively. Rather than absenteeism, the number should be attendance. Rather than percent with defects, the number should be percent perfect.

7. Scorecards are most powerful when visually displayed. Often performance graphs have a great deal of impact because they are easy to read. Past trends, current performance, and goals can be seen at a glance. Put your important performance measures on your scorecard.

Building a Scorecard

A team scorecard is composed of five to ten key measures that reflect the team's performance. Teams must balance the demands of their customers with delivering their outputs as cost effectively as possible. In building a scorecard, teams should consider measures that include both business and financial results as well as customer satisfaction. Total quality must include the team's ability to compete in business. This means delivering what the customer wants while staying as profitable as possible. In other words you might produce the highest quality shoes in the world with absolute perfection in all materials and workmanship; however, your rate of production might be so low and your costs so high that no one could afford to pay for them. You would be out of business quickly. It is important that teams take a total view of their performance. Therefore each team is encouraged to have a balanced scorecard.

Business and Financial Measures

The first measure of business results is revenue. Many teams are now receiving balance sheets for their team's area of responsibility. Teams with responsibility for broad processes can usually define revenue measures; those with a more narrow focus may not.

Many team members are not accustomed to looking at the costs of their operation. This task has traditionally been the manager's job. Unfortunately both managers and employees have accepted this situation. The assumption that employees always want to spend money to buy a new piece of equipment or add another person to their staff, and that managers are always seeking to reduce their costs, guarantees an adversarial relationship between employees and managers.

When employees are given good information, they will act to improve costs just as they will act to improve quality. It is our experience that employees will become more cost conscious

and often more conservative than managers if they are given this responsibility. This responsibility often requires a change in the system of sharing information. This system change is essential to achieve total quality and total involvement.

Quantity, also known as rate of output or productivity, should not be ignored as an important measure. Several years ago there was great attention paid to productivity improvement. In recent years quality has been the most important focus. However quality and productivity should be viewed as equal partners. Both are components of total quality. The ability to produce efficiently is just as important today as it was in the past.

Customer Satisfaction Measures

Every process has a cycle time. The cycle time begins when input enters the first step or activity of the process and continues until the process is completed. Long cycle times often result in cost overruns and missed deadlines to customers. Reducing cycle time often enables you to respond more quickly to customer demands.

In the previous chapter we discussed the importance of defining quality in terms of customer satisfaction and specifications of the customer's requirements. If you have not done so, your team should consider developing a customer survey or establishing some other type of direct feedback from your internal and external customers.

The most traditional view of quality has been that of meeting defined specifications or standards for product attributes or characteristics. The importance of conforming to specifications has not diminished. You may produce a product or service that meets design and production specifications but does not meet customer requirements. An automobile may be perfectly reliable, but accelerate only from zero to sixty in fifteen seconds, which is sluggish performance. Every car of that make and model is identical, and all specifications as defined by engineers are being met. In other words there are no defects. The problem is that the customer's requirements are not met. First you must know the customer's requirements, and then you must define specifications that meet those requirements. Meeting specifications then becomes the key element of quality.

Building A Scorecard

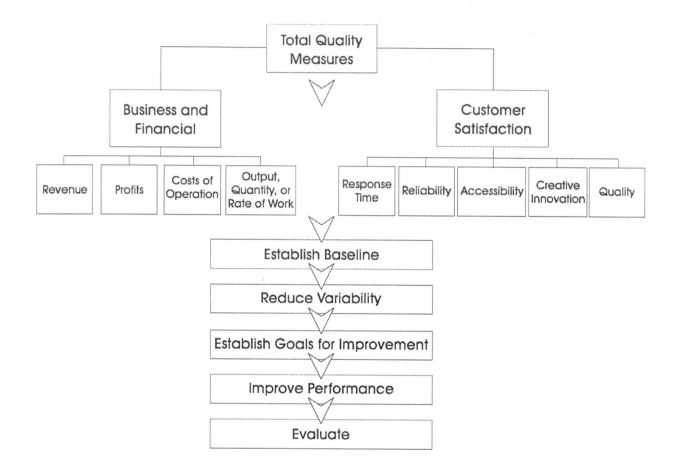

Where to Start Building Your Scorecard

Look at any of the current methods you have for measuring your team's work. Assess your current performance measures to see if they fit the criteria listed on page seventy-five for developing effective team scorecards. Once you start building your team's scorecard, you will have a better sense of how to translate your customer feedback into performance measures. *Don't wait until you've completed all your customer interviews and analyzed your key work processes to begin building your scorecard.* Many of these steps in the team process can occur simultaneously.

Most teams already know something about one half of their balanced scorecard. They generally have some measure of their team's output and the costs associated with it. This will give you a place to begin your visual display of team performance.

Quantitative & Qualitative Scores

When we think of scorecards, we are most likely to think of quantitative scores. Numbers are a wonderful thing. They appear to be so objective. Our score went from ninety-five to ninety-eight! An increase of three points is clear and unarguable.

While this is true, there are other facts just as important and just as factual, yet not so easily quantifiable. If a customer in a restaurant "feels" that the service was poor, it may be the result of many things. It may be the result of a waiter or waitress who did not smile or did not look the customer in the eye when talking to him. The customer may not be sure why he felt the service was poor; yet the way the customer "feels" is just as important as any number.

Of course we could gather quantifiable numbers on how many people felt this way; then we would have numbers, and we could put them on a graph. However those numbers would not define the problem. We would have to analyze the behavior that led to the feeling of discomfort on the part of the customer. It would be best if we had this information from the first customer who felt this way.

Sources of Information

From Customers

In the previous chapter you identified your customers and initiated a process of defining customer needs and gathering feedback from your customers. If you did not do this, you should return to the assignment in chapter three. Your team's success depends on it!

Remember that your customer is the answer to the question, "Where does my work go, and why is it important?" Your customers may be either internal or external, and feedback from both is important. Often your internal customers have the best feedback on the results of your team's performance because they have the clearest view of that work. If they have to touch your product, add to it, bottle, package, or combine your product, they will have far better knowledge of your work than the final or external customer. The external customer sees the result of the combined work of many teams. While feedback for the external customer is valuable, it is likely to be less specific and immediate than feedback from the internal customer.

The total work process is a chain of customers and suppliers. You are one link in that chain. The breaking of one link is a break in the entire chain. To keep your link strong, there are three things you must do. First ensure that you are giving your suppliers good feedback so they can improve their process; second improve your own process; and third ask for feedback from your customers.

Results of the Process/Outputs

The most traditional form of quality checking is to measure the results of your entire process before your output ever reaches the external customer. The work is completed and then checked at the end of the production line. Reliance on this process alone fails to catch errors as they happen, so how can team members take responsibility for improving their own work? Still we should not rule out use of inspection at the end of the process.

Honda of America, a company well known for high quality, has a quality checking process at the end of the assembly line. They do find defects that need correcting after some cars are produced. However they have relatively few of these "after process" failures because every "associate" or team member is responsible for finding and correcting problems on the line <u>within</u> the process. The more this responsibility is accepted, the fewer defects are found at the end of the process.

Within the Process

Teams should not wait for someone to find problems after their process is complete. They should monitor and collect scores on each step in the process. If each step is free of variation, there will be few performance problems at the end of the process. If they are improving each operation, the entire process will be improved.

Imagine that you are building an engine. There are the measurements of how well the engine runs once it is completely built. However when the piston rings are placed around the pistons, the tightness can be measured. When the pistons are placed within the cylinder block, the resistance when they move up and down the cylinder can be measured. Virtually every step in the process of building the engine can be measured, statistics gathered to determine whether or not the process is in control, and feedback provided to those doing the work or to the supplier at the previous operation.

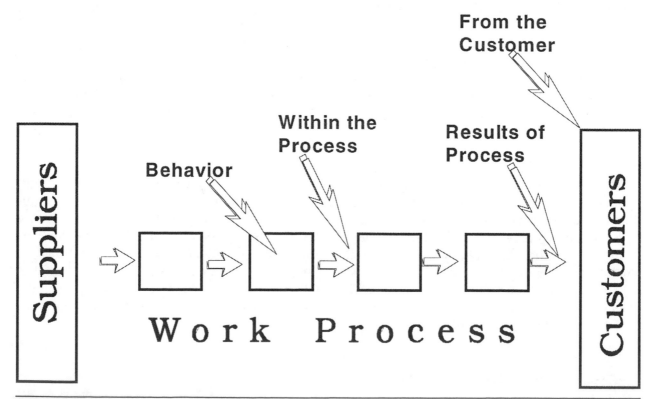

Your team should discuss each operation or step in your total process. Where is the greatest opportunity for improvement? What measures would be most useful?

Behavior or Activity

In some cases it is most helpful to give feedback on actual behavior rather than the effect of that behavior on an operation. For example if you have a team of waiters and waitresses, you may have feedback on the customer's feelings about the service they received. This feedback is helpful, but it may not pinpoint the behavior which may need to be changed. The trained manager or team member may see that a waiter never smiles, never jokes, or does not offer suggestions. These are specific behaviors that the customer may never identify. They are, however, the most useful type of feedback for the waiter if the goal is to help him improve.

Behavioral feedback is often the most useful in sales organizations. The manager or another team member may accompany a salesperson on a call. The result of the process is the decision by the customer. However the decision is the result of many things, including the behavior of the salesperson.

Whether or not the salesperson nods his head in agreement, offers suggestions, asks open-ended questions, and asks for the order are all important behaviors that result in success. It is not helpful for the coach who observes the sales call simply to say, "You just didn't seem that interested in the order," or "You didn't seem very enthusiastic." It is more helpful to know exactly what you did or did not do that would change these impressions.

This is also true in technical operations. How information is computed, how engineers draw plans, or how researchers compile information are all specific behaviors. If the success or failure of your work output is highly dependent on how well your team works together, you might want to track the effectiveness of your team meetings as an element of your scorecard.

Your team should discuss which behaviors are critical in your operation and those for which it would be helpful to have feedback.

BUILDING A BALANCED SCORECARD
WORKSHEET

Business Indices:

Performance Indicator	Measure for Team	Source of Data	Comparison/ Goal
1. Volume	lbs/hour	Production report	2,000 lbs/hour
2. Costs	$/man-hour	MIS report	20% reduction

Customer Satisfaction Indices:

Performance Indicator	Measure for Team	Source of Data	Goal
1. Turnaround time	# of hours request is in department	Log sheet	Avg. of two hours turnaround per request
2. Project completion on-time within budget	Man-hours and milestone completion	Project planning timeline and hours logged	To come in on-time, under budget

The Practical Side of Scorecards

In building your teams scorecards, don't expect to find five or six "perfect" measures that tell the complete story of your work output. Realize that the team will need to look at the scorecard as a "family of measures" that needs examination as a whole to get a complete picture. Try out different performance measures and experiment until you find a set that are meaningful to your team.

White Collar Measurement Systems

Often development of scorecards for teams of white collar workers, especially the "knowledge" worker, poses special problems. While some white collar jobs are very consistent with the factory floor because the work itself follows a repetitive process and is measurable, there are other jobs that are non-repetitive and are very difficult to measure. For example measuring the work of a team of claims processors in an insurance company would be significantly easier than measuring the work of a new product development team in a computer company. White collar work falls into five categories:

The **"Factory"** which includes work such as processing functions and data entry.

The **"Support Functions"** which include work such as planning, scheduling, training, marketing, and maintenance.

"Recurring Projects" which include such things as monthly reports, billing, accounting, and payroll.

"Quick Response Projects" such as special reports, ad campaigns, or customer service response.

"Long-Term Projects" such as research, product development, and exploration.

Each of the categories requires different types of measurement systems. To give you some ideas of where to begin thinking about these areas, we offer some examples of measures for each category:

The Factory
Output Per Hour
Unit Cost of Processing
Errors/Rejects
Time

The Support Function
On-Time Delivery of Service
Response Rates
Customer Results/Satisfaction
Customer Complaints

Recurring Projects
Time of Task Completion
Quality/Accuracy
Rework
Complaints
Staff Utilization

Quick Response Projects
Frequency of Utilization
Backlog of Requests
Errors
Customer Satisfaction
Timeliness
Response Time
Cost of Service
Cost to Plan

Long-Term Projects
Project Schedule Adherence
Budget Compliance
Customer Satisfaction
Errors in Completion Steps/Rework
Cycle Time for Decisions

Maximizing the Effectiveness of Your Scorecards

Deciding how best to present your performance data is important to making your scorecards meaningful and motivational to your team. The following should help the team determine how to best gather and present the data so that it is helpful in continuously improving their performance.

Sources of Comparison

System Performance

Every system, whether it is a restaurant making pizza, an airline flying airplanes, or a sales organization, produces a pattern of data. Teams must understand this pattern to analyze their performance.

No team produces "straight line" performance. In other words a sales organization may average one hundred sales per day, but it will be a rare day on which they will sell one hundred units. And it will be almost impossible for them to sell one hundred units each and every day. One day they will sell one hundred and five, the next ninety-seven, the next one hundred and two, the next ninety-three, and so forth. It averages one hundred. The pattern within this system is a normal distribution or normal variability. This variability typically forms a bell-shaped curve with approximately half of the days falling below the mean of one hundred and about half above with the greatest number of days falling close to 100.

The normal, random causes of variation within this system we call "common cause." In other words if the manager asks, "But how come today the sales team only sold ninety-seven units if the mean is one hundred? It is obviously poor performance." The only sensible answer is that nothing is wrong; it is normal variability within the system. It is simply random performance. In other words if everything is held constant and there are no changes or anything unusual influencing performance, you will see this amount of variation. It is also true that when the performance is at one hundred and five, there is nothing especially good happening either. It too is random performance within the system.

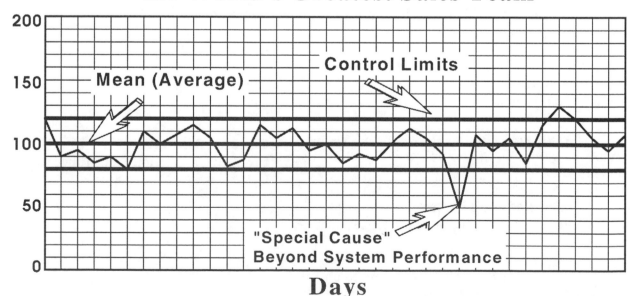

Number of Units Sold by the World's Greatest Sales Team

It is useful to compare performance in units of time (hours, days, weeks, or months) regularly to understand the normal distribution. This is the essence of statistical process control. Knowing the normative statistics, the distribution, you can define upper and lower control limits. For example if our sales organization one day sells fifty units when the pattern generally falls between ninety and one hundred and ten, it is clear that this performance indicates that something outside of the system has occurred. There is a variance, a special cause. Something abnormal has influenced the performance of this system.

Now it will make sense to problem solve the cause of this "special cause" variance. Why has it happened? It cannot be explained by the common cause variation within the system.

There are two types of improvements in performance. First is the elimination of special causes or variances from system performance. The second type is improvement in the system to raise the mean or normative standard of performance, often called a "breakthrough." In both cases, it will be helpful to have information that lets you know what is normal for the system.

Competitive Benchmarks

Even though your system may be perfectly under control, and you have eliminated all special causes of variation, performance may still be mediocre compared to competitive organizations. You may have a football team on which every running back averages 2.8 yards per carry. In fact they run this amount on practically every play. This is certainly good information to have. But, is it adequate performance? Is it great performance? No!

In order to know whether your team's performance is great, you need sources of com-

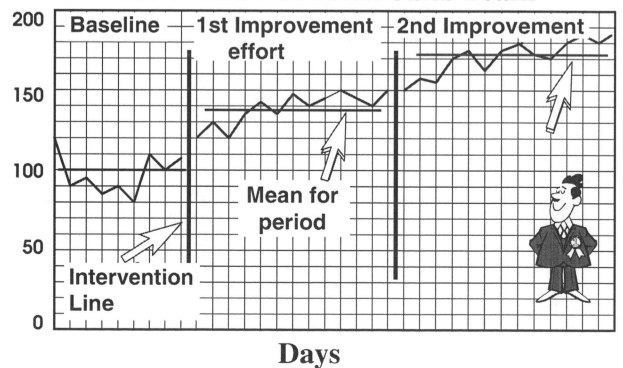

Number of Units Sold by the World's Greatest Sales Team

parison. The best sources of comparison are benchmarks from the highest quality companies or teams doing similar work. If you discover that some other team doing similar work has figured out a way to achieve superior performance, your team then needs to learn why and then seek to better their own performance. You can gain important benchmarking information from your customers, from research sources, and often from the competition themselves!

Previous Performance

Another very useful source of comparison will be comparing your own team's performance over time. A run chart plots performance on a daily or weekly basis. Every team will want to develop a couple of charts with their key performance variables (quality, productivity, and cost) and maintain these charts over time to determine whether their performance is improving or not.

While comparing your performance with others is interesting, everyone, even the best, can improve. If you are far below other teams, you should not focus your energies on how far below you are. Rather, focus on improving over your own previous performance. Improving your own performance is the most realistic focus for any team.

Visual Display

The idea of visually displaying performance is so simple it seems that it would be worth little discussion. However displays are one of the most powerful influences on performance, one of the most powerful ways to provide feedback, and one of the most powerful ways to help the team improve its performance.

A graph is easy to understand. We have worked in manufacturing plants where many of the employees could not read or write. Yet they could easily understand a graph that displayed the rise and fall of performance figures. They could get excited about improvement and feel unhappy about declines in performance.

Every issue of *The Wall Street Journal* contains charts and graphs. Every financial report uses graphs. Why? The reason is not because the readers are incapable of reading and understanding lists of numbers but because a graph can be understood immediately! It simply communicates more effectively than numbers or words alone.

Graphs create an emotional reaction. When performance declines, the team will have an emotional reaction. When it goes up, they will be prompted to celebrate.

The larger, more colorful the graph, the greater the impact on performance. We have all seen the United Way thermometer in front of our community bank or in the lobby of our work place. This is a good example of a graph designed to create motivation. Imagine if it were only black and white, and a small 8" x 11" graph posted on a cluttered bulletin board.

If the graph represents important performance, it is important for people to see it vividly presented and often. One company with which we worked was striving to reach a billion dollar revenue goal. Is it possible to involve every employee in excitement around reaching such a revenue goal? Most of the employees in this organization worked on computer terminals. Each morning when they turned the computer on there was a picture of a mountain, Mt. Billion, with a little mountain climber climbing up the side of the mountain. His progress up the summit equated with the company's progress toward the one billion dollar goal.

Graphs focus our attention on trends (upward or downward movement) and ranges (spreads between the highest and lowest points). Focusing on trends allows us to evaluate performance in the context of past performance and to predict future performance. Focusing on ranges lets us determine how stable or variable our performance is.

Graphs help us look at relationships between events and performance. Does training help a particular performance? We should be able to determine an answer by graphing baseline data, providing training, then observing the trend of the performance data following this interven-

tion. If training is effective in this case, the graph should show a positive change following training. If training is ineffective, the trend or performance should not change. Graphs make the relationships between such interventions and performance very apparent.

Graphs help us think clearly!

There are thousands of creative ways to make performance visible. The most common and practical in most work settings is simply posting graphs of the team's performance in the team's work area. They should have immediate access to their graphs. It is their performance, and it should be immediately visible to them.

Tips on Graphing

Graphs should be clear and simple. A graph with more than two or three lines becomes difficult to read.

If possible, a graph should be designed so that "up is good." Improvement in performance should result in an upward trend on the graph.

If the performance graph is to be used as a feedback device, it should be big and colorful. Low-tech graphs done with markers on flipcharts are often more effective than spreadsheet generated graphs. A good test is can the graph be read at a glance from anywhere in the work area?

If you are posting a feedback graph, be sure to explain what its purpose is and how to read it. Also be sure to post a feedback graph in a well-traveled area where people will see it.

Since the graph will be used to provide feedback, the scale should be drawn so that small increases and decreases are easily noticeable.

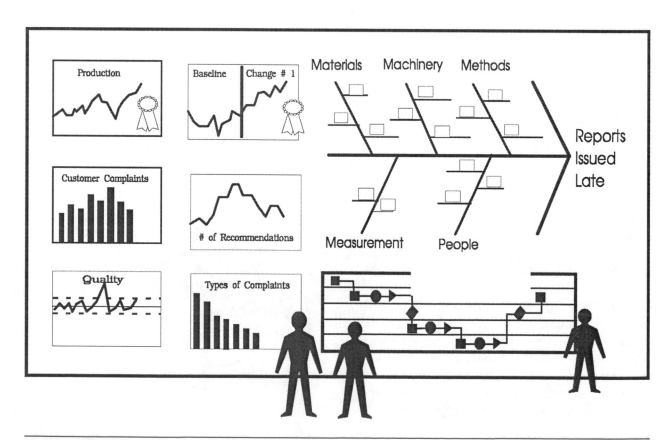

A good model to follow for designing your feedback graphs is:

1. **Title of graph**. Every graph should have a title.

2. **The vertical axis** of the graph is usually for the performance.

3. **The horizontal axis** of the graph has the time intervals of the measurement.

4. **The baseline data** is the data collected before the intervention in order to identify the current level of performance.

5. **The baseline average**. The mean average of the baseline data can be calculated for easy reference.

6. **The intervention line**. The intervention line is the heavy vertical line drawn on the graph to mark the date on which an intervention was begun.

7. **The goal line**, labeled with the numeric goal, shows the desired level of performance.

8. **Control limits**. If appropriate, control limits should be added to the graph.

Different Types of Graphs

Trend Charts

Most of the graphs and charts that you have seen are probably trend charts. If you look in the financial section of the newspaper, you will often see trend charts of economic indicators such as inflation or stock prices charted over time. In the workplace, you may see trend charts of company orders, orders sent out on time, attendance, and other performance measures.

By looking at a trend chart, you can immediately gain an understanding of the essential characteristics of that performance. Is it going up or down? Have there been periodic changes, such as seasonal changes? Does it vary greatly or slightly? All of these questions can be answered almost immediately by looking at a trend chart. Trend charts can help a team further analyze a problem. It will also help a team determine whether the problem has been solved.

A trend chart...

Is a graph that visually represents performance over time.

Lets us know how the environment is affecting performance to date.

Shows us baseline performance.

Shows us the trends and variability of performance.

Control Charts

Below you can see a statistical control chart. A control chart plots the data over time and indicates a mean for that set of data. For example the number of phone calls answered each working hour; the number of parts produced per day, week, or month; or the percentage of on-time shipments or deliveries can all be plotted with the mean indicated. A quick glance at a control chart can tell you a great deal. You can see the normal range within which the data points fall. Within three standard deviations is generally performance within the systems' capability. The upper (UCL) and lower (LCL) control limits are plotted so that you can quickly see if a data point is outside of the range which is considered normal system performance.

If performance is occurring outside of the control limits, we can say there is a problem that must be solved. If the system is in control, we can then ask how the system performance can be improved, either by reducing the variability, or by increasing the overall level of performance.

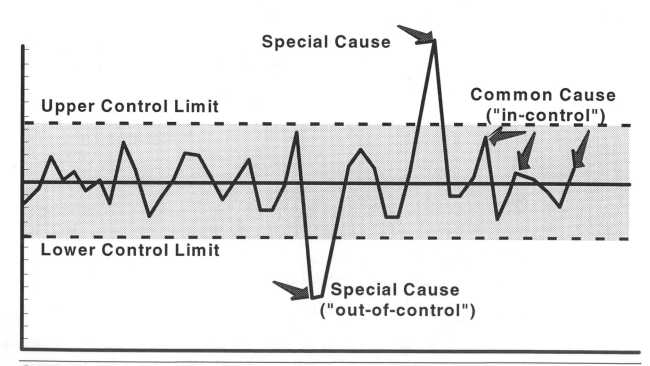

© 1994 Miller/Howard Consulting Group, Inc.

Using Scorecards In Team Meetings

The scorecards that are developed for the team should become the focus of each team meeting. The meetings are designed to enable the teams to do a more effective job of managing their piece of the business by continuously improving their work processes.

These scorecards, whether tracking outputs, costs, behaviors, or processes, all serve as indicators of how the team is performing. The team meetings are designed to allocate specific time for the group to work on analyzing and improving their work.

A Note to Management

Integration of Team Scorecards

Once the teams have made their initial attempts at a balanced scorecard, it is then important that there be some integration and alignment. This should be done in two primary ways: horizontal and vertical alignment.

Vertical

The most senior team develops their critical success areas for the business and for the way that their team will measure these. These will generally fall into the categories of productivity (volume, sales, etc.), profitability (return on capital employed), and customer satisfaction (quality of product, speed of delivery, responsiveness of service). Then each team throughout the organization will pick measures that will impact these areas and eventually "roll-up" to cause the entire organization to meet their goals.

Horizontal

Because the work process typically flows from one department to the next in a supplier-customer chain, it is important that the scorecards of each horizontal link are also aligned. These links make the customer-supplier teams become "partners" in serving an external customer.

In this analysis of horizontal and vertical integration, there often surfaces structure and system misalignment. The senior managers of the organization often have to make decisions about restructuring some teams and determining if there are unnecessary layers of management or redundancies of work. Structure and system misalignments can be addressed throughout the implementation of the team process or by introducing a design team (see Miller's *Whole System Architecture* manual).

Action Assignment

1. Have your team name five to eight key measures they feel reflect a balanced view of their work. They should include both business and customer satisfaction measures.

_____

_____

_____

_____

_____

_____

_____

_____

2. Using the **Building a Balanced Scorecard** worksheet, determine the performance indicator, measure, source of data, and goal for your team's scorecard.

3. Determine a tracking method and design a visual display for each of your key performance scores to review in your team meetings.

Implementation Tips

Whether working with white collar knowledge workers or employees on the factory floor, follow these steps to build a team scorecard.

1. **Define the team**, process, or project which will have its progress tracked. The focus is on the team rather than the individual.

2. Identify the **purpose** of the measurement system. What is being tracked and why? How does it fit into the business strategy and meet customers' needs?

3. Teams should be **involved** in identifying their own measures. Teams should meet to brainstorm and reach consensus on the team's measures.

4. Teams should identify their measures in the context of their **purpose and key objectives.** The purpose and objectives should clearly describe what the team should accomplish (effectiveness) and the resources which the team uses (efficiency). Upper-level teams and customers should be involved in defining the team's purpose and objectives. The definition of purpose and customer interviews should help the team's identification of its measures.

5. The team should expect to identify a **family of measures**, each of which describes an element of the team's performance rather than a single, all-encompassing measure. The family of measures should reflect quality, customer service, productivity, cost, timeliness, and other elements linked to the team's objectives.

6. Teams should focus on **ratios** as indicators of team performance. For example percent of milestones completed (number completed / number planned) vs. number of milestones completed.

7. Teams should review the **trend** of their performance over time as well as the **magnitude, direction, and trend** of the variances from the performance levels targeted in their objectives.

8. The team should choose the types of performance measures depending on its objectives and current problems. The types of performance measures include **behaviors, outputs, outcomes, point systems,** and **customer feedback surveys.**

9. Measures should be **customer** oriented, (not just focused on internal performance indicators), and as **objective** as possible.

10. Teams should **verify** the usefulness and clarity of their measures with their customers and the teams above them for **integration and alignment with the strategic business plan.**

Note: This is a critical step to getting teams focused on performance. Don't get bogged down in debate over individual measures or how many to track. Keep in mind the principles behind this: creating common focus; motivating the team; and improving performance.

Chapter Five

Managing the Process

Each team is responsible for a process which adds value to a final product or service. Each team must know and continuously improve its process in order to satisfy their customers.

Objectives

1. To define the process by which our team creates added value.

2. To analyze our process to eliminate quality variances.

3. To initiate the continuous improvement in our work process.

How Do We Do Our Work?

This seemingly simple question is the beginning of managing for quality. Once you have identified what work you are doing by talking to your customers and identifying your key products and services, then you can define how you are doing your work. What is our process? Before a team can improve its work, it must understand how its work is accomplished today. Then it must analyze the steps in the process to identify opportunities for improvement. Look to continuously improve the process rather than a single perfect solution.

What is a Process?

A process is a set of related work activities that are based on a set of inputs and result in outputs that have added value. In other words it is <u>how</u> we do our work.

Almost all work requires inputs. Stockbrokers require orders and information (inputs) in order to do their work (process) of making recommendations and placing orders. An engineering team requires the input of metallurgical or chemical specifications and statistics in order to do their work (process) of designing, calculating, or engineering their projects. Weavers in a textile weave room require the warp and bobbins of yarn and well-maintained equipment (inputs) in order to do their work (process) of weaving cloth.

Everyone engages in a work process. Presidents of corporations and countries, scientists, teachers, production workers, sales representatives, and homemakers - all have a work process. When the President of the United States is preparing his State of the Union address (output), he gathers opinions from his advisors (input), consults the opinion polls (input) and other sources of information, and then makes notes as to his priorities (process step 1). He then discusses his thoughts with his speech writer (step 2), who then develops a draft (step 3), etc. No one's work is too lofty or too menial to be defined as a process and analyzed for possible improvement.

Basic Elements of Any System

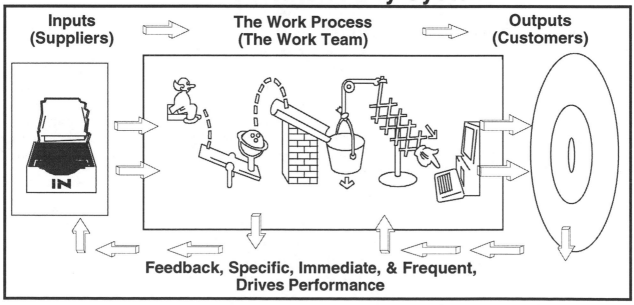

Inputs (Suppliers) → **The Work Process (The Work Team)** → **Outputs (Customers)**

Feedback, Specific, Immediate, & Frequent, Drives Performance

Focus on the Process, Not the Person

Almost always, people want to do a good job. When there is a problem, it may be the result of an individual who has inadequate skills or knowledge and who may need help to improve. However the need for improvement is often beyond the behavior of one person. More often it is the nature of the work process and of how people work together. For example, an exploration manager wants a report on his desk within two weeks. The geologist needs at least three weeks to analyze data which is frequently late getting to him from the field. By meeting the two week requirement, the information is limited and frequently incorrect. Also the process cannot be improved by blaming, punishing, or rewarding. It can be improved only by studying, analyzing, modifying, and studying further. It is usually individuals who are blamed. It requires a team working together to improve the work process.

Blaming creates fear, which reduces improvement efforts. Studying the process creates knowledge which increases improvement efforts. Improving the process is one of the most fundamental purposes of the team.

Macro Processes

The entire corporation is a process. Capital is received from the sale of stocks and bonds which is then invested in plants, equipment, and people, etc. Satisfied customers are the final result of the corporation's "macro" process.

Major activities such as how the corporation develops new products, how it develops people, and how it makes decisions to invest in new businesses all can be analyzed as a process.

It is an unfortunate fact of corporate life that the most important processes that determine the fate of the corporation and thousands of jobs are often among the most dysfunctional processes. In many cases, more effort has gone into analyzing how workers on the shop floor assemble widgets than how decisions are made to invest millions of dollars which may affect the business for a decade.

We worked with the senior team of financial officers of one of the top twenty largest industrial corporations to help them define the current process of developing the annual budget plan, which included spending billions of dollars. When these officers looked at the process which had been visually mapped out on the wall with all of the "recycles" identified and the nine months of time required, they all shook their heads in amazement and said, "Who designed this process? This is incredible; no wonder we can't get the budget done until the year is half over!"

This experience is common. No one designed their process! It just happened! Years of habits and individual decisions to add this person in the loop, add another check, add another report, add another review, obtain another signature, caused the system to gradually evolve without any real rationale. No one liked it, and everyone blamed someone else. No one was to blame. Everyone went along because, *"That's the way it's supposed to be done,"* or because, *"We've always done it that way."* These are the two most common and fatalistic explanations for a poor process.

These managers were able to redesign their process, reduce it to a few months, eliminate much wasted effort, recycling and redundancies, and produce a higher quality product at the same time. They found that when they eliminated wasted, non value-adding activity, they also eliminated causes of quality problems. This is true with management processes as well production processes.

This financial team presented their new process to the operating committee of the board of directors of the corporation for their approval. This company is rapidly gaining a reputation as a leader in the quality improvement field.

Current State Budget Process

1. Corporate planning staff tells the presidents of each division what financial contribution they are expected to make to the corporation.

2. The president reviews the budget and gives it to his planning staff to make allocations to each group V.P.

3. Planning group decides how to allocate the dollars and gives the figures to each V.P.

4. Group V.P.'s review numbers and decide they are unreasonable.

5. Group V.P.'s call in business unit managers to discuss numbers so they can determine what's accurate.

6. Business unit managers don't want to commit until they talk to their planning group.

7. Business unit managers meet with planning group and redraft budgets.

8. Budget is returned to V.P.

9. V.P. reviews new numbers with his planning group and makes more revisions.

10. New draft goes to division president.

11. Division president rejects new plan because it doesn't meet corporate goals.

12. Returns to V.P.'s to rework their numbers.

13. V.P.'s revise with business unit managers.

14. Business unit managers revise with planning group.

15. V.P. approves.

16. V.P.'s send to division president for approval.

17. President sends to corporate for approval.

Current Budget Process

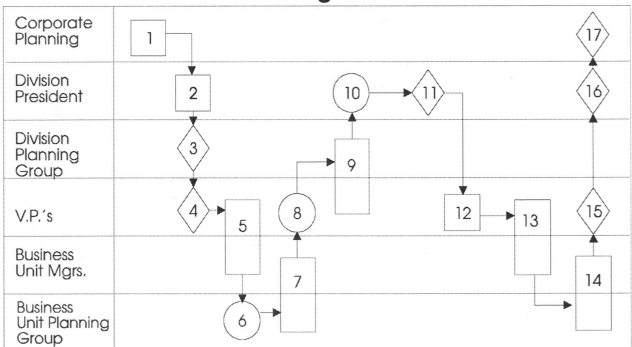

*Note: See page 105 for definitions of symbols

Redesigned Budget Process

1. At the end of the third quarter of the current year the corporation issues their requirements to each division president for the following year.

2. The division president meets with the corporate planning department, the group V.P.s, the business unit managers and their planners to review the requirements. In this meeting they agree to get input from their units as to forecasts and expenditures expected for the following year.

3. Business unit managers prepare document from their units and compile it for V.P.'s.

4. V.P.'s and president meet with corporate planning department for a day to review plans and compile document.

5. Compiled document is distributed for final review to all parties.

6. Final revisions are made by division Planners and sent to corporate.

7. The budget is approved by corporate.

Redesigned Budget Process

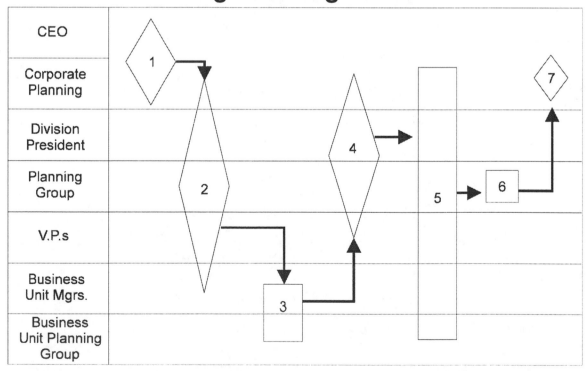

Process Improvement

The following list outlines the steps to process improvement:

1. Define customer requirements for team output.

⬇

2. Define input requirements.

⬇

3. Define the value-adding state changes.

⬇

4. Flowchart current activity steps.

⬇

5. Analyze variances and brainstorm solutions.

⬇

6. Analyze cycle times and eliminate waste.

⬇

7. Analyze for conformance to principles.

⬇

8. Define and implement new process.

⬇

9. Continuously improve.

⬇

1. Define Customer Requirements for Team Output

In chapter three you worked to define the customer's requirements. When you developed these requirements, you defined what it is that you do that adds value. All work groups should do something to add value to a product or service for an end user. By transforming inputs to outputs, something of greater value is created.

When identifying key processes of your team, analyze your customer feedback to determining what is of most importance to them. Then brainstorm all the processes of your team that add value to the customer. Apply the 80/20 rule (what 20% of work has 80% of impact on customer) to determine which processes to map first.

What is it about accounting reports that make them of value to their customer? What exactly is it about an engineering drawing that is most valuable? How is your product used that makes it of value?

These questions are important because they define what your process is supposed to do. You cannot study a process without knowing what you want that process to accomplish. This is the process output.

Let us take an example of a simple process that we can all understand. Cooking a meal is a work process that we have all participated in at some time. If we are going to cook a meal, we will first want to identify the customers. Who will eat the meal? You may be cooking it for yourself. If you are this makes defining requirements easy. Perhaps you are having your neighbors over for dinner. Do they have any dietary restrictions? Do they have children? It is obvious that we need to know the answer to these questions before we can even consider the value of the process. We might design a process that would make the world's greatest shrimp and crab casserole only to find out that the entire family is allergic to shellfish!

Let us assume that we have inquired about our guest's preferences, and they love Italian food. We happen to make fantastic spaghetti.

2. Define Input Requirements

To make our spaghetti, there are several key ingredients or inputs required for the process. There is the spaghetti itself. It may be thin or thick, short or long. Is there a preference?

There are numerous ingredients to the sauce, the heart of any spaghetti meal. There are requirements for each. The store is our supplier, and someone will go to the store to purchase our ingredients. When more than one person is participating in a process, quality problems can occur by simply not specifying the requirements for the input. There are many types and specifications for meat, vegetables, etc. Those who are expert in the process and the customer's requirements of the process must specify the inputs.

Too many times we hear employees (including plant managers and division vice presidents) say, "We know we have a problem with input, but purchasing controls that!" For whom does purchasing purchase? Purchasing is nothing more than a supplier to the manufacturing process as well as to the executives with financial responsibility. By buying based on price alone, they often increase costs by creating production problems.

If you purchase meat on Monday morning because it is on sale after the weekend, imagine what shape it will be in on Friday when you want to cook your sauce. You will have created waste, not a satisfied customer.

A specification sheet will be helpful in being certain that you are covering the right attributes with your supplier. Of course there are many different types of beef, onions, green peppers, and other ingredients. Even within a type there may be specifications that are important. Specifications may include dimensions, weight, thickness, or other criteria. The need to state the quantity is obvious.

The need to state the time as a requirement may be less obvious, but it is one of the most critical requirements for a supplier. It is a requirement that corporate purchasing is likely to ignore because they have no knowledge of the process itself, and are often uninformed.

We do not want the meat purchased five days before it will be cooked. We do not want it purchased in quantities of twenty pounds on the idea that it is cheaper in large lots. Buying in bulk increases our need for space, which is expensive. When we purchase large lots, we are also increasing the difficulty of correcting problems.

For example a manufacturing plant had corrugated boxes stacked all over the plant. You could not see what was going on due to the canyons of stacked boxes. These would all be used eventually as they boxed their outgoing product. The plant manager complained that he, "needed more space and that everything would be fine as soon as the corporate executives got off their rears and authorized the expansion of the plant!" Within two hundred yards of the plant gate was another plant which produced corrugated boxes. Across town there was another plant that also produced corrugated boxes.

The plant manager explained that corporate purchasing had worked out a wonderful contract with the manufacturer of corrugated boxes. They got the lowest possible price, but they had to take months of supply. Purchasing was praised for saving the company money. The plant manager argued for more space. He was blamed for failing to hold his costs down! Actually the purchasing process was at fault. The process by which input is purchased must also be designed intelligently.

The supplier of boxes argued that he had to produce large lots to be efficient and sell at a low cost. This supplier is operating on the theory of mass production and will soon go out of business himself as a competitor adopts the practices of total quality, lean production, and team management. There is no reason why he cannot produce small lots efficiently.

From these examples you can see why just-in-time input is critical. You want your input of meat for your spaghetti sauce just in time. The plant manager, his employees, and customers will all be better off if he can receive boxes just in time. Just-in-time shipments will increase his space, reduce costs, and improve quality.

Every team must contribute to defining the requirements for their input. You cannot be held accountable for quality, costs, and speed if you are suffering under a system that provides input that does not meet your requirements.

3. Define the Value-Adding State Changes

The key steps in a process reflect "state changes." State changes occur when the product or process changes form or "transforms." Your work process is a transformational process. For example, the accounting process transforms incoming numbers and pieces of paper into numbers and reports that are of added value. The numbers must change state if they are to be of greater value. For example 1) information is received by an accounting department; 2) they organize the information; 3) they input the information into a computer; 4) the computer further organizes and calculates the information; 5) reports are printed out; and 6) reports are sent to customers within the organization. These six steps represent the major steps in the work process of an accounting department.

Back to our spaghetti. We have our raw material. The first state change is when we take one large onion and cut the onion into small pieces. The onion has changed state.

This state change can be measured. How large are the pieces? How consistent are the

pieces? You may desire very large pieces or small pieces. What are the requirements? Does the cook know the requirements?

The next state change is when the onions are placed in a frying pan and browned in oil. Here again the onions change state. Again, the state change can be measured. How brown do you want them? Are all of the pieces browned identically? Of course not. There is variability in the browning of onions as there is in any process. Look into any frying pan of onions and you will see that some are more brown than others. You stir them to reduce the variability. If you never stirred them, you might find that some are burned while others are not brown at all. You are working to reduce the variability in the process.

Here you see the idea of statistical process control. What is "in control?" You can see that if you were cooking spaghetti sauce as a commercial product, you would want to define specifications and create a process that reduced variability and was a stable process. In other words the cook knew to stir the onions every two minutes through a ten-minute cooking cycle with the pan temperature the same each time. In this way you would work to stabilize the process.

Knowing your state changes and developing measures is critical to managing a process for quality.

Spaghetti Sauce State Changes

1. **Onions and green pepper in small pieces.**

2. **Browned onions.**

3. **Browned meat.**

4. **Mixed onions, meat, green pepper, tomato sauce, stewed tomatoes, and spices.**

5. **Cooked mixture.**

6. **Cool.**

4. Flowchart Current Activity Steps

Activities or work steps revolve around state changes. A flowchart illustrates what we do in what order to create the transformation.

An easy way to create a flowchart is to have the members of the team write down all of the activities on 5" x 8" cards and tape them on the wall in order of occurrence. In this manner you will develop a flowchart of your process. It is very helpful for the team to see the process in front of them. Analyzing the process will become much easier.

After the initial state change analysis you may need to breakdown individual steps within each state change. For example, looking at the accounting work process, step two has many activities within it. A clerk a) sorts expense reports by department; b) sorts those that are within expense limits and those which are not; c) sorts those with proper signatures; d) sends back to department manager those not in expense limits or without signatures; e) makes a list of entertainment, travel, lodging, and miscellaneous from all reports; and, f) makes a list of expenses that are billable to clients. Then the process goes to step three.

You can see from this more detailed definition of the process that opportunities for improvement begin to become evident. Is all this sorting necessary? Does it really add any value? Can the recycles for signatures be eliminated? "Re" means a return step resulting in waste or scrap. In other words it was not done right the first time. Each time the clerk sorts information, there is the possibility of an error. These errors then create more wasted time and effort. Only by detailing their current process can they begin to study where opportunities for improvement may exist.

When flowcharting, it is helpful to use symbols to describe different types of activities. The following are symbols that are commonly used and may be helpful. For your own purpose you may wish to decide on additional or different symbols for specific types of activities in your work. The important thing to remember is to flowchart the process as it currently works, not the way the team thinks it <u>should</u>.

Accounting Work Process

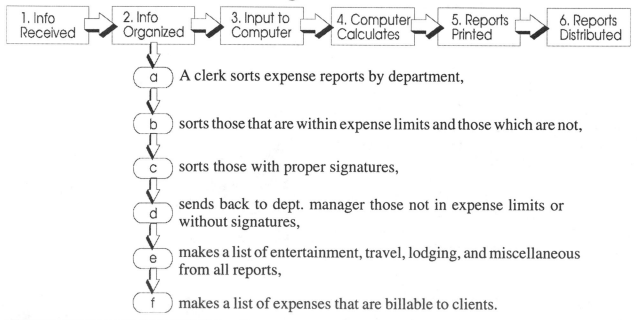

Process Map Symbols

Transporting
Product movement between steps/vessels with no state change.
Movement from one department to another.

Decisions
Choice between alternatives that will impact product movement.
Approvals to support process activities.

Delays
Waiting for something to happen (tanks heating up/cooling down, reports).
No state change to product.

Work Activities
Adding to product/process.
Starting up or shutting down of equipment.
Filling out reports, data entry.

Inspection
Samples, lab tests, quality reports, weighing material (mechanical and manual).

Work Activity/Transporting
Retrieving or getting materials or supplies.
Pre-mixing of materials before usage in process.

Here is the flowchart or process map of making spaghetti sauce:

1. Decide on menu.

2. Decide on ingredients.

3. Go shopping.

4. Wait until Friday night.

5. Take ingredients from storage.

6. Oil and heat pan.

7. Cut onions and green pepper into small pieces.

8. Brown onions.

9. Inspect in ten minutes.

10. Brown meat.

11. Drain fat.

12. Mix onions, meat, green pepper, tomato sauce, tomatoes, and spices.

13. Reduce heat to low flame.

14. Stir every fifteen minutes.

15. Cook for one hour.

16. Remove from flame.

17. Cool.

Another way to develop a flowchart is called a relationship map. This type of map is constructed as a set of relations and illustrates the flow across individuals, departments, or even companies. A relationship map is helpful because it illustrates all of the different parties involved, and in what sequence. You will often see the recycles or rework on a relationship chart or map.

On the following page you will see a relationship map of a manufacturing plant's production scheduling process. This is a weekly process. Essentially every week this activity takes place. The "re" loops are almost always followed at least once, sometimes two or three times, during the week. Much of the activity takes place between Thursday and Friday afternoons. This process frequently results in employees being told late Friday afternoon that they will have to work overtime on the weekend. Just as often they are told that there will be layoffs the next week due to lack of orders even though they have worked overtime the week before.

It is well-known to all employees in this plant that their product is used by the customer in a very consistent manner. The inconsistency is not in orders! It is in the scheduling process!

You can see how an inconsistent process destroys the morale and motivation of employees, thereby hurting quality.

Examine this process, and you may wish to discuss how you might redesign this process to eliminate wasted effort.

The following steps and flowchart describe the processes of production scheduling in a manufacturing plant:

1. The customer calls, faxes, or mails an order request to the sales representative.

2. The sales representative enters the order in the order book, fills out an order report, and puts it on the sales manager's desk.

3. The sales manager reviews and approves the order.

4. The credit department within corporate accounting must approve the order prior to forwarding to corporate engineering or the plant.

5. If the order requires engineering modifications or approval, it is forwarded to the engineering department.

6. The engineering department forwards the drawing (usually by fax or Federal Express) to the plant.

7. Corporate engineering may complete, modify, or originate technical drawings.

8. Plant manager reviews the order, and his secretary then gives it to the accounting department.

9. Accounting reviews the order, enters it on the accounting books, and gives it to the scheduling clerk.

10. Scheduling clerk will often then call sales or corporate engineering to clarify the priority, to determine the true required date, or to discuss the current schedule. If it appears that fulfillment will be a problem, she will also call Tom Rush in the pattern shop if a new pattern is required, or will call Jack Elliott in casting if there is a pattern in stock for this order. This clarification process often requires several calls and the salesman may have to call the customer for clarification or extension of the date.

Relationship Map

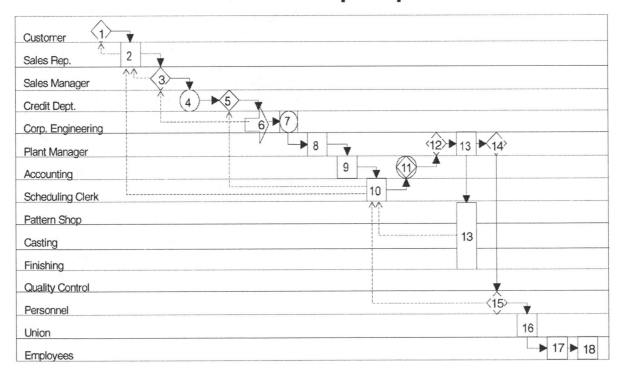

11. Susan will develop the following week's production schedule and give it to her manager.

12. The accounting manager will approve the schedule and give it to the plant manager.

13. The plant manager will call in Tom Rush and Jack Elliott (department managers) to discuss manpower requirements for the coming week. As the schedule changes on Friday, this discussion may be held several times.

14. The plant manager will call in the human resource manager to discuss manpower requirements for the coming week. They will decide on the work schedule, layoffs, or overtime.

15. Human resources manager will contact the union representative to inform him of the manpower requirements for the coming week.

16. The employees will be informed about the work schedule, overtime, or layoffs for the coming week.

17. The employees arrange their personal schedules and....

18. Arrive to complete the work.

5. Analyze Variances and Brainstorm Solutions

A variance is the gap between how things are and how they could or should be. A variance is a deviation from standards. ***Any quality problem is a variance.*** Any variance is an opportunity for improvement.

A bakery produces cakes. Once in a while a cake comes out of the oven that did not rise. This is considered a variance from specifications or standard performance. What is it about the process of work that causes this?

Computer programmers in a corporate information systems' department write programs to assist the highly-skilled engineers employed by this company. Frequently the engineers complain that the programmers have not listened or responded to their needs, and the programs will not perform to meet their needs. This is a variance from customer requirements. What is it in the process of developing computer programs that causes these variances to occur?

A variance is different than variability. Every system produces some variability, and that variability is not necessarily a quality problem. A gun placed in a vice and held still, aimed at a target one hundred yards off, will not produce shots that fall in exactly the same place. There will be a pattern on the target. This is normal variability that results from this system. Even the most expensive, best-maintained rifle fired by the world's greatest marksman will produce shots that vary. This is normal and no amount of adjusting will alter this fact.

Weather patterns vary. Everyone listens to and observes statistics on weather. We know the statistics. Because we know that variability is normal both within and between seasons, we do not ask, "Why is it getting colder? Who is responsible for this weather?" We understand that the changing weather is simply normal performance within the system.

A variance is something beyond the system's normal performance. If it failed to get cooler one winter (in the Northern Hemisphere of course), we would say that something is "wrong." The weather has "varied" outside the range of the normal variability.

There are two kinds of variances; one is *variance from normal system performance* which was just described, the other is *variance from customer requirements*. You may produce a calculator that works perfectly. Each one is exactly the same. They all work according to the established standards for this type of calculator. The only problem is that other calculator companies are producing new ones that perform twice as many functions at the same price. These other companies have created new customer expectations, and you are losing customers. Your product now "varies" from customer requirements.

When your product no longer meets the requirements of the customer this, too, is a quality problem. It is not a defect in the traditional thinking of quality problems. However your product is not perceived by the customer to be a "quality" product because it is inferior in function. This is a variance and must be corrected if you are to stay in business.

In chapter nine we will discuss problem analysis and how to examine statistics more closely to identify variances.

For now your team may wish to brainstorm all of the variances with which they are familiar. Consider variances from standard or system performance and variances from customer requirements.

On the next two pages you will find the Variance Analysis Worksheet and the Variance Solution Worksheet we used to problem solve our spaghetti sauce-making process. Following that example is a case study of requesting a computer for you to practice using the Variance Analysis Worksheets.

After you map your current state and do a variance analysis, begin fresh with a blank sheet of paper asking your team to design an improved process using the following questions.

➢ *How can we improve customer satisfaction?*

➢ *How can we eliminate waste and rework?*

➢ *How can a different process increase employee satisfaction?*

➢ *How can we eliminate interruptions and "wait time?"*

➢ *How can we eliminate or combine steps?*

➢ *Can we control quality earlier in the process?*

➢ *Which steps can be simplified?*

➢ *Should the order of the steps be rearranged?*

Variance Analysis Worksheet

Work Process:

Key Variance	Cause	Where It's Found	Where It's Fixed	Who Controls It
Sauce too bland	Insufficient spices.	During the meal. Testing stage.	When measuring and adding spices.	Cooks
	Not cooked long enough.			Cooks
	Wrong spices.		Testing stage.	Cooks
	Bad spices.		Mixing stage. Purchasing.	Cooks/Vendor
	Cook didn't test.		Testing stage.	Cooks
	Cook not trained adequately.		Certification assessment.	Trainer or Master Chef
	Wrong specs.		Writing recipe.	Master Chef
Sauce too watery	Added too much water.	During the meal. At mixing stage. Testing stage.	When measuring prior to mixing.	Cooks
	Not cooked long enough.		Testing stage.	Cooks
	Different tastes.		Testing stage.	Cooks/guests
	Cook didn't inspect.		Testing stage.	Cooks
	Cook not trained.		Training.	Trainer or Master Chef
	Tomatoes were too watery.		Purchasing stage.	Cooks/Vendor

Variance Solution Worksheet

Key Variance: *Sauce too bland.*

Cause	Changes in Supply	Changes in Work Process	Changes in Tools, Equip.	Changes in the Social Systems
Insufficient spice	Order more. Buy stronger spices.	Add more spice. Redefine the specs. Add taste test.	Calibrated measuring devices.	New training to teach desired taste. Provide more feedback to the cooks on customer reaction and preferences.

Exercise: Buying a Computer

Practice using the Variance Analysis and Variance Solution Worksheets on this example.

Scenario: Our team has decided that in order to improve cycle time in our customer response time, laptop computers would be a possible solution. We decided to order one computer to try out as a pilot and analyze for cycle time reduction.

We followed this process:

1. Defined output requirements: a laptop computer for our team.

2. Input requirements:

> **Input** - Paperwork and proper approvals for purchase of computer.
> **Supplier** - To be determined by purchasing department.
> **Specifications** - 386, less than seven pounds.
> **Quantity** - One.
> **When** - By end of year.

Our planned process: (macro view)

1. Prepare and submit paperwork.

2. Purchasing processes order.

3. Supplier delivers computer.

Several months later, after our computer was (finally) delivered, our team mapped the actual process to analyze for improvement.

We mapped our current state using a relationship map.

1. Fill out requisition.
2. Send requisition to purchasing department.
3. Purchasing department gets requisition.
4. Purchasing department sends requisition to manager for approval.
5. Manager gets requisition.
6. Manager reads requisition.
7. Manager gives requisition to secretary with request for letter to be written describing need for computer.
8. Secretary gets request and requisition.
9. Secretary sends written note to our team describing manager's request.
10. Our team gets note from secretary.
11. Team leader reads note to team at meeting.
12. Team member volunteers for action item to call manager to clarify and write the letter he requested.
13. Team member calls manager for clarification.
14. Member leaves message for manager.
15. Manager returns call and clarifies request.
16. Team member writes letter.
17. Team member sends letter with requisition.
18. Manager gets letter.
19. Manager signs (approves requisition).
20. Manager gives requisition to secretary.
21. Secretary sends requisition to purchasing department.
22. Purchasing records requisition.
23. Purchasing gives requisition to (personal computer) committee.
24. Committee gets request.
25. Committee considers request.
26. Committee approves request.
27. Committee sends request to purchasing department.
28. Purchasing gets request.
29. Purchasing researches suppliers.
30. Purchasing chooses supplier.
31. Purchasing issues purchase order.
32. Supplier gets order.
33. Supplier processes order.
34. Supplier delivers computer.
35. Supply room gets computer.
36. Supply room calls our team to notify.
37. Team members pick up computer at supply room.
38. Team member carries computer to work location.

Buying a Computer: Current State

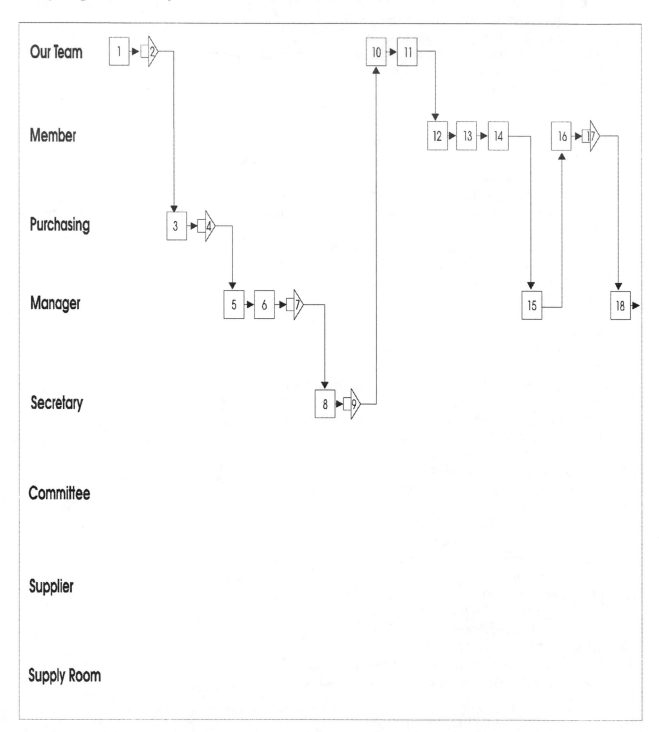

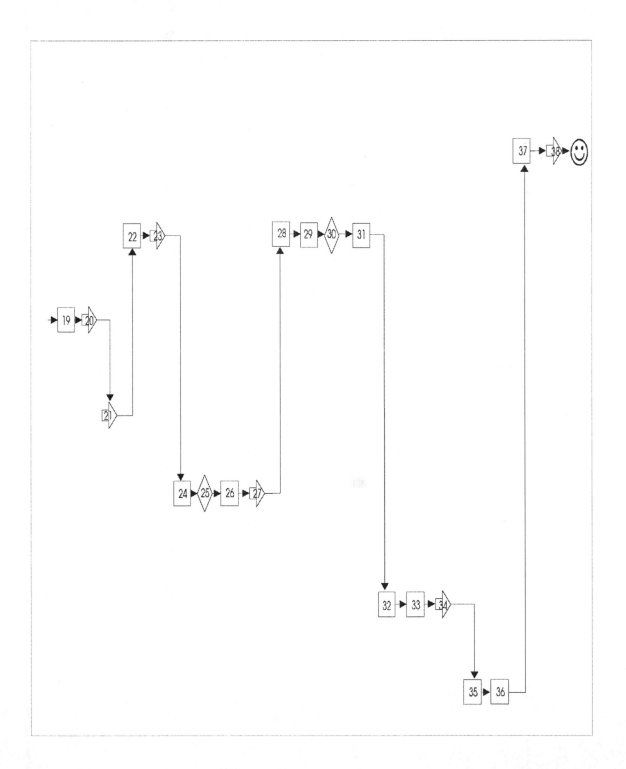

Variance Analysis Worksheet

Work Process: **Example**

Key Variance	Cause	Where It's Found	Where It's Fixed	Who Controls It
Requisition sits on purchasing manager's desk for three days.	Purchasing manager is at three-day workshop.	Purchasing department.	Purchasing department.	Purchasing manager.

Variance Solution Worksheet

Key Variance: Example

Cause	Changes in Supply	Changes in Work Process	Changes in Tools, Equip.	Changes in the Social Systems
Purchasing manager at three-day workshop.		Purchasing manager delegates approval to someone while he is gone.	Use E-Mail to request and receive approval authority - eliminate paper forms.	Change approval authority so that team can order computer without purchaser's approval.

Variance Analysis Worksheet				
Work Process:				
Key Variance	Cause	Where It's Found	Where It's Fixed	Who Controls It

Variance Solution Worksheet

Key Variance:

Cause	Changes in Supply	Changes in Work Process	Changes in Tools, Equip.	Changes in the Social Systems

6. Analyze Cycle Times and Eliminate Waste

In the old days managers sought to make workers more productive. They did "time-and-motion studies" to determine *"standards"* which were then imposed on the workers. This system assumed a static work process. In other words the focus was not on improving the work process but on controlling the workers. Changing the process would just distort the standards requiring another time-and-motion study to develop an up-to-date standard.

This system was demotivating to workers. It also placed supervisors in the position of policing the workers to make sure they were doing their work according to the prescribed method at the prescribed rate. Supervisors also became victims of this system since they were placed in a system that conflicted with their natural desire to improve the process.

This system is dead! What has proven much more successful in many organizations is to work on improving the work process itself. A great example of this is the Toyota Production System which gives the employees the responsibility for improving the system. Quality and productivity improve simultaneously when the employees focus on eliminating waste. Therefore standards are not needed.

Eliminating waste and improving the speed of the work process are highly correlated. In other words *when you eliminate waste, you increase speed. To increase speed, you must eliminate waste.*

Increasing speed has nothing to do with workers working faster!

Imagine a pit crew at an automobile race. During the course of the race there are three pit stops to add fuel and change tires. Crew "A" completes each pit stop on an average of fourteen seconds. Crew "B" takes sixteen seconds. Car "A" wins the race by six seconds. At one hundred and fifty miles per hour, a car can travel some significant distance in six seconds, the total difference in the two cars' pit stops.

It is very common in auto racing for races to be won or lost in the pits. Clearly, crew "B" must improve its performance. Here are two possible approaches. Which do you think will be most successful?

The owner or manager of the team can meet with his pit crew and explain the facts to them. "You guys have lost the race because of your poor pit performance. Obviously the other crew just wanted it deep in their gut more than you guys did. They had more character, more intensity, more desire, more motivation. At the next race I want to see you guys dig deep. I want to see you guys fly over that pit wall. I want to see those wrenches spinning in your hands. I don't want to see anything but a cloud of dust! I don't want just two seconds off each pit stop. I want five seconds off. And, if you aren't man enough to handle it, I'll find crew members who are!"

Or, would the manager do better to say: "Guys, we ran a good race. I know you did your best. But let's face it; someone else is doing something better than we are. Let's put our heads together, study what we're doing, what our competitor is doing, and let's figure out the best possible process." With that he shows them a video played in slow motion of their pit stop. He then shows another videotape, again in slow motion, of their competitor. They go over the tapes ten times. Each time they stop and discuss as a team the differences they see. Together they reach agreement on five specific modifications in their process, each of which they believe will eliminate some wasted time or effort.

The first approach is typical of the "macho manager to the rescue" image that comes from watching too many Vince Lombardi films. It assumes the problem is a motivation problem within the workers rather than a problem within the system of work. It transfers the guilt from the manager to the worker. This pit crew is not only likely to do little better; they are also likely to place the driver's life at risk (a definite quality variance!). The second crew is becoming smarter, feeling more confident with greater knowledge. They do not feel guilty; they feel responsible because they have been asked to gain knowledge and change the system. They will now go practice their new procedures. They are much more likely to improve their speed and quality.

Speed is improved in all work processes not by calling upon the workers to work faster but by eliminating waste and studying the process.

There are many different kinds of waste that occur in a work process:

Wasted effort.
Rework, restudy, replan, reconsider, review.
Wasted space.
Unnecessary travel.
Wasted product in inventory.
Memos sitting in in-boxes.
Wasted product in process.
PC's that are never turned on.
Product defects.
Ineffective meetings.
Excessive approval levels.
Poor decision making.

Cycle time is the time from input to output of materials, information, or other resources used in the process. For example in the production of aluminum cans large rolls of aluminum sheets are received at the plant loading dock on Friday morning at 10:00 a.m. The aluminum roll goes into the incoming inventory warehouse. Eight days later the roll is called out of inventory and goes to the first stage of production. At the first operation it is unrolled and washed. This process takes three hours. It then is "in-process inventory," where it waits an average of three hours for the next operation. The cutting operation for an entire role requires about one hour. The thin strips of aluminum are then ready for the operation that rotates the aluminum, cuts the sheets into strips, and welds the seam into a body. The strips are stacked on a pallet where they wait an average of two hours. The actual operation that transforms these strips into cans requires about ten minutes per strip.

If you simply examine these steps in this operation or in one of your own, you will see that as the material flows through the process, it spends much more time in waiting than in actual production. Most of this waiting is waste! A great deal of the waste in work processes is wasted time. There is wasted time of people and wasted time of materials. Both destroy quality. An interruption-free, continuous process eliminates all of these delays.

Just-in-time inventory systems are based on creating an interruption-free flow, both within production sites and between production sites. Speed of operations increases as delays are removed. Imagine if the pit crew had an operation where the workers got in place and then had to wait for tires to be delivered. Then they had to wait for gas to be delivered. Obviously they could never win a race! They must have an interruption-free, just-in-time, continuous-flow operation if they are to win the race. The only way they will accomplish this type of operation is for the team to take responsibility for improving its process.

Speed is not only an issue in the factory. How long does it take your organization to make a decision on capital expenditures? How long does it take to hire a new employee? How long does it take to get a piece of equipment repaired? How long does it take to change a process that employees know does not work well? How long does it take to answer a customer's request? How long does it take to develop a new computer program?

All employees engage in work processes, and all processes have a cycle time. All process cycle times can be studied, waste can be eliminated, and speed can be improved. When waste is eliminated, not only does speed improve, but quality improves. Waste is often justified on the argument that the extra reviews, restudies, or inventory is needed to make sure nothing goes wrong. This extra material or work simply tends to hide a bad process and bad quality at the cost of additional labor, space, and inventory. The more bad quality and bad processes are hidden, the slower they improve, again causing more quality problems.

To analyze the cycle time of your process, simply place the steps in your process on the Process Cycle Time Evaluation sheet on the next page. Be sure to include all delays. Account for all of the time, from the time the process begins to the time it arrives at the customer. Identify where the greatest waste is. Redesign the process to eliminate this waste.

Process Cycle Time Evaluation

Process:

Step	Process Description	Time Consumed

Process Cycle Time Evaluation

1. **What is the total number of time units (minutes, hours, days)?**

   ◇ **A. Time in Decision-Making?**

   ☐ **B. Time in Work Operations?**

   ▷ **C. Time in Inspection?**

   ◯ **D. Time in Delay?**

   ⇒ **E. Time in Movement?**

2. **Total number of current process steps?**

3. **Target process cycle time?**

4. **Which steps can be *eliminated*?**

5. **Which steps can be *combined*?**

6. **Which steps can be completed *faster*?**

7. **Which steps can be *simplified*?**

8. **Which steps can be *rearranged*?**

Now develop an Ideal Process Flow.

7. Analyze for conformance to principles

During your initial team meetings you reviewed your principles and the principles of the team process. A process must conform to principles. Principles must lead to an effective process.

Principles are stated values that become operational. For example a person may state the value with the utmost sincerity that, "I believe in giving to charity. From the bottom of my heart I can honestly say that I do believe I will give this year." Then when asked the question, "When did you last give?" the same person may reply, "Well, I can't remember; it has been a number of years. I've been quite busy."

Stated values and operational values (what you do or what you say) are often not the same. Your words should match your deeds. "Walk as you talk," or "do as you say." We have all heard these expressions. They all state the obvious principles that how we behave should conform to our principles. This is the purpose of principles.

The process of work when seen as a flowchart or relationship map visually illustrates the operating values in the system. We may say that we trust employees to make decisions about their work, but the flowchart reveals checks upon checks. We may say that we value teamwork, but when the process is examined, paper is passed from one person to the next with signatures and comments; the people never sit down face-to-face to consult with one another.

These processes must be redesigned to be aligned with or conform to the stated principles. If the processes are not going to be aligned with the principles, what is the point in having principles?

We have great principles such as "freedom of speech, press, and religion." But if our processes fail to conform to these statements, the statements themselves would soon come to have little value. Analyzing the process against stated principles is a "reality check."

Look at your flowchart, and take each principle in your statement of team principles and walk through each process step, asking the question, "Is this step consistent with our principle?" As you work through the chart, brainstorm a list of things your team could do to cause the process to represent more effectively your principles.

8. Define and implement a new process

Once you have mapped the current state of your work process and you have analyzed it for variances from normal system requirements, variances from customer expectations, cycle times, and for conformance to principles, you are now ready to redesign your process.

Many processes can be incrementally improved by applying the solutions to the variance analysis you did in step five. Some processes are too faulty to be improved in this manner, and the team would do better to ask itself if there is an entirely different, more efficient way to complete this process. Your team scorecard is a useful tool to determine how broken your process is. If the performance gap between actual and desired performance is so large that adjusting the current process will not achieve the desired level of performance, it is time to "nuke" the existing process and start with a blank slate.

When your team reaches a consensus on an improvement in your process, you will try it out. You should attempt all changes with a scientific attitude. In other words each change is an experiment. The scientist does not have his ego invested in any one possible solution to a problem. He doesn't try to make his solution work because it is his solution. Rather, he simply says, "This is one possible solution; let's try it and see what the data says." If your improvement works, you should see the improvement in measurable results on you scorecard such as improvements in quality or speed.

As soon as you decide on an improvement, the question of decision-making authority will arise. Does your team have the authority to make the improvement alone, or is additional approval or coordination required? It may be the responsibility of the team leader to seek approval at the level above. It may be someone's responsibility to coordinate the change with other teams. If equipment is to be rearranged, it may affect others outside your team.

This type of coordination is normal for significant changes in process. As soon as you become aware that you are pursuing a process that has links with other teams, you will do well to involve members of that team in your analysis and problem solving. Involving other members shares the ownership with them and increases their cooperation.

You may find that some improvements are within the decision-making "boundaries" of your team, and some are not. It is always wise to focus your efforts on those things which you can control. This increases your ability to make the improvements yourself. However major improvements usually involve others.

9. Continuously improve

Your team will be continually analyzing its process to find opportunities for improvement. You will maintain a current flow chart that will define current procedures. However each time a problem is discovered, you will study the causes and determine whether the cause is in the process, in a lack of skill, poor materials, etc.

Improvements build on each other. The internal combustion engine was an improvement over steam engines. But it led to the development of the transmission. The transmission led to other developments. The engine itself has seen thousands of improvements.

Never think that you have found the one best way. You will only be holding up progress. Be proud of your improvements, but then be prepared for further improvements that will inevitably make your current process look like the "horse-and-buggy."

The most important task of the team is continuous improvement. The most important measure is the rate of improvement.

Process Analysis for Non-Linear Work

Although similar in nature to the previously described "linear" work flows, the mapping process for knowledge workers has some nuances which require a different mind-set and approach.

Outcomes for knowledge workers are usually ideas or decisions that are intangible, emergent, or ill-defined. Frequently the goals are unclear, long term in nature, difficult (but not impossible) to measure, and feedback is usually delayed.

When trying to define the transformation process, you quickly understand that the creative thought process is non-linear, asequential, and has multiple concurrent processes. There is no single "right way" so progression is disorderly. As a result it is difficult to optimize the process in the same manner one can in a linear, routine process.

For non-linear work to be effective, we must understand that knowledge in this instance is the most important technology. The organization must be able to effectively generate, transfer, and utilize the knowledge in a productive way.

The criteria of success for knowledge workers is effectiveness, not efficiency. The services provided must demonstrate sufficient value to the company in helping them meet their mission and objectives. Quality, timeliness, and innovation are more important than efficiency.

The steps to consider for mapping the technical system for knowledge workers are to map the processes for generating and utilizing knowledge, the procedures for sharing knowledge and information, and the sequence of complex interlocking deliberations (discussions, considerations) leading to decisions.

The following demonstrates the steps in process analysis for non-linear knowledge workers. Although they are numbered, you may find that it is easier to do some of the steps in a different sequence. All steps may not be necessary for every mapping procedure. Decide which ones make the most sense. You don't have to do them all.

I.   Scope of the Process

A.   Define the boundaries of the process.

   1.   Broad phases of the process (decisions, made in what order, etc.).
   2.   Identify the sub functions/processes/systems.

II.   Identify Your Customers

A.   Identify each major customer (there may be only one).

III.   Identify Outputs (Results) for Each Customer

A.   What are the results of your work? What products or services will you provide for your customers?

IV.   Define Specifications

A.   What requirements do the customers have? (accuracy, format, timing, responsiveness, creativity)

V.   Define Inputs

A.   What key inputs (information, tools, etc.) are needed for each phase of the work?

VI.   Throughput (State Changes)

A.   What are the major steps during the process?

VII.   Variance Analysis

A.   Do a variance analysis for each state change identifying the key major variances (20% of the variances causing 80% of the problems).

Examples might be:
- Efforts going in the wrong direction
- Erratic starting and stopping
- Critical components missing
- Incorrect information
- Delays in getting information
- Excluding knowledge
- Group too homogenous
- Infrequent deliberations
- Conflict in group
- Continual delays and committees

> ➤ Misdirected energy
> ➤ Team not composed of correct membership
> ➤ Delays in getting decisions
> ➤ Unclear goals

B.   Do a cause and effect analysis for each key variance.

Look for things such as:
> ➤ Too many needs
> ➤ Unclear vision
> ➤ Changing goals
> ➤ No priorities
> ➤ Insufficient knowledge
> ➤ Information ignored

VIII.   Deliberation Analysis

The key is to identify deliberations which are critical to the work flow.

For key decisions in the work flow, you will:
   1.   Determine what work will be performed: don't get too micro.
   2.   Determine how the work will be performed: minimum specifications.
   3.   Determine who will be involved.

A.   Identify what outcomes are required for this phase.
B.   Identify what input is required.
C.   From whom is the input required?
D.   What decisions must be made and when should they be made?
E.   What knowledge, skills, and abilities are needed?
F.   Do a player analysis.
   1.   Who should be involved?
   2.   What do they bring?
   3.   What do they lack?

IX.   Essential and Non-Essential Activities

A.   For each state change, analyze what essential activities must be performed to be successful.

B.   Identify non-essential activities.

X.   Solution Analysis

A.   Once key causes are identified, do a solution analysis with appropriate action plans.

B.   Redraw the map if necessary.

Example for Non-linear Work

Situation: Team consultant has requested help with a difficult team leader and wants recommendations on ways to help the team leader.

Scope of Process Analysis From the time I am ready to analyze data until I give the recommendation to the Team Consultant

Customer Team Consultant

Outputs Recommendations

Specifications Timely, helpful, practical, easy to apply

Inputs
Accurate description of team leader behavior
Accurate written information
Organizational chart
Willingness to listen
Commitment to follow through

Throughputs
Analyze data
Design a strategy
Deliver the strategy
Evaluate the results

Deliberation Analysis
May need to decide:
- do I need help diagnosing
- do I have the knowledge or experience for this problem
- who should be involved to help me

Essential/Non-Essential Activities Read data, condense information, brainstorm possible solutions, pick best scenario, make decisions, etc.

Variance Analysis
Misunderstanding the data
Wrong conclusions
Wrong or poorly stated solutions
Untimely feedback
Unrealistic recommendation
Incomplete data

Solution Analysis Recommendations

Action Assignment

As a team 1) identify one of your major work processes. 2) Develop a flowchart of this process. 3) Define the cycle time and variances which occur in the process. 4) Redesign the process to reduce cycle time and eliminate causes of quality variances.

Implementation Tips

1. Identifying the team's key processes is critical to improvement but also seems to bog teams down in detail. Start with one or two <u>key</u> processes. (What would shut down the business if you quit doing it?)

2. When your team maps "current state" of a key process, stay macro in the beginning. Getting too detailed results in never <u>fixing</u> anything because the team is too consumed in analyzing its current state. Continuous improvement means you return to your processes time and time again to look for more opportunities.

3. Most initial improvement opportunities are very obvious. Go ahead and let your team fix some things that are blatantly obvious regardless of where you are in meeting your team milestones. Success breeds enthusiasm.

4. You may want your team's coach to facilitate your first mapping process. It sometimes helps to have an objective outsider walk you through the mapping analysis.

5. Don't get bogged down in the tools of process analysis. They are there to be helpful but if team members waste time arguing over which symbol to use (Is that step an activity or a decision?) you may lose valuable energy.

6. Some processes don't need improvement, they need elimination! Be prepared to ask the ultimate question of "do we need to be doing this at all?"

Chapter Six

Managing Human Performance

Teams learn to manage and motivate themselves, earning the right to self-management.

Objectives

1. To focus the efforts of the team on important performance.

2. To develop the skills of increasing desirable behavior and decreasing undesirable behavior.

3. To establish a performance management system so that teams continuously improve their service to their customers.

Understanding Human Performance

For teams to maximize their effectiveness it is critically important to understand motivation, what makes people tick. Human performance can always be improved just as machinery, materials, and other elements of the total system can be improved. However many efforts to improve human performance are based on mistaken ideas about why people may not be performing their best. Among some of the mistaken ideas are the following examples:

"People around here just have bad attitudes." The idea that people just have a bad attitude assumes that this is a random event with no explanation. There is an explanation. Something in the environment now or in the past has influenced the thoughts, feelings, and behavior of these people. These same events can be changed to change attitudes. If we manage the system in which people work, we can have a positive influence on their attitudes.

"The problem is that the people are not motivated. People just don't care." It may be that people are not motivated. But again the problem is not necessarily the internal chemistry of the people. The problem is in the system or the environment which is influencing those people.

"We have a training problem." Without a doubt sometimes there is a training problem. However people often assume that a human performance problem is the problem of the training department. We must learn to analyze whether a problem is a skill or knowledge problem which requires training, or a motivation problem. Actually most problems, whether skill or motivation, reflect problems in the work system or social system, and it is these that must be changed.

"That's just the way things are done around here. That's the way it has always been." This is another statement that says, "I can't do anything about it." It is a form of giving up. If performance is to improve, then the way things are done around here is exactly what must change.

"He's always been that way. You'll never change him." We have heard this prediction in every location we have worked to improve performance. This person has always been that way because the system in which he has worked has always been that way. It is amazing how people can change when the system changes.

These explanations of performance deficiencies are not useful because they do not suggest clear actions to address the problems. It is important that the team members are able to examine human performance without blaming, accusing, or expressing other emotions that make problems worse. It is important that they discuss actions they can take to have a positive impact on how their fellow team members feel and act.

A useful first step is the Mager Model. Robert Mager and Peter Pipe have contributed a great deal to analyzing the causes of performance deficiencies by developing a performance analysis model.

Mager and Pipe's model helps you determine whether the problem is caused by a lack of *skill* or a lack of *motivation*. It looks for the specific factor that may have caused the problem. Understanding the performance deficiency helps you identify the appropriate corrective action.

Mager and Pipe suggest the following series of steps in analyzing problems in human performance:

Pinpoint the performance deficiency.

A performance deficiency is a discrepancy between the behaviors that you would like the individual or team to exhibit and the actual behavior. Remember to ask yourself the questions,

"What behaviors do I want and what behaviors are current?" Describe what you want by using pinpointed behaviors. Avoid references to traits and personalities such as "attitude" or "laziness." A pinpointed behavior is one which can be observed and recorded. For example, if you define a team's problem as "lack of creativity" it is hard to determine improvement. If you pinpointed the "number of new ideas suggested" by the team, it would be possible to track progress. Pinpointing is critical to clear communication.

Is it important?

Decide if the problem is worth the effort of addressing. Ask yourself, "How important is this behavior?" "Is it critical to the team's performance?" "Will it make any difference to the customer?"

Is it competency or motivation?

Decide if the problem is a skill (competency) deficiency or a motivation deficiency. Ask yourself this hypothetical question, "If I offered this person $1,000,000 or if his life depended on it, would he or she improve this performance?" If $1,000,000 would not improve the performance, it is a "Can't Do" problem. If $1,000,000 would improve the performance, it is a "Won't Do" problem.

Determining whether it is a competency or motivation problem is the most important question in the analysis of performance problems. You will do completely different things to im-

The Mager Performance Analysis Model

Pinpoint the Performance Problem

Is it Important?

If Their Life Depended on it, Would They Perform as Desired?

No
(Can't Do - Capability)   **Yes**
(Won't Do - Motivation)

Analyze Capability
+
Learned Competence   **Analyze Obstacles**
+
Goals & Expectations
Feedback & Reinforcement

prove problems that are competency problems versus motivation problems. If a person cannot type fifty words per minute, it is a complete waste of time to offer incentives to type faster. In fact it is destructive to motivation. On the other hand if someone already has the skill, offering additional training is also a waste.

Identify corrective action.

"Can't Do" Actions

If you have a **"Can't Do"** performance problem, follow steps "A" through "E" to identify possible causes and determine appropriate solutions:

A. Has the person ever been trained? If a person has a skill deficiency and has never been skillful in the past, the person probably requires training to perform well. The solution to a lack of training is to provide on-the-job training, formal training, or individual coaching.

B. Does the person get feedback? A person may lose his skill in performing a particular task because no one comments positively or negatively on his performance. Without feedback the person may develop bad habits or gradually lower performance standards. For example a person may receive coaching to raise his voice and vary inflection to improve his public speaking skills but without continued feedback is likely to revert to his original speaking habits. The solution to a lack of feedback is to increase the frequency or specificity of the feedback which the person receives.

C. Does the person get practice? A person can become less competent if he or she does not get a chance to practice the skill. For example a team member learns to operate a computer program. A year goes by, however, and she never has the opportunity to use this computer program. At the end of the year she cannot demonstrate the skill any longer. Her competence has decreased through lack of practice.

The solution to a lack of practice is to provide opportunities to practice and review rarely-used skills.

D. Is there an easier way to do it? Sometimes a person cannot do the task as it is currently arranged, but a slight change in the methods or some type of job aid may resolve the problem. For example if a job originally required ten steps and the procedure can be reduced to four, it is more likely that the employee will be able to do the job correctly.

E. Does the person have potential capability? If the job cannot be changed or made easier in any way and the employee has been involved in comprehensive training, practice, and feedback and still cannot do the task, she may not have the necessary capability for this skill. In this case the team leader and team member should discuss alternatives.

"Won't Do" Actions

If you have a **"Won't Do"** performance problem, follow steps "A" through "D" to identify possible causes and determine appropriate solutions:

A. Is good performance punished? Sometimes an individual's good performance has unpleasant results. For example, an employee completes a project quickly and efficiently, then is given another very difficult task. The employee may become less motivated to work quickly and efficiently.

B. Is poor performance reinforced? If a person encounters pleasant consequences for poor performance, he or she may become less motivated. For example an individual runs into difficulty on a project and complains rather than tries to solve the difficulty. Her manager relents and tackles the task herself. The employee may stop trying to solve problems herself.

C. Is good performance ignored? People may become less motivated if their performance does not receive any attention at all. For example a maintenance technician begins making quality checks on critical gauges but no one comments. He starts making fewer checks; incorrect gauge readings increase, but still no one says anything. The technician may continue to make fewer checks, believing incorrect readings don't matter to anyone.

D. Are there obstacles for good performance? People may become less motivated if obstacles make performance more difficult or if expectations for performance are vague or confusing. For example operators are expected to complete control logs for each job. It frequently takes twenty minutes or more to complete the log for each job. The operators, therefore, may gradually stop completing the log because it is difficult and time consuming.

Once you have diagnosed whether the performance problem is a **"Can't Do"** or **"Won't Do"** problem, you can move on towards designing a solution.

The "Won't Do" problems tend to require additional analysis as human behavior is often more complex than it appears on the surface.

Exercise: Analyzing Performance Deficiencies

Label the following performance problems as "Can't Do" or "Won't Do" problems and suggest a possible course of action for correcting the problem.

1. Team members perform inconsistently on priority jobs.

_____

_____

_____

_____

2. Team members repeatedly end up arguing about a problem rather than using problem-solving techniques.

_____

_____

_____

3. A team does not graph the number of completed jobs that conform to specifications.

_____

_____

_____

_____

Attitudes & Behaviors

Perhaps the most difficult job of a team leader or facilitator is to manage behavior in a team meeting. The purpose is to bring out the best in all of the team members. The leader or facilitator is like a coach who encourages and brings out the talents of each member. This is the key to a winning team.

For generations philosophers and students of human conduct have debated the causes of behavior. Does it come from within? Is it the result of the external environment? Is it the ego or id or bad parents or the neighborhood? Is the employee driven from a deep inner "need" to succeed or motivated by the manager and reward systems?

We do not need to resolve or enter into this debate. There is dynamic relationship between the inner emotional or psychic states, the person's external behavior, and the environment.

The only question we need to address is what the team leader should think about and act upon when individuals behave in ways that are either constructive or destructive to the group process.

Rather than focusing on an individual's **attitude** (subjective), it is more constructive to focus on the person's **behavior** (objective).

Imagine a member of your team comes to the meeting and sits with his arms folded for the first ten minutes. He then takes out a newspaper and starts to work on a crossword puzzle. A few minutes later he gets up and walks out to make a phone call.

How might we describe this person's behavior? We might say that he has a bad "attitude," does not care about the team's objectives, lacks enthusiasm, or is "impolite." Have you seen his "attitude" to determine whether it is good or bad? Have you seen, touched, or measured his caring or enthusiasm? No.

Can you imagine trying to change this person's "attitude?" It would be very difficult. What we do know about and what we can change is the specific, pinpointed behavior of doing a crossword puzzle, reading a newspaper, speaking with his neighbor, and leaving the room. We will have much more success if we focus on changing these pinpointed behaviors.

The A-B-C Model

It will be helpful to our discussion of managing behavior if we have a simple model that can help us understand why people behave the way they do and what we can do to influence the behavior of ourselves and others.

Each member of the team influences each other. We either encourage or discourage each other to make positive contributions or to behave in negative ways. In this respect every team member is facilitating the behavior of other members.

The A-B-C Model is a way of defining all of these influences on behavior.

Activators

Some influences come before behavior. These are **Antecedents** or **Activators**. They are *cues*, *triggers*, or *stimuli* that get behavior going. A fire alarm is an activator to leaving the building. A red traffic light is an activator to putting your foot on the brake. Observing a graph indicating performance that just dropped downward is an activator to a discussion about improvement.

The environment is constantly providing activators to behave. Every time we see a clock, look outside at the weather, or listen to the sound of a machine running, we are experiencing activators. In a team meeting the agenda is an antecedent for an orderly discussion and for staying on the topic. The Code of Conduct is an activator to desirable meeting behavior. A question from the team leader such as, "What do you feel would be the best way to handle this situation?" is an activator to discussion.

Behavior

The "B" in the A-B-C Model stands for the pinpointed **Behavior** which the activator has evoked. Pinpointed behavior is performance which can be measured, counted, and recorded.

The A-B-C Model

Antecedent ⟹ Behaviors ⟸ Consequences

Consequences

The best systems of managing performance provide **Consequences** for desired behavior. Consequences to behavior follow the behavior and determine whether or not the behavior will continue, increase, or decrease. All behavior is a function of its consequences. In other words if behaviors continue, they have been reinforced in some way. No behavior continues unless there is some desirable consequence. All behavior pays off in some way.

There are three kinds of consequences, each with a different effect on behavior:

Reinforcement

Positive reinforcement is a desirable consequence that results in an increased rate of response. Reinforcement resembles a reward; though rewards are typically tangible such as money or prizes, reinforcement can be either tangible or social, such as a verbal "thank you."

There are many types of reinforcers: approval from our team members or manager, seeing the results of our efforts, pride in our own work, money, or recognition in our community.

It is important to recognize that reinforcement is individualized. In other words what is reinforcing to one person may be punishing to another. The same is true for teams. The determination of the consequence is in the eyes of the receiver.

The Three Types of CONSEQUENCES

Reinforcement

Punishment

Neutral Consequences

Neutral Consequences

Imagine that you have been given a project to work on by your boss. You work for three weeks. You work late. You take work home and work on weekends. You are enthusiastic, and you consider the project important. When you complete the project, you turn in a report to your boss. A week goes by. Two weeks. Three. Four. Nothing. With each passing day, are you now more or less likely to work hard on future projects? Clearly you are less likely to work as hard in the future.

Behavior that is ignored will "extinguish," much like a fire deprived of oxygen. At first an individual may try harder and behave at a faster pace in order to achieve the expected reward, but soon the behavior will come to an end.

Punishment

Punishment is a consequence of behavior that results in a decreased rate of response. In other words if something undesirable happens after a behavior, the rate of that behavior will decrease.

We can use punishment often to stop behavior we do not like. However there are side effects to punishment that must be considered. If you punish frequently, others will come to see *YOU* as punishing. A work environment in which there is a great deal of punishment is an unpleasant place to work. It is also an environment in which there will be little risk-taking. People are always computing the probability of reinforcement versus punishment, which is risk analysis. If the probability of punishment is high and reinforcement low, they will take few risks.

This effect of punishment is very important to understand. Many of our work places have seen high rates of punishment and, therefore, little risk-taking or initiative by employees. The purpose of the team management process is to enhance involvement, initiative, and risk-taking. This is impossible if there is a high probability of punishment and low probability of reinforcement. As a team leader or team member, you bear some of the responsibility for increasing positive reinforcement for desirable behavior and decreasing punishment.

There are often multiple consequences to a given behavior. Therefore you must analyze the balance of these various consequences. At any one time there may be five or ten different kinds of consequences acting on a behavior. "I want to solve this problem, and it will be reinforcing to reach a solution. However I wish this meeting would end so I could get home to my family. I know my contribution is appreciated by the team, but the way this other team member keeps yapping, we will never get out of here!" Here the positive consequence of staying at the meeting outweighs the need to go home. This is called the balance of consequences.

Remember that you can often tip the scales. Even the most subtle behavior on the part of the leader or other members can tip the scale between an individual's sharing an idea or not sharing an idea. Your reaction to other's suggestions may determine what they say next. Consequences are a very powerful impact on all of us.

Exercise: A-B-C Analysis

1.   Select a behavior of a person that you would like to see <u>increased</u>.

   A)   Define the behavior in pinpointed terms (observable and measurable).

   B)   What events/actions do you feel often elicit that behavior (activators)?

   C)   What consequences do you think currently reward that behavior?
   What consequences currently suppress or punish that behavior?

2.   Conduct the same analysis of a behavior that you would like to see <u>decrease</u> in frequency.

   A)   Define the behavior in pinpointed terms (observable and measurable).

   B)   What events/actions do you feel often elicit that behavior (activators)?

   C)   What consequences do you think currently reward that behavior?
   What consequences currently suppress or punish that behavior?

Encouraging Desirable Behavior

Now that you've learned to analyze why a behavior is occurring under the current conditions, let's look at ways to increase desirable behavior in the team environment.

Activators

The most common reaction to changing a person's behavior is to change the activators. Managers traditionally decide to increase performance by setting more challenging goals, giving motivational talks, and offering frequent reminders: "The customer comes first!", "Quality is job one!". While these techniques do often result in temporary improvement, they rarely produce lasting behavior change. For example choosing a controversial problem for a team to solve may result in increased participation at that particular meeting, but the involvement of team members will not be sustained unless the problem gets addressed.

The most potent way to have sustained behavior change and performance improvement is through positive reinforcement.

Positive Reinforcement

Positive reinforcement is a situation in which a person receives a desired consequence following a behavior.

Examples of positive reinforcement are verbal responses such as "good idea," body language such as head nods and smiles, and written notes that say "good job."

An example is "I want to thank everybody for completing his action items this week. We are making progress on problems that have been around for a long time." Or "Thanks for coming to the meeting prepared. That is some of the best discussion of our goals we have ever had."

It is worth consulting with your team on how you can make meetings more enjoyable. The meetings themselves should be reinforcing to team participation. If the meetings are punishing, members will not want to attend.

You may also want to discuss how you can reinforce the entire team for meeting performance goals. For example if you set a goal to achieve a fifty percent reduction in errors going to your customer, you may want to provide some reinforcer for achieving this goal.

You might have your next team meeting after hours at the local pizza restaurant, or you may agree to meet over at a member's house for a party.

The members of the team are the "world's greatest experts" on what they would find reinforcing. Do not guess. Ask them.

Some points to remember when you reinforce your team are:

Frequent

The more people experience positive reinforcement, the more positive they will feel about the workplace. Reinforce frequently! <u>Look</u> for people doing good things; **catch people doing something right!** In fact it is known that the best ratio for behavior change is 4:1. Four positive consequences to every punishment issued. Now while this need not be applied on an individual basis, it is an excellent guideline for team leaders (and members) to work toward in their daily interactions. (Try tracking the number of positives you deliver in a day vs. negatives!)

Free

Contrary to popular opinion, the most effective positive consequences are free. The type of reinforcement that best fits all of these criteria is typically social reinforcement. Social reinforcement is generally positive interaction between people or symbols of recognition and appreciation. While people are most often more comfortable giving tangible reinforcement (plaques, buttons, jackets, etc.), social can have more lasting impact. Before you go out and buy awards, try saying, "Thank you," writing a personal note, making a quick phone call to his/her family, sharing your appreciation at a team meeting, or putting your recognition in a company newsletter or bulletin board. When delivering reinforcement, people should have some guidelines to maximizing their effectiveness. Try following the SIP model.

Sincere

The sincerity of the reinforcement is critical. If a person is perceived to be "giving away recognition to everyone who walks by," it diminishes the power of the reinforcer. Also be sure not to use a positive introduction to "soften up" someone before you ask him to do additional work. Keep your recognition clear and concise so the person recognizes it for what it is: appreciation for his behavior.

Specific

If a leader wants to reinforce improved team performance, he might say, "You have done a great job during the past couple of weeks!" That is fine, but do they actually know in what way they have been successful and why it is great? It is important that the leader lets the team know that, "During the past several weeks we have reduced the error rate from .03 to .015, and the customers called to let us know that they appreciate this." Now the team knows what to keep on doing or do more of in the future.

Immediately Reinforce

The longer the delay between behavior and consequence, the less effective the consequence. Imagine that you worked for four weeks collecting data on a quality variance, and the team did not talk about it for six months.

Individualize

We do not all like the same things. Some like time off; others would rather work extra hours to earn overtime. Identify what is reinforcing to individual team members.

Effective Reinforcement Is ....

SPECIFIC
SINCERE

IMMEDIATE
INDIVIDUALIZED

PERSONALIZED
PROPORTIONAL

Personalize

Telling the person why his behavior is meaningful <u>to you</u> often makes the recognition more powerful. For example saying, "Joanne, I really appreciated your staying late and covering the telephone for me so I could go to my son's softball game," is often more meaningful than, "Joanne, your dedication to this company is an inspiration to us all!"

Proportional

Being proportional in choosing your reinforcement simply means that the value of the consequence should be consistent with the value of the performance. For example it would be just as inappropriate to award a week's paid vacation to someone who had perfect attendance for a month as it would to give movie tickets to someone who had created millions of dollars for the company with a new product launch.

Exercise: Identifying Possible Reinforcers

I. Mark the possible reinforcers which you believe would be effective and practical in your work environment.

Intangible or Activity Reinforcers

_____ Praise.
_____ Letter or memo of commendation.
_____ Increased responsibility or autonomy.
_____ Passing on positive comments heard within the organization.
_____ Announcement of accomplishment at a meeting.
_____ Allowing a person to present results to an upper-level group.
_____ Choice of work assignments.
_____ Novel and interesting work assignment.
_____ Opportunity to attend special training or meetings.
_____ Telephone call from V.I.P.
_____ Visit by V.I.P.
_____ Unit or department-wide lunch or dinner.
_____ Employee or team of the week (or month or quarter).
_____ Unit or department-wide picnic.
_____ Lunch or dinner with top manager.
_____ Free dinner with spouse.

Tangible Reinforcers

_____ Accomplishments posted on bulletin board.
_____ Posting of customer compliments.
_____ Picture of individual or team posted on bulletin board.
_____ Positive comment and initials written on graph or chart.
_____ Article describing accomplishments in company newspaper.
_____ Status symbols such as best equipment or new tools.
_____ Coffee and donuts.
_____ Stationery or stickers saying, "Super!" or "Good job!"
_____ Department or unit banners.
_____ Awards, trophies, pins, ribbons.
_____ Jackets, caps, T-shirts.
_____ Gift certificate.
_____ Tickets to sports or entertainment event.
_____ New tools or equipment.
_____ Raffle tickets for drawing.

II. Create your own. Add your own ideas about possible reinforcers to the list. Be creative! (Think about social, intangible, tangible, activities, etc.)

Dealing with Poor Performance

Most performance problems are the result of a poorly-designed system. The individual lacks information, skills or any reinforcement for good performance. When these are provided, and when the individual is part of a team working together to improve performance, there are few problems with individuals who do not want to perform well.

However, because people are imperfect, there will be times when the team leader or members may need to address specific individual performance problems.

When attempting to correct a problem of poor performance, always assume that the individual wants to perform well. If you make negative assumptions, you will "blame" or "condemn" the individual. This always results in a negative counter reaction that becomes a larger problem.

If poor performance is not addressed effectively, the morale of all team members will decrease until people become accustomed to mediocre standards. Effective correcting can help morale.

Team members are often more motivated to correct poor performance than managers. They are often most directly connected to the poor performance. It is important that team members or team leaders provide negative feedback in a manner that is most helpful.

Guidelines for Effective Negative Feedback

Before discussing the poor performance, be sure your "stage" is properly set. Provide negative feedback in <u>private</u>. You will set yourself up for success if you remember to <u>listen first</u>. Determine the other person's point of view. Iden-

tify the reasons for the undesirable behavior. Getting all the facts by listening to the other side will help you avoid "putting your foot in your mouth!"

Just as with reinforcement, the critical guidelines in correcting behavior follow the SIP model.

1. Be specific. Describe behaviors which are undesirable, not traits. Always pinpoint the desired new behavior. The goal is for the person to remember what he or she should do differently in the future.

2. Correct as immediately as possible following undesirable behavior. Do not wait for the "ideal moment" to correct. The best time is as soon as possible, unless you are angry and feel you should cool down before meeting with the other person. Catch the problem while it is still small.

3. Individualize. Describe the benefits of the desired behavior whenever possible. We change our behavior more readily if we see possible benefits to us.

4. Proportional. It may help keep you on track to remember your ultimate objective is to get agreement on future behavior. Don't dwell on the problem or blow it out of proportion.

5. Personalize. Most people care how you feel about their behavior. It is often appropriate in correcting situations to tell the person how you feel about his or her behavior, or the results of that behavior.

6. Avoid emotional pitfalls. Don't attack, whine, blame, or be defensive. Don't use this discussion as a chance to vent pent-up emotions or to make yourself look good. Speak calmly and firmly and act as though the other person is a well-intentioned, responsible adult like yourself.

A Model for Helpful Correcting

1. Pinpoint the undesirable behavior. Describe actions, not personality traits. "When you are lazy you cause problems," will produce much more defensiveness than, "When you don't finish a task on time, the whole team misses its project deadline."

2. Describe the negative outcomes or results of the undesirable behavior. People often do not realize the problems which their behavior produces. They certainly do not have your perspective on the problems.

3. Your feelings often have significant impact on other people's behavior. You should share your feelings unless you believe the other person truly does not care about them. In that case, skip this step.

4. It is very important to state the new behavior you would like to see in the future. Involve the other person in this step if you are not sure what new action would solve the problem or if several alternatives are possible.

5. State the benefits of the new behavior. How will this new behavior benefit the person, the department, or the company? This step can help you "sell" the desired behavior and thereby increase the likelihood of its occurrence in the future.

6. Check it out. To get a commitment to the new behavior and to get the other person's reaction ask, "What do you think?" Using an open-ended question here helps you find out how they feel. When you both verbalize what the future behavior will be, you increase the chances of success.

Setting Goals and Expectations

When employees feel responsible for their work and have control over their work process, they will want to set goals and expectations. If you play golf, it is natural to set a goal for how many shots will be required to complete the 18 holes as you tee off. If you are a runner, you probably set goals and track your performance in terms of the number of miles per week, minutes per mile, or days per month on which you run.

This goal setting establishes the basis upon which we feel self-satisfaction. Meeting goals is a reinforcing experience.

Dr. Deming has argued that we should eliminate *management-by-objectives* or *management-by-the-numbers*. His reason for this has to do with another principle, that of driving out fear. In many organizations, the process of objective setting has become a top-down process of intimidation and fear. Peter Drucker, in his book The Practice of Management, published in 1954, included a chapter titled *Self-Management By Objectives*, one of the first advocating management-by-objectives. The original idea, as advocated by Peter Drucker, was that employees would be motivated if they set their own objectives. This became distorted and bureaucratized into a system of top-down control.

We believe that the most useful objectives are those set by those who must perform.

When developing a goal-setting process, you should review the scorekeeping system you developed during the previous chapters. Each of these measures can be a subject of goal setting.

Goals can be set on many different levels in an organization. You may be aware of **company goals** for achieving market share levels, revenue levels, quality performance and recognition, or creating new products or services. The company establishes an annual plan as well as a strategic plan. The annual plan represents the company's plan for the next year and the strategic plan represents the company's goals for three, five, or ten years. Both are useful for establishing the company's direction and coordinating efforts toward a common purpose.

Team goals fulfill the same purpose. **Team goals** may also be short term, months or weeks; and they may be more strategic, for a period of a year or more. Obviously, in a large company you have little control over the company goals. However you can have a great deal of impact on your team's goals.

Highly successful people are most often individuals who set their own **personal goals**. These may be goals for further education, learning new skills, achieving financial objectives, or other events important to the individual. Personal goals are an important aspect of individual continuous improvement. There is always a gap between who we are today and what we can do today, and who we could be tomorrow or what we could do tomorrow. Personal excellence is the personal pursuit of continuous improvement.

Effective Goal Setting

Setting goals is one of the oldest, well-proven methods of improving and managing performance. Athletes set goals. This does not contradict the concept of continuous improvement, it simply fills a human need of satisfaction for reaching some specific point.

The following are some guidelines that will help you keep your goals understandable and useful.

Goals should be challenging.

It is fun and exciting to attain a performance level that represents excellence. To attain average performance is rarely exciting.

Goals should be attainable.

This is the balance to the previous statement. Goals should be both challenging and attainable. If goals are set too high, the team members will become discouraged. Attainable goals are motivating. Goals that are perceived to be unattainable are demotivating. This is a case where perception is reality. If the team does not perceive the goal to be attainable, then it is demotivating to them. This is one of the reasons why teams should set their own goals. They are the world's greatest experts on the level of performance they consider to be challenging and attainable.

The team needs to have "line of site."

This means that goals should be written at the team's own level and should be meaningful and measurable in terms of the team's job responsibilities.

K.I.S.S.

"Keep It Short and Simple." Goals should be as clear and brief as possible, and should avoid technical jargon or complexity.

Goals should be based on team measures.

Goals should be set for each team measure. Some additional goals may be set that are necessary but not based on the key performance measures. For example, a team may have a goal to install a new system by a specific date even though it does not directly affect any of their key outcomes.

Goals and measures should be adjusted periodically.

A sales dollar measure can increase when there is an increase in sales price per unit. Goals should also be adjusted by the team when they no longer represent a challenge.

How to Write Clearly-Defined Goals

Goals should be written specifically and with time frames. For example, "To reduce the number of customer complaints on quality by three percent by July 15."

The statement of a goal should include the following:

To + Action Verb + Measurable Output + Quantity (goal) + Time Frame

Here are some examples of goals that include these elements:

To decrease the number of customer job failures from 50 per month to 30 per month by March 31.

To increase the number of patent suggestions accepted by the Patent Committee by 10% by December 31.

To decrease the average turnaround time for requests for parts to one day by June 30.

To complete the top five user requested projects by January 1.

Exercise:

Choose a behavior or performance area that you would like to see improved by your team (or supplier, or customer!) and design a behavior change plan to reward improved performance.

Follow these steps:

1. Pinpoint the desired behavior.

2. Define the goal or standard you would like to see met.

3. Discuss this desired outcome with the person or team.

4. Determine several forms of reinforcement you could use to reward improvement.

5. Apply positive consequences as they improve.

6. Check your data to see if desired performance is sustained.

Action Assignment

Review your scorecard with your team. For those performance areas:

1) in which you are improving, plan a celebration for goal attainment and recognize the team's improvement efforts.

2) in which you are maintaining acceptable performance, give yourselves recognition, but also ask if there are more opportunities for incremental or major improvements.

3) in which you are not performing acceptably, assess your goals, are they appropriate? Review your action plan, is it being implemented? Talk to your customers and suppliers, do they have observations to share?

Implementation Tips

1. Much of managing human performance is common sense; doing what we know we should, but don't. Don't under estimate the power of recognition to elicit a person's best work.

2. Team members need to feel equal responsibility for recognition to their peers and team leaders. This is not a boss-to-subordinate technique.

3. We too often assume the "no news is good news" mentality. If no one is complaining, we must be okay. This does not create a culture of performance excellence.

4. One of the most powerful ways to "drive fear out" of the organization is through recognition of taking risks. Try giving awards for "bold trys" (things that sounded good but didn't work). Design an "innovation fair" where people can present their ideas to the rest of the organization without going through formal approval levels.

5. Recognize that not everyone's reinforced by the same thing. Talk to team members about what is reinforcing to them. For example some people would be thrilled to present a project review to a senior executive team while others may be terrified. Be sure the consequence does, in fact, strengthen the behavior.

6. While focus should be in team performance, outstanding individual achievement should also be recognized. One does not preclude the other.

Chapter Seven

Having Effective Team Meetings

The success of the team meeting is often determined before the meeting begins through preparation and planning.

Objectives

1. To understand why teams should meet and what should occur in the meetings.

2. To plan for effective team meetings, including the physical setting, agenda, and roles and responsibilities of those attending.

3. To learn skills that help ensure participation in meetings such as asking questions, rephrasing, and showing empathy.

4. To establish ground rules with the team for appropriate meeting behavior.

Why Have Team Meetings?

Teams need to meet in order to benefit from the collective wisdom of the group. While some decisions can probably still be made effectively in the hallway or by phone, if the organization truly wants to maximize its people's talents, then people need to meet.

The team meetings are designed to offer a forum to make the necessary decisions to run a team's particular portion of the business. Therefore they must meet often enough to make the routine decisions required to manage effectively as well as to address more long-term significant problems.

The complexion of the meetings will change over time and vary according to how the team is performing. Initially teams will be struggling to apply continuous improvement techniques such as identifying customers and mapping processes. Later the teams may have their performance under good control and will be spending their time looking for new applications, techniques, or innovative ideas for their future.

In any event, the team needs to learn to work well together and to run their meetings as effectively as possible.

Effective Team Meetings

The key to success in an athletic contest, military assault, or business activity is often in the preparation. Likewise the success of the team process and each team meeting are based on preparation. When you are prepared, you are confident and comfortable. Ensuring this confidence and success is the purpose of this session.

Meetings can be one of the most powerful management tools or one of the most abused. Common complaints about meetings include the following examples: they last too long; they are boring; nothing ever gets accomplished; there is never any follow-up; there is no control; people ramble on about their own particular issues; and people arrive late, creating the need to repeat information that has already been covered.

The team process should be fun and productive. There is, however, a feeling that meetings in business are not fun, too often a waste of time, and too often unproductive. This is "committee-itis," and it is the result of poor team leader and team member skills.

Both team leaders and team members need to work at making their meetings efficient and productive. Just as teams improve their work process, they need to develop the process of functioning as a team. The team meeting is the key event in their team's effectiveness. If the meetings are of poor quality, the team will have great difficulty achieving their goals. This chapter will deal with how to plan and prepare for a successful team meeting as well as the facilitation skills needed to get the most out of the team members during the meeting.

Many people wish to jump into their team meetings without planning properly, defining desired results, or anticipating obstacles. Like successful coaches, managers need to realize that much of the success comes from good planning before the game. Plan ahead so that the cards are stacked on the side of success.

Although these terms are used differently in some literature, we will use the following definitions throughout our training manuals:

Team Leader — the line manager or project manager responsible for the output of the team.

Team Facilitator — the person who prepares agendas and leads the team process. (may be a team leader or member)

Team Coach or **Internal Consultant** — the person who is not a member of the team but gives assistance and advice to the team during the implementation phase of the quality process.

Subject Matter Experts — SMEs are people who have or acquire a particular expertise necessary for the team members to address their key performance measures. These may be team members or may be people invited to the team meeting to assist with problem solving.

Team Member — the people who participate on the team on an ongoing basis. Team members are peers who "own" the process they are working to improve.

Team Roles & Responsibilities

➢ **Team Members**
➢ **Team Leader**
➢ **Subject Matter Experts**
➢ **Outside Experts & Advisors**
➢ **Customers & Suppliers**
➢ **Guest Managers**

Exercise:

Consider what elements make a meeting effective. What are the "drivers" or antecedents for a good meeting and what are the obstacles or restraints to an effective meeting?

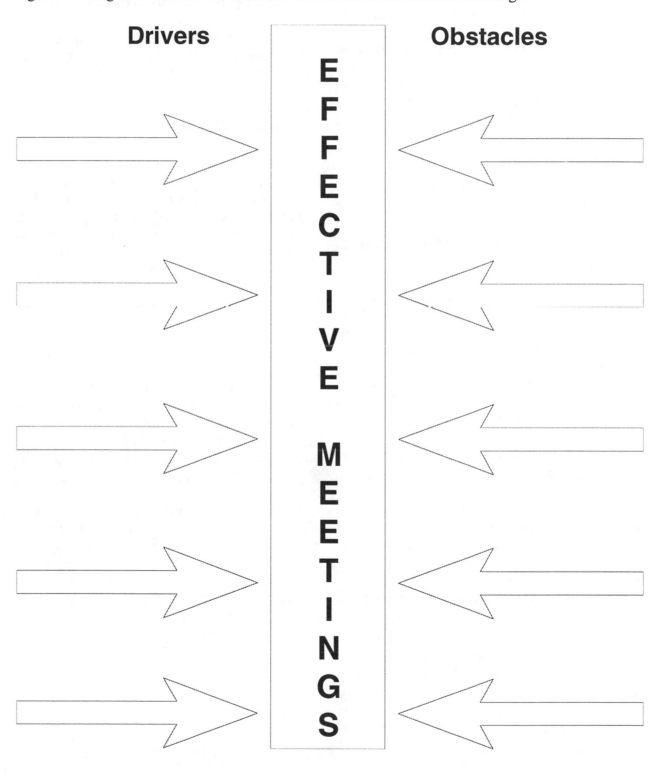

Drivers   **Obstacles**

E
F
F
E
C
T
I
V
E

M
E
E
T
I
N
G
S

Planning the Environment

Where

Increase your chances of a successful meeting by planning and designing a physical environment that is conducive to listening and concentrating on the topic being discussed. The team management process will be an ongoing component of the permanent work environment. The meeting environment is worth thinking through carefully. It is also worth discussing with your team members.

Here are some guidelines for choosing your meeting location:

Find a designated time and place.

Consistency is helpful, and having one room where the team always meets will be helpful. This will prevent the team leader from having to write a weekly memo on the time and place of the meeting. If meetings are consistently held in the same place, attendance and timeliness will become habit much more quickly. You want your team meeting to become a part of your normal business routine.

Try to find a room with minimal distractions.

If your work area is in a noisy environment with equipment operating, you will want to find a meeting room without distractions if at all possible.

Find a place where there will be no interruptions.

If necessary, put a "Do Not Disturb; Meeting in Progress" sign on the door of the meeting room. It should be agreed upon that others will not interrupt meetings unless there is a genuine emergency. If others feel free to interrupt to ask questions, relay messages, or call members to the phone, the effectiveness of the team will be diminished.

Set up the room for comfort.

Have good lighting, minimal noise, and comfortable seating so that team meetings can be as pleasant as possible for everyone concerned.

Arranging the Room

The seating arrangements will have a significant impact on team members' behavior. Do you remember when you were in school? The teacher was the center of attention. She or he spoke most of the time, and the students listened obediently. The students were there to listen and learn, not to participate in mutual decision-making. The physical arrangement of the classroom defined roles and responsibilities between teacher and students.

The definition of roles and responsibilities in a team meeting are very different from the classroom, and the arrangement of tables and chairs should reflect the difference. The leader or facilitator of the meeting is not teaching. He or she is not "controlling" the meeting. The team leader should not be the dominant personality or speaker.

The leader's job is to encourage team members to participate. The seating arrangement should signify equal participation and responsibility. Avoid having the leader sit or stand on a higher platform, behind a desk, or in any other way appear to be the "general" in charge.

When to Hold Meetings

Football teams play each week during the season. Choirs and bands often practice several times each week. There is wisdom in these schedules. They reflect the basic need for frequency of interaction and frequency of performance review for a group to feel and act like a team.

There is no one right answer to how often or how long teams should meet. We do not have a cookbook to give the perfect ratios of ingredients for length and frequency of meetings. However, it is critical to remember that team meetings are focused on managing performance. Teams need to meet frequently enough and long enough to make good business decisions about how to run their unit of the operation. When teams meet infrequently or for too short a time period, they deteriorate into status reports by the members or top-down direction by the team leader.

The most common schedule for successful meetings is once a week for about an hour. But there are many options.

Options to Consider

Daily: Ten to twenty minutes. Some organizations have found that the most valuable meeting time for their first-line teams is every day for ten to twenty minutes before their work day begins. Obviously, in-depth problem solving would have to be addressed in a different meeting, but daily operational measures can be reviewed each morning and decisions made on how to proceed for the rest of the shift.

Weekly: Forty-five minutes to one hour. This is the most common schedule for team meetings. A weekly one-hour meeting will allow the team to cover all agenda items and still have some active participation in decision-making and problem solving during the meeting itself.

Biweekly: One to two hours. Some organizations have chosen to meet every two weeks due to their rotating shift schedules or the frequency at which performance data is received. Obviously it means that individuals will have to make more decisions without team members' input. However meeting biweekly allows the team more time to get into broader issues when it does meet.

When & How Long to Hold Team Meetings

Discuss with the Team
Weekly or Bi-Weekly
Be Consistent
Begin & End on Time
Appoint Timekeeper
When the Members Aren't Too Tired

Monthly: Half day to an entire day. The only time monthly meetings are appropriate is when geography or travel schedules are a major obstacle for the team. This is most common in sales organizations in which team members cover large territories. In these situations we recommend more frequent written communication, conference calls, voicemail, and computer network discussions to share ideas between meetings.

Making Best Use of Time

People do not like to have their time wasted. We all like to feel that we are productive and making effective use of our time. The following guidelines will help make effective use of meeting time:

It is better to schedule meetings early in the day or shift. People are generally most refreshed and can focus their energies on the team meeting if you get them together before they have put in a full day of work.

Get the team members involved in making the decision about what time is best for them. This is a good exercise for your team's first consensus decision, and they will feel more committed to being there if they made the decision.

Be consistent. Keep the beginning and ending time of your meeting consistent. In your first team meeting, you might discuss the schedule and make this team decision with the members committing to consistency.

Appoint a timekeeper to keep the meeting on schedule. If you are having trouble keeping your meetings within the allotted time, a timekeeper will enable the team leader to remain focused on the content being discussed. Timekeepers track the allotted time for each agenda item in addition to the time for the entire meeting.

Always start and finish on time. This way team members can honor other commitments they have made following the meeting. It also teaches discipline in following team commitments.

Planning Meeting Content

When planning a team meeting one must first determine the purpose of the meeting. What do you want to accomplish? In general the purposes of a team meeting are as follows:

➤ **Review the team's performance.**

➤ **Recognize/reward/reinforce progress.**

➤ **Discuss problems and look for solutions to improve the team's performance.**

➤ **Plan action steps for upcoming work and for implementing solutions.**

➤ **Share important information.**

You also need to consider what you are going to do during the meeting to accomplish your objectives. For example the team may decide that a particular problem should be discussed at the next team meeting. Possible activities for that discussion would be analyzing data related to the problem, identifying possible causes of the problem, or brainstorming potential solutions.

Questions you might ask before each team meeting are as follows:

What are the main things we want to accomplish at this meeting?

For example you may have a primary objective of communicating some critical business information that will impact your team's direction, or you may have a particular performance problem that needs to be addressed immediately. Identify your most important objectives to enable you to prioritize your agenda.

How are we going to accomplish our objectives?

For example if you were going to attack an important problem, you may decide that you will analyze data related to the problem and identify causes in this meeting. If you wanted to address several problems, you might decide to divide the team into two task forces to discuss separate issues.

What are we going to do to ensure participation from the team?

For example you may want to assign a particular team member to be prepared to present information on a certain topic, or you may want to offer a couple of unusual ideas to get the group to start a brainstorming session, or you may ask another team member to lead the discussion.

Planning the Agenda

The purpose of the agenda is to organize the meeting, plan what you want to accomplish, and keep the meeting on track. Meetings without agendas are usually disorganized and end with participants wondering what was accomplished. Remember that the agenda is not only for the team leader; it is to help all members of the team participate, plan their own input, and stay on the topic.

Once you have identified the purpose of the meeting, you are ready to plan your agenda. As you are planning, keep the following in mind:

Prioritize the agenda. Since you may not have time to discuss every issue, it is important that the most urgent and important issues are addressed first. Deciding what color the office walls will be painted may not be vitally important to the business, but because the painters are coming in tomorrow, that topic may be at the top of the agenda. However, it is also important not to let debate over wall color consume too much valuable time when a critical performance problem also needs to be discussed. Allocating time limits to each item helps control the meeting and ensures every item gets adequate coverage.

Organize the sequence of decision-making. For example it makes no sense to discuss individual work assignments before discussing scheduling and workload.

Ask team members to add items to the agenda. People should have the opportunity to raise issues that they would like addressed during the meeting. One way to handle this is to ask for contributions to next week's agenda at the end of each meeting. Also be sure to ask how long the subject should take. Usually issues raised that are not on the agenda for the current meeting can be added to the agenda the following week.

Planning Your Agenda

❋ **Review Agreed-on Actions from Previous Meetings**

❋ **Prioritize & Sequence**

❋ **Send Out - In Advance**

❋ **Ask Team Members for Input**

❋ **Make Agenda Visible During Meeting**

Publicize the agenda. This will allow participants to think about the items to be discussed and come to the meeting prepared with any necessary information. *Note any preparation that is required of the team members.* This will prompt them to do their homework and read any background information or prepare their thoughts on a complicated topic.

Make the agenda visible to all members during the meeting so that each item can be checked off as it is completed. A visible agenda allows members to cooperate in helping the team leader complete all of the meeting objectives. If they do not know the objectives in the beginning of the meeting, they are more likely to overwork whatever subject is on the table at the moment.

Stick to the agenda to which the team agreed. If you must deviate, first ask the group's permission.

Sample Agenda

There are eight critical ingredients to designing a good agenda for team meetings. The order does not always have to be the same; in fact some team leaders prefer to get the most difficult items covered first and save the easiest for the end of the meeting. The core ingredients are as follows:

1. Review the Agenda/Set Time Limits for Agenda Items

Get input before the meeting begins to see if anyone has something to add to this agenda or if there are issues that can wait until the next meeting agenda.

A Sample Agenda

Review Agenda
Recognize Members
Review Action Plan
Review Performance
Share Information
Solve Problems
Develop Action Plan
Plan Next Agenda

2. Recognize Team Members

An important piece of the meeting is to recognize something good that someone has done since the last meeting. Recognition is an important habit to acquire. The team leader can share accomplishments, or team members can take time to recognize one of their team members. Positive recognition establishes the proper spirit and sets a positive tone for the rest of the meeting.

3. Review Existing Action Plan

To use your team meetings as a source of accountability, you should review commitments made in prior meetings. Each person who committed to carry out a task should be asked the status of his/her activities. If they are completed or proceeding as planned, the individual should be recognized by the team. If they are having difficulty, the team should help them devise a strategy to complete the task.

4. Review Performance

The team should review their three to five key performance measures. This is probably the most important part of the team meeting. This information determines what problems the team chooses to solve. Teams should be reinforced for improvement and goal attainment of these performance measures. Managers should reinforce improvements, too!

5. Share Information

The team leader shares information from the meeting he attended with his peers. Because of this process of disseminating information, it is best if the most senior team meets at the beginning of the week so that the information can filter down through the team system as each level has their meetings. Information needs to move upward through the organization as well.

6. Problem Solving

The problem-solving process should be used to address performance areas which need quality improvement. Unless it is a "quick fix" problem, or the entire meeting is devoted to the process, you will be able to cover only a few of the steps in the problem-solving process. It is often the case that one meeting may be devoted to defining the problem and brainstorming causes, and then team members take time to research the causes between meetings.

7. Develop an Action Plan

When the team makes a decision or finds a solution to a problem, the last step is to define action steps to implement the decision or solution. Team members should volunteer or be assigned an action item to be completed by a specific date.

8. Review Action Steps and Plan Next Agenda

The last step of the meeting is to review all decisions made and any action steps that have been devised during the meeting. This will clarify who is accountable for carrying out tasks and is helpful to determine what items will be on the agenda for the next meeting. Most agenda items will be determined at this point though everyone should feel free to go to the team leader before the next meeting and request that items be added to the agenda. It is a good idea to have the agenda finalized and circulated (or posted) twenty-four hours prior to the next meeting.

Agenda Format

Agendas can vary in format and detail. The following sample agendas can give you some options. In general, the longer and more complex the meeting, the more detailed the agenda needs to be. This is primarily to ensure that people come prepared, they know what the objective of each topic is, and it's clear who is responsible for facilitating discussion.

Sample Agenda

Topic	Purpose	Presenter or Facilitator	Time Allocated	Preparation Required	Outcome/ Decision

Team Meeting Agenda

I.   **Review Agenda**   (Time Frame: _____min.)

II.   **Recognize Team Members**   (Time Frame: _____min.)

III.   **Review Performance**   (Time Frame: _____min.)

IV.   **Review Existing Action Items**   (Time Frame: _____min.)

V.   **Solve Problems**   (Time Frame: _____min.)

VI.   **Plan Action Items**   (Time Frame: _____min.)

VII.   **Share Information**   (Time Frame: _____min.)

VIII.   **Plan Next Team Meeting Agenda**   (Time Frame: _____min.)

TEAM MEETING CHECKLIST

Use the following checklist to be sure you have not forgotten anything for your team meeting:

_____ 1.   Have you planned what the team should accomplish at the meeting?

_____ 2.   Have you decided what type of activities the team is going to do during the meeting to accomplish your objectives?

_____ 3.   Have you planned what you are going to do to ensure participation from your team?

_____ 4.   Do you have a written agenda?

_____ 5.   Has the agenda been circulated in advance of the meeting?

_____ 6.   Have the agenda topics been prioritized?

_____ 7.   Have time limits been set for each agenda item?

_____ 8.   Did you allow participants to add items to the agenda?

_____ 9.   Do you have necessary information collected for the meeting? Do team members know what information they should bring with them?

_____ 10. Have you invited all of the necessary people?

_____ 11. Have you selected a meeting time? Can everyone on your team meet at this time?

_____ 12. Is there an appropriate space set aside to conduct the meeting with a "do not disturb" order issued for the duration of the meeting?

_____ 13. Does everyone on your team know when , where, and how long the meeting will last?

Team Process

Now that we're altogether, what do we do? To really capitalize on the thinking of each team member and to synthesize their ideas into a group conclusion is a challenge. Being an effective facilitator is a critical skills for all team leaders.

That's interesting. How did you feel about the new contract?

Well, I guess I felt proud of what our team did.

Skills of Facilitation

To "facilitate" a discussion means to make it easier for others to participate. The facilitator of a group has the responsibility and function of removing obstacles to participation. The facilitator of a team may be the team leader, the manager, or any individual who agrees to act in this role. It is also important to understand that every team member can use the skills of facilitation to help others participate and to improve his own communication skills.

The effective team is one where effective communication occurs. Contrary to popular perception, the best communicators are the best listeners, not the best talkers. They are effective communicators because they ask good questions, show genuine interest in the other person, and respond positively to the contribution of others. If everyone feels comfortable sharing his ideas, he will enjoy the conversation, enjoy being in the company of the listener, and enjoy participating on the team.

Effective listening skills are far more important to running good meetings than are speaking skills. This is particularly true if you are trying to increase the participation of your team members. Effective listening is also critical in resolving conflicts between members and helping the group problem solve and reach consensus.

Capitalizing on Differences

If you grew up in a tiny remote village and never saw a television, you might well think that the norms of behavior within this village were the norms of behavior for all people. If in this village people always ate with sticks, you would be puzzled, perhaps even suspicious, of someone who picked up a fork and ate his meat with this strange instrument.

Similarly if in this remote village it were normal for groups of people to get together and sit with their heads down for long periods of time to think about a subject before speaking, you would consider this normal behavior. You might be puzzled and perhaps suspicious of someone who spoke about a subject immediately, sounding very authoritative, even though he had not taken time to bow his head and think.

We are all villagers. We have all grown up in a culture and have accepted most of the norms of communication of that culture.

One of the great virtues and strengths of the United States is its cultural diversity. Decision-making groups from the Constitutional Convention to this day have been faced with creating unity of purpose and action from cultural diversity. Your team most likely is also characterized by cultural diversity.

Men and women may have different cultural communication patterns. Different ethnic, religious, and regional cultures all have different norms of communication. Some will speak up immediately and argue their point in a loud and commanding voice. Others will wait to be called upon and speak softly. These different styles have nothing to do with the value of the ideas commu-nicated. The person who speaks the most softly may have the most powerful and useful idea.

These cultural differences should be discussed during the team meeting. Each member should share how they prefer to communicate and the team should decide how best to accommodate individual differences.

The facilitator is faced with the challenge of giving everyone equal opportunity to participate, to be heard, and to listen regardless of cultural differences. This means you will have to treat people differently. The loud and fast talkers will not require you to ask many open-ended questions. The quiet and soft-spoken may not contribute until you invite them by name to share their thoughts. You will need to be sensitive to their patterns of communication and help them make their best contribution. This means treating all team members equitably but not necessarily the same.

Facilitation skills include

Asking questions
Empathy
Rephrasing
Silence

Exercise

Discuss one of the three following *profiles*. The people profiled are on a new product development team. They are employed by a cosmetics company and are working on an anti-aging cream.

In three groups discuss the following: How would this person likely behave? How would she express herself? How would he attack problem situations? What would you predict his reaction to conflict to be? What type of biases might this person have?

After each group develops their expectations of the profile described, present these to the larger group. Discuss with the larger group the following: How could the team leader deal with these differences? How can the team build on and benefit from these differences? What value might these individual differences bring to the team? How might you deal with the fact that your expectations of these people are wrong? What is the impact of "self-fulfilling prophecy" on people's behavior?

Profile # 1

Jim grew up in a small rural town in the Southeast. His father has a high school diploma and works as an auto mechanic, his mother is a secretary at their church. Jim is going to school at night to finish his last year of college to complete his engineering degree. He has two children and his wife teaches elementary school.

Profile # 2

Martin grew up in Brooklyn, New York. His father worked in Manhattan in the garment district selling men's suits, his mother is a CPA. Martin has a graduate degree in finance from a college in New England. He is married to an attorney and has no children.

Profile # 3

Sarah was raised in California. Her father is an engineer and her mother a computer programmer. Sarah is a chemist and went to school in southern California. She is a single parent of one teenage daughter.

Active Versus Passive Listening

Confusion in communication often occurs as a result of passive listening. When a message is delivered by the speaker, the listener mentally translates the spoken word into a particular message. This may or may not be the message intended by the speaker. The passive listener accepts his translation to be accurate. The active listener reflects back to the speaker his understanding of the message to receive verification, clarification, or more information.

The chance for confusion in a meeting is magnified because there are many "listeners" for every idea and, therefore, many potential translations. It is critical that the team leader use these active-listening skills frequently during the meeting.

Asking Questions

The first skill of an effective facilitator is to ask effective questions. There are two broad types of questions: **closed-ended questions** and **open-ended questions.**

A closed-ended question can be answered with a one-word answer: Yes or No.

"Would you like to collect this information this week?" is a closed-ended question. It could be answered with "yes" or "no." On the other hand, "What information would you like to collect this week?" requires some explanation. This is an open-ended question.

Asking closed-ended questions does not elicit as much participation as asking open-ended questions. However, it is an appropriate technique for fact finding, to narrow down focus to

The Best Communicators Are The Best Listeners

"It sounds as if you are really concerned about..."

specifics and to "shut down" an excessive talker. Open-ended questions cannot be answered with a yes or no. The best conversationalists at a party are those who ask many open-ended questions, providing the opportunity for the other person to talk about those things that interest him. They elicit participation. Those teams which have the most participation are those with facilitators who are skilled at asking open-ended questions.

Open-ended questions usually begin with

> **What?**
> **Where?**
> **Why?**
> **How?**

Open-ended questions tend to prompt more information. One of the problems with closed-ended questions is that they are often leading. For example, "Don't you think this is a good idea?" is very leading! Therefore, you can never be sure if the answer is truly what the person thinks, or simply what you led him to say. If, however, the question is phrased, "What are your thoughts on this idea?" your chances of finding out where the person actually stands are much greater.

Open-ended questions are very useful for facilitating discussion in team meetings. They can be used to:

Start a discussion: "What do you think about the new project priority list the Finance Department developed?"

Ask a specific member for his opinion: "What is your opinion about our new quality program, Jack?"

Bring a conversation back on task: "What other information do we need to solve this problem?"

Make transitions from one agenda item to the next: "What other comments do you have before we move on to the next agenda item?"

The Key Facilitation Skills

Asking Questions

"What do you feel are the most important issues?" (open)
"Can you get that data to the team in time to run the analysis?" (closed)

Empathy Statements

"It must feel disappointing that..."

Rephrasing

"In other words you would like to..."

Exercise:

Habits of communication change only with practice. With a partner practice asking open-ended questions. Try having one person think of something that is bothering him or her. The other person can then try to find out what it is. First, ask your partner three closed-ended question about what is bothering him. Then ask three open-ended questions beginning with what, why, how, or where. Note the difference in information you receive.

Remember, both of these types of questions are useful facilitation skills but they tend to have very different impact on the talker.

Empathy

With an empathy statement you express how you think the other person feels and why. Showing empathy toward another person helps that person feel like a part of the group; it helps him share his feelings and ideas. It helps him feel understood. We all want to be understood, and we all participate more frankly when we feel the other person is genuinely listening to our point of view.

An example would be, "It sounds like you're upset because you feel you were left out of that discussion when I didn't ask for your opinion." In this example the upset feeling was being left out, and the reason was because I did not ask for your opinion. This empathy statement should make the person feel that you understand him/her better, thus improving communication.

Empathy is not the same as sympathy. *Empathy* means that you can identify with the other person's feeling whether you agree with the feeling, or not. Sympathy means that you agree with the person's feelings and that you share them. *Sympathy* also suggests sorrow or sadness. Empathy can be happy, excited, thrilled, or angry.

As a team leader you can use empathy statements:

To help reduce strong emotions that can stand in the way of rational thinking. Making an empathy statement to someone who is expressing anger can often diffuse some feelings about an issue. An example would be, "I can see that you are furious about being embarrassed in front of your peers."

To encourage other people to listen to you. If they feel you are genuinely recognizing their emotions, they are more likely to listen to what you are trying to say.

To relieve some of the anxiety being felt about discussing a problem publicly. An example is, "I can understand why it would be very awkward for you to get that phone call from the customer when only a month ago you promised him we would deliver every shipment on time in the future."

Note that in both the above examples, the empathy statement did not include the word *but*. We are usually trying to help with phrases such as, "But once you get used to it, it won't be so bad." Unfortunately, the *but* often sounds like you are challenging the person's feelings, saying he is not right or should not feel that way. This tends to escalate the emotion instead of reducing it, so that the benefit of the empathy statement is lost. An alternative is to explore thoroughly the other person's feelings and position on the subject before presenting your opinion. Use phrases such as, "Another way to look at that is....," or, "In my opinion....," or, "At the same time, my view is...."

"I can understand that this makes you feel a bit anxious."

Some models for empathy statements are:

"It sounds as if you feel...(feeling word) because........(reason)."

"It sounds as if you feel anxious because you have to make that presentation tomorrow."

"It must be....(feeling word) when....(reason)."

"It must be annoying when he doesn't return your calls."

"I can understand that ....(reason) would make you ....(feeling word)."

"I can understand that getting that project would make you feel excited."

Exercise:

Form into groups and practice making empathy statements. One person should present a situation that caused some emotional response, and the other person should express empathy with that other person, then switch roles.

Rephrasing

Rephrasing or reflective listening is a way of verifying what you think the other person has said. It is much like holding up a mirror and saying, "This is what I understood you to be saying. Is that right?" The other person will confirm your understanding and will then feel that you understand him. Then, if necessary, the other person will provide clarifying information.

Rephrasing is restating the speaker's message *in your own words*. It can be very useful for clarification of people's ideas during discussions and decision-making. Its primary function is to demonstrate the listener's understanding of what the speaker is saying.

As a team leader, you can use rephrasing:

To clarify a team member's statements. A example is, "It sounds as if you think we are spending too much time creating programs for specialized reports."

To resolve conflicts between two team members. "It sounds as if John thinks we should continue hiring inexperienced programmers, and Sara thinks we should consider hiring experienced programmers. What do the rest of you think?" (Note: In this example an open-ended question is used in conjunction with rephrasing to open the discussion up to the rest of the team.)

To help someone express his emotions. "What I hear you saying is that you feel very strongly about this issue, and it has caused you some real pain."

To get at deeper issues than those being expressed. Some issues are hard to talk about. The first expression of a concern may be only the superficial expression, skirting around the issue. The person may hope that you will try to understand him so he will feel free to express his greater, deeper concerns.

Rephrasing statements start with phrases such as:

What I'm hearing is ...
So in other words ...
So it sounds as if ...
Let me make sure I've got this right ...

Exercise:

Rephrase the following statements. Try simply stating in your own words what you think the person really means.

1. "I think Steve Brown should be assigned to that project immediately because he has the drive to ensure that the group finally produces a successful project."

_____

_____

_____

2. "I think you should begin work on this project right away and put the other things on hold; it may pay higher dividends."

_____

_____

_____

3. "I think everyone should be able to work at his/her own pace."

_____

_____

_____

4. "I think Jim is a real team player."

_____

_____

_____

5. "I think the instructor should change his/her teaching style."

_____

_____

_____

6. "I don't believe that 'the customer is always right.'"

_____

_____

_____

Getting the Most from Your Team

The purpose of all of these facilitation skills is to increase the participation in your team meetings.

Your success with your team will be magnified if people are reinforced (recognized and appreciated) for their participation. Be careful not to inadvertently punish someone for participating. For example if a team member offers a suggestion which is immediately shot down, the team will quickly learn that participation is dangerous. Furthermore it is important to remember that sometimes people have nothing new to contribute. Pressing a member to say something can be very embarrassing and punishing. The sensitive team leader also knows when to leave a member alone.

Your meetings will be more successful if you keep them upbeat with plenty of active listening to draw out everyone's ideas and to reinforce creativity and cooperation.

Getting the most from your team can be enhanced by having the team members "contract" or reach agreement with each other about how they want to be treated during the meeting and as a team. This can be done in one of your first team meetings by setting ground rules together.

Ground Rules

One of the best ways to share the responsibility of meeting behavior being productive is to have each team develop a set of ground rules or a "Code of Conduct" to describe how they want to treat each other.

Developing Ground Rules

This is a list of guidelines for appropriate meeting behavior. It is important that the team develop their own guidelines. No one else will manage the behavior of the team. If they can agree on their own guidelines, they will feel that these are mutual agreements, not "rules" imposed upon them by someone else.

These guidelines can be posted in the meeting room, reviewed at the beginning of the meeting, and referred to during the meeting when inappropriate behavior occurs.

Why should we develop ground rules?

1. To create common expectations and understanding among team members.

2. To encourage desirable behavior from individual team members.

3. To enhance the self management of the team.

4. To keep a written record of guidelines.

The group will be more committed to conforming to the code if they establish it as a group. You may find it helpful to provide a "sample" ground rules as a model. For example:

1. Stick to the topic at hand. If you have other issues to discuss, wait until the one being discussed is resolved.

2. Make criticism constructive. Avoid value judgments and try to suggest alternatives.

3. Arrive on time and end on time.

4. Pay attention to whomever is speaking. Be a good listener.

5. One person talks at a time.

6. No gossip! Keep discussions on issues over which the group has control.

7. Everyone has the responsibility to contribute.

8. Ideas belong to the group, not the individual.

9. Be frank and honest.

10. The team speaks with one voice after the decision is made. Leave united.

11. Respect differences in communication, thinking, and decision-making styles. We are all wired differently!

Although developing ground rules is a rather simple matter, you will find that it is a key ingredient in the success of a team.

Action Assignment

1. In one of your early team meetings have the group discuss and reach agreement on its ground rules or code of conduct. Practice good listening skills to draw out participation from all members.

How did you do? What happened when you tried this? How do you think the other person reacted?

_____

_____

_____

Was it effective?

_____

_____

_____

If you had it to do over again, what might you do differently?

_____

_____

_____

2. Practice good listening skills at home or with friends. See what you can learn.

Implementation Tips

1. While team meetings are a critical piece of the quality effort working it is important to remind people that quality pervades <u>everything</u> at work and should be happening all the time, not just in team meetings.

2. Be aware of teams becoming consumed in meeting "mechanics" versus getting to the core of their work. It's better to have a sloppy meeting and be working on improving customer satisfaction than vice versa!

3. Most of meeting effectiveness is related to behavior change. This requires a lot of work from the team's coach, who will be observing the process and getting feedback to both the team and the team leader.

4. Every meeting should end with a debriefing. As the team "matures" they will be able to give themselves feedback. Early in the process, that will be the coaches' job.

5. Be prepared for frustration in the early phases, "Why are we doing this?" "When can we quit meeting?" Until the team experiences some success in improving results it will feel like "all cost and no benefit" to the team.

6. The success and failure of meeting effectiveness most often falls on people issues: truly listening, being open to new ideas, working to reach consensus, and resolving conflicts. This is going to be increasingly true as the workforce becomes more and more diverse. It will require more work and effort on everyone's part to respond openly to different communication patterns. Discuss these issues within your teams and really use your Code of Conduct as a working, breathing contract!

Chapter Eight

Making Decisions in Teams

There are different methods of decision-making for different times. As teams develop, they will take more responsibility for decision-making.

Objectives

1. To understand different decision-making styles.

2. To establish clear expectations for when to use various styles.

3. To provide guidelines for teams to reach consensus.

Decision-Making

When organizations implement team management, one of the biggest sources of confusion is who has the responsibility and authority for which decisions. Management often thinks that the team is responsible for the process automatically take charge of the process and should start making appropriate decisions. Teams usually believe that the manager will continue to make the decisions until they, the team members, are told differently. Team members are often afraid of making a mistake, of overstepping their authority, or are still waiting to be told what to do because they don't believe that things have really changed. Very important decisions can fall through the cracks or not get made in a timely manner.

There is no one right way to make decisions. The best style of decision-making is determined by the situation. The best managers and teams know when and how to make decisions based on an understanding of the environment, the people, and the priorities. In this chapter we will explore the different styles and the times to use them. Your team will want to reach agreement on the *who, how,* and *when* of decision-making.

Today's organization faces a highly unpredictable environment with a turbulent economy, increasing competition, and a demanding consumer. On top of all this the average employee is often one who desires and sometimes expects to be consulted on issues that affect his work life. Today employees recognize that they have more options than in the past. Their expectations for job satisfaction and involvement in meaningful decision-making are much higher than ever before. A skilled employee will shop around for more meaningful work if she becomes dissatisfied with her job. How decisions are made is a major factor in the satisfaction or dissatisfaction with work.

The difficulty and strain are often greatest on the veteran manager who came into his position during a different era. The image of the effective manager has evolved from one who is all-knowing, tough, and single-minded to one who can motivate and challenge his associates to be creative and competent and who can participate in team decision-making. Today managers do not stand alone. They stand on a field as members of a team, sometimes leading and sometimes participating. This is a difficult transition for many managers to make.

Turning decisions over to teams initially can be confusing and threatening. A manager may feel that she alone should make all of the decisions because she is ultimately responsible for results. Also it is natural for a manager to want to use the experience and skill she has developed over the years to make decisions. If she is not making decisions, why is she a manager?

The transition to a team-based organization and the acceptance of team decision-making will take time. So, too, will the development of the team's decision-making skills and the trust that managers are willing to place in teams. This will be true whether the teams are at the senior management level or at the first-level employee.

Not all decisions are appropriate for teams. Some decisions are best made by an individual alone, sometimes with input from others and sometimes without. One of the marks of the successful, modern-day manager or team is competence at determining which decisions fall into which category. Boundaries should be determined for each level of team, indicating which types of decisions should be made in each style. This will prevent the frustration which arises when decisions get made without the involvement of people who expect to be consulted.

It is not lack of involvement that is frustrating but conflict with expectations for involvement.

Effective decision-making is not a mysterious process. Decisions can be made by a variety of methods which take into consideration such

---

issues as time constraints and information availability. Another consideration is the question of who is expected to execute the decision. It is the objective of this session to help you consider these issues and determine the best way to make each of your decisions.

Why Bother with Team Decision-Making

The quickest, most efficient decisions are made by the individual on-the-spot without consulting anyone else. It is not only time-consuming to involve others; it is often frustrating. People join the discussion with all kinds of strange ideas, misunderstandings, biases, self-interest, and commitment to their own course of action! Why bother?

It is often true that involving others in decision-making is a bother and a cost in time and resources, and it must be justified by some benefit. In fact every one of these objections are reasons for teams to make decisions.

They bring strange ideas. In other words they have ideas that are different than your own. These may conflict with yours. If they did not bring different ideas, then what possible good would team decision-making be? These ideas are added to the stew, and the result can incorporate and greatly benefit from many different alternatives.

They bring misunderstandings. Team members often perceive a problem from their own personal points of view. It is difficult to get buy in to the implementation of the decision without clear and consistent understanding from all team members. What better way to clarify points of view than through discussions of the decision alternatives.

They bring biases that are hard to overcome. It is true. People are biased. They are biased by their previous experience. They prefer what has worked for them in the past or what they have seen succeed. They are against that which they have seen fail. But is this wrong? It is perfectly natural and logical. In truth we can learn from these biases. They should be taken into account. The person with biases should be heard so that he can feel a shared ownership for the final decision, and we can all benefit from each other's expectations.

They all have their own self-interests. Everyone comes into a meeting concerned about how decisions will affect <u>him</u>. Each one wants what will be best for him. However is it so harmful if the team is comprised of those who do the work, who feel a responsibility to their customers, who know their process, and who are keeping their own scores? This self-interest is the same as a motivation to see things improved. It can work to help the team reach effective decisions.

They already are committed to a course of action. Sometimes this is true. But most often members of a team along with the team leader are looking for a way to improve and are open to alternatives. As they learn to work in teams, they will learn to remain open to alternatives and allow the magic of group brainstorming to work. Sometimes they are committed to a course of action. When they are, it is important to listen to the course of action. Why are they committed to this course? What facts, experience, and reasoning have gone into their commitment? This information is important. It will also be important to get this same person committed to a new course of action. There is no better way than involvement in the decision-making process.

The following examples are some of the other reasons to engage in team decision-making:

Increased learning and personal growth. When you participate in decision-making, you are challenged to think. You try to understand facts, alternatives, and the ways different jobs affect one another. The brain comes alive! Participation in decision-making increases learning.

Increased job challenge. Challenge is excitement and motivation. Confronting problems and seeking improvement can make even repetitive work much more interesting.

Increased employee autonomy. Employees require less management time when they accept responsibility for their own work. This frees managers to do higher level problem solving and creative work for which they often cannot find time.

More employee receptivity and trust of the management decisions. When you are involved in decision-making, you understand that solutions are not as simple as they might otherwise appear. You understand the difficulties in choosing between different options. You then become more accepting of the decisions made by others. Also if someone listens to you and takes your opinion into account, you are then more likely to respect his opinion and judgment.

Better quality decisions. Two heads are better than one. Ten are even better! If the decision-making process is effective, team decision-making brings out the knowledge and experience of all and allows the whole to become greater than the sum of all the parts. The best decisions are made when the opinion and input of all are taken into account.

Improved teamwork. Most decisions will need the cooperation of more than one person to implement. Teamwork begins when the decision is being made. The longer you wait to involve others, the harder it will be to gain their cooperation in the implementation of the decision.

Discussion

Which of the benefits would be most valuable to your team?

_____

_____

_____

_____

_____

Which of the benefits do you think are most likely to impact your organization?

_____

_____

_____

_____

_____

Decision-Making Styles

There are four possible decision-making methods or styles. Each is legitimate and has its place. <u>Management and decision-making in particular are situational.</u> The skilled manager is not only able to use these styles well; he knows <u>when</u> to use each style.

It is important that team members have clear expectations. In other words if employees have been given the expectation that they will be involved in a particular decision, that expectation should not be violated. You do not want to establish unrealistic expectations. It is helpful to discuss the different styles of decision-making with your team and reach a mutual understanding as to which style of decision-making will be used in different situations.

Command

Command decisions are decisions made by an individual without consulting others. For example if there is an irate customer on the phone, it is not the time to gather the team together and involve them in a group decision regarding how to please the customer. It is preferable that the person who knows the answer take charge. In this case command decision-making is desirable. One of its advantages is eliciting a quick response from others in a crisis.

Appropriate situations for command decision-making are when time is a major factor or when only one individual has knowledge and competency in the area of the decision. Command does not stimulate creativity. It stimulates conformity, and in crisis conformity, 'doing it by the numbers', is often desirable. This is why command has always been the primary mode of decision-making in the military. As long as the military was the dominant organization in society, command was habitually valued as a decision-making style. The function of defense for thousands of years was the primary reason for organizing. Leaders were almost all military leaders. It is a recent turn of history, only the past few hundred years, when we have had large organizations for any other purpose. Now the primary purpose of most organizations is not defense but rather to create and distribute wealth. This requires that other styles become dominant.

A weakness of command leadership is that it fails to elicit the input and contribution of others. Without the participation of others in the decision, commitment to its implementation is likely to be at risk. Command decision-making also fails to develop subordinates' decision-making competence. It preserves that competence for the designated leaders. This does not lead an organization to effective self management.

Consultative

In consultative decision-making the manager or individual team member obtains the advice and involvement of others who have relevant knowledge or who will be impacted by the decision. After considering this input, the individual makes the decision. In the day-to-day world of business the majority of decisions that must be made are not crisis decisions, nor are they decisions that require the effort and time of team discussion and consensus. The manager presents the problem to others, asks for advice, and weighs the various alternatives. This informal involvement is often unnoticed and occurs every day. It is the method most frequently used by most managers. A strength of consultative decision-making is that it is a quick and flexible process for obtaining information. In addition it involves

team members, thereby increasing their commitment and experience in decision-making. A potential disadvantage of consultative decision-making is that an individual's input may be rejected in the final decision, thus discouraging future involvement.

Consensus

Consensus decision-making occurs when the team comes together, fully considers the facts and alternatives, takes ownership for the decision as a united team, and agrees on a course of action. Consensus does not necessarily mean that there is 100% agreement that a given solution is the one best solution. It does mean that everyone can agree to the benefits of the solution and, therefore, support it. The responsibility and the decision belong to the team, not any one person. If the decision is successful, the team is  to be congratulated. If it fails, there is no one to whom a finger can be pointed other than the team.

Consensus decisions are most appropriate for strategic issues, issues that will impact everyone, that are complex and require in-depth analysis by more than one individual, and that require the commitment and ownership of the entire team. There are strategic issues at every level of the organization. At the level of the hourly employee, issues regarding the methods and organization of the work on his team are strategic issues. Two strengths of consensus decision-making are increased commitment by the team and increased likelihood of quality decisions. A disadvantage is the increased time and effort invested in the consensus process.

Delegation

Delegation is the decision to allow someone else to decide. The person or team to whom the decision and responsibility are delegated may then choose to employ command, consultative, or consensus as a method of decision-making. It is desirable to delegate decision-making as far down the chain of command as possible. This gains the commitment of those who will do the work and frees the manager to devote his energies to other value-adding activities. Another strength of delegation is that it develops the subordinates' decision-making skills. A possible disadvantage of delegation is the risk of a poor decision. However managers can delegate without abdication. It is still the managers' job to ensure his team has the time, skill, and ability to make a good decision.

Those most qualified to make a decision are those "on-the-spot" with their hands on the work. Unfortunately we tend to push decisions up the organization away from those with true knowledge and experi-  ence most relevant to the decision. In this manner we demotivate those who must deal with the work process immediately, and we make poor decisions.

The core idea behind the team process is that when employees who have their hands on the work take responsibility for improving their work, quality improves and waste declines. It is also important to recognize that ***all employees are decision-makers***. First-level employees answer the phone and decide how to respond to a customer. A factory worker *decides* that a machine needs repair. Team members are constantly making decisions. It is important that they have the tools and techniques to make the best decision possible.

Exercise:

Discuss the advantages, disadvantages, and appropriate situations for each decision-making style.

Style	Advantages	Disadvantages	Situations
Command: Individual makes the decision alone.			
Consultative: Individual asks for input from others.			
Consensus: The team reaches a joint decision.			
Delegation: The manager gives away the decision- making authority.			

Increasing Involvement In Decision-Making: Issues to Consider

Information

Before team members become involved in decision-making, consider whether they have the training and information to make the decisions. If your team lacks the necessary information, how can the information distribution be changed to provide team members with the necessary background to make informed decisions?

Time

Turning decision-making over to a group almost always results in its taking more time to reach the decision. So you must consider the benefits derived against the time spent. The decision-making time will decrease as the team becomes more competent and efficient through the practice of thinking together.

Authority

A manager cannot give away more authority or freedom than he has. It is important that managers and team members consider which decisions they actually have the authority to make. Get agreement at the level above on the types of decisions you would like your team to make.

Involvement

Passing decision-making down does not necessarily mean that the manager no longer has input. Teams are often composed of managers and their subordinates. Together they comprise a decision-making team. It is important to recognize that a manager may have been assigned and accountable for performance in an area. He, therefore, cannot give up all interest in decision-making. He may also have knowledge that the team may lack. Therefore the team members must be sensitive to the actual responsibility, knowledge, and experience possessed by their managers.

Integrity

A manager should also never pretend to be giving up decision-making if she already has her mind made up. All participants must be completely honest about their actual roles and expectations for the decision-making process.

Responsibility & Accountability

Taking on decision-making authority brings with it a great deal of responsibility. As teams begin to make more decisions, they must demonstrate the maturity to respect differing ideas of each other and to uphold decisions they commit to as a team. If the decision made turns out to be a mistake, they must assume the same responsibility/ownership as their team leader!

Setting & Expanding Decision Boundaries

Once teams have successfully made the decisions within their original decision-making boundaries, it's time to delegate more authority to them. Soon after their decision-making boundaries are originally set, management needs to plan how to expand the decision-making boundaries of the teams. This ensures that more authority for improving the process actually continues to get moved to the people closest to the work. The plan also lets teams know that there is an organized method for turning the process over to them. The team members can anticipate and prepare for increasing their knowledge and skills. They know that management is serious about continuing everyone's role in managing quality.

Absolute Frankness & Honesty

Are we truly honest with one another? Often we are not. We withhold information or opinions because of our fear that we will be "put down" or ignored. We color our views based on what we feel the group will accept. This is not being absolutely frank and honest, and it cheats the team out of the best input.

Unity & Diversity

We are all different. Diversity among team members is never more apparent than during decision-making. It is becoming increasingly more critical to recognize, acknowledge, and deal with diverse points of view as our companies hire people from different cultural, economic, and historical backgrounds. Look at this as enriching the opportunity for innovation and growth rather than slowing down the process. It is difficult sometimes not to reject ideas from those who think differently or have different values. We need to treat each other with complete courtesy and respect to achieve total participation. This can be particularly difficult during a decision making process as some people like to "think out loud" while others need to leave a problem and come back to it later after some "digesting time."

It is important for the team to discuss their differences and needs for good decision-making and to reach agreement on how to accommodate people's various thinking styles. Everyone will have to make compromises, but no one should feel "bullied" into a decision.

Once we recognize and build on our diversity, it is critical to realize we have a common purpose as a team. When we have listened to the opinions of others and when we have been respectfully listened to, we are then ready to be unified in a decision. If you commit to the decision, it is necessary to execute it as though it were your own decision in complete unity even when the group makes a decision with which you don't totally agree. Just as when a football team leaves the huddle, they all work for the success of the team's play.

Pitfalls to Avoid in Decision-Making

There are many things that influence our decision-making which we should examine as we begin to involve individuals in working together towards a decision. Be careful to avoid these potential pitfalls in team decision-making.

Individual Bias

Often times decisions are made based on our individual or collective bias or preferences with little regard for the facts or alternative benefits. For example if given a choice between the following magazines which one would you choose?

Sports Illustrated	*Fortune*
People	*Money*
Ebony	*National Geographic*
Cosmopolitan	*Rolling Stone*

Why did you select this magazine?

Why didn't you select the others?

Your choice would be based on your personal interests, experiences, or values. This could result in a lowered probability of breaking out of your decision-making paradigms and consideration of alternative solutions or information sources. This is one of the dangers of a lack of diversity between members of a team. It can also occur where there is diversity, but the minority opinion is not heard.

Positions of Influence

Meeting expectations of those in a position of influence can often times determine the outcome of a decision. This approach to the decision-making process is aimed at pleasing others more than on solving the problem. In these situations you will often hear someone say, "It was the politically correct thing to do." The decisions made using this approach may or may not solve the problem and may increase the risk of a wrong decision. Individuals or groups may feel pressured to go along with a decision even though they do not personally or collectively agree with it. This type of decision-making is often based on impact considerations and not on the existing information for problem resolution.

Popularity Rules

Perhaps the most common approach to decision-making is the vote or "majority rules" method. The advantage to this approach to decision-making assures that the majority position will be selected and implemented by the team. The disadvantage of this approach is that it may result in division within the team or the ideas of some members not being fully heard or evaluated as to their merit. When team members know their point of view is not popular and will not be supported by the majority, they tend not to share their true opinions.

Over Using Consensus

Frequently, as companies move toward team-based organizations and employee involvement, there is the mistaken assumption that all decisions should suddenly be made by teams reaching consensus. This would be a disaster. The organization would come to a grinding halt with angry customers, missed deadlines, and frustrated employees. As we will discuss later in the chapter, *consensus is only one style of decision making and probably should only occur about 10% - 15% of the time decisions are made.*

When you do use consensus, you will find that one of the major benefits of pushing decision-making down is the employee's commitment to the decision. If ownership is critical, consensus decision-making is likely to be worth the time, investment, and training necessary to do it correctly. If ownership of the solution is not critical, it may be more efficient for an individual to make the decision alone.

Exercise:

Which influences do you see most prevalent on your team?

_____

_____

_____

_____

_____

_____

What do you think could be done to moderate these influences?

_____

_____

_____

_____

_____

_____

Choosing a Decision-Making Style

There are specific issues that must be considered in choosing which decision-making style fits a given situation. When choosing a style, a team should consider the following ideas:

Speed

How critical is it that the decision be made quickly? Obviously if it must be made on the spot, command is most appropriate. If it can wait, perhaps another decision-making style should be used.

Shared Ownership

How critical is it to the decision's success that the team members feel it is their own? Some decisions people willingly accept and/or execute without any contribution to making it (such as adjusting equipment); for others it is more critical to have participation (such as systems changes).

Investment in Finding a Solution

In some instances team members are not concerned enough about the decision to take the time to participate. There are some decisions that a team will not feel are important, yet may be important to a manager or technical expert. In this case it will be appropriate for the manager or expert to make the decision.

Competence in Making a Decision

Choosing a decision-making style should also include the issue of competency. If the team members have little understanding or knowledge of a certain topic, use the consultative or command decision-making style to involve those who do have knowledge or competence or provide the training and education to get all of the team members competent.

Autonomy and Self-Direction

If a manager wants to encourage autonomy among her team, she should lean toward delegation and consensus decision-making. The less dominant the leader, the more the team is encouraged to be self-directed. In some cases, such as newly-formed teams of novice workers or teams which are having significant performance problems, stronger direction may be appropriate. In these instances command or consultative decision-making should be used.

Availability of Necessary Information

In many instances when managers start to be more participative, they forget to provide adequate information to their team to make good decisions. For example if the team leader wants to include her team members in goal setting for the first time, be sure they have all the data necessary to make an intelligent decision. Some exceptions to providing information might be if the discussions are too complex or technical in nature or if it is highly confidential. In those instances consultation or command decision-making styles would be more appropriate.

Exercise: Choosing a Decision-Making Style

To help determine whether a decision is better made by a team or by the team leader (or a subject matter expert on the team), we have broken down the characteristics of decision-making into six categories. Review the following scales, and assess a specific decision that needs to be made in the next thirty days. Place a mark on the scales according to what you feel accurately reflects the ingredients of the decision. Add your scores, divide by six and place a mark on the top scale to determine which style is most appropriate to this decision. If the score falls in *"consultative,"* *"consensus,"* or *"delegation,"* the decision may be appropriate for your team meeting.

Characteristics of Decision-Making

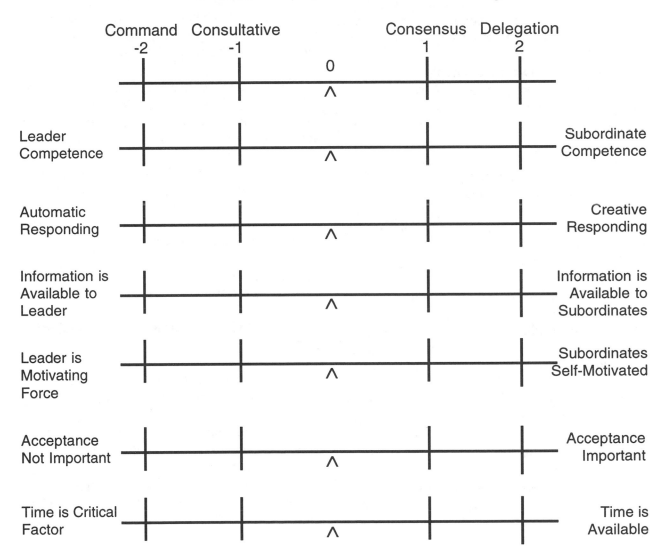

Bringing a Team to Consensus

Once you have discovered which decisions should appropriately be made by team consensus, you are faced with how to get there. Since this is the most complex style to use, let's explore it further.

Let's start by defining what consensus is.

A consensus is the result of a group's coming to the willing acceptance and support of a decision by all members of the team.

There are two different views of what a consensus is. One view is a *pure* or *ideal* consensus. In ideal consensus after talking about a problem and considering alternatives, the entire group will eventually become of one mind with common understanding and agreement. In the view of pure consensus there is no disagreement when consensus is reached. This can be quite common when teams are dealing with routine or simple matters. It is less common when dealing with complex issues or issues that produce strong feelings on the part of team members.

Some writers, particularly those whose primary experience is in academia, argue that the team should continue discussing the issue until it reaches pure consensus. Unfortunately in the real world of organizational life, decisions must be made whether there is a pure consensus or not. For example a customer may have called with a complaint and requested that a correction be made. Time is important to the customer. You cannot tell the customer that he must wait until your team reaches a pure consensus! That might require weeks when the customer needs action in hours. In this case the team members must make their best decision and take action even if there is not pure consensus.

Instead of a pure consensus a *practical* consensus may be reached. A practical consensus is one in which there is a prevailing view held by a majority of team members, and the minority is willing to *act in a unified manner because they recognize that the decision meets the needs of the majority of the team and their customers.*

Democratic governments operate on this principle. Imagine that the President and his cabinet could not decide until everyone is of one mind. This would lead to very poor performance, and the group would tend to revert to autocratic command decision-making in their frustration with the "committee-itis," (the inability of a group to take action). Your team has a responsibility to your customers. Therefore if you cannot reach pure consensus, you may decide to act on the prevailing view.

In practical consensus dissent is welcome, encouraged, and supported. Yet once the time to make a decision comes, the group must take action following the predominant view.

Ideal or practical consensus exists only when the following conditions have been met:

1. All members have been heard fully, frankly, and respectfully.

2. All members have been honest in their views and feelings.

3. All views have been considered without prejudice.

4. All relevant information has been shared equally among the group.

5. There has been a genuine search for new, creative alternative solutions.

6. Members are willing to sacrifice their personal position for the sake of the whole team.

7. Members act as if the decision were their own.

Principles of Consensus

There are two absolutely essential ingredients required for a team to reach consensus.

The first is **absolute frankness and honesty**. This sounds easier than it is. Frankness and honesty are the solution to what has been called **groupthink** in which members of a team "sense" which way the discussion is heading, which way most people will approve, and which way to go along by giving in to the direction of the group. When a team is trying to reach consensus, it is absolutely critical that every member of the team state his true and honest feelings about the best course of action.

It is common for several people to offer the same solutions and then agree on a course of action. A fifth person is then asked his view. He honestly believes another course would be better but does not want to cause conflict or have to argue against what appears to be a consensus so he nods his head and goes along with the previous statements.

This person has just cheated his team members! He has been dishonest with himself and his team. He has given in to groupthink! If he had been honest and stated his views about another course of action which he felt would be better, the other team members would ask "why?" He would then give his view. Perhaps this person has information, experience, insight, or intuition that the other members do not have. They listen respectfully. They consider this new information. Suddenly the entire course of discussion changes, and a new course of action becomes evident!

It is not always easy to be honest and frank, but it is the commitment we make to our team members when reaching consensus. You never know whether your view will be the one that will stimulate an idea in someone else's brain that may be the key to the best solution. Remember that team problem solving in a free and frank manner is like a chemical reaction.

One person's ideas may act as a catalyst that sparks a new idea in another team member, thus resulting in a breakthrough for the team. Your ideas are just single molecules in the total chemical solution.

Why don't people state their frank and honest views? The reason is because they have experienced punishment from groups in the past. They are anxious that someone will think that they have said something dumb. This is why it is so important that we always listen with respect and concern to our team members. This makes it possible for others to be frank and honest.

The second most important ingredient in reaching consensus is that once a decision is made, all members of the team leave the meeting and **act as if it were their personal decision.**

Consensus does not mean that everyone would have selected the final solution. It means that everyone has been heard respectfully. It means that all possible solutions have been presented and discussed. It means that the team has made its best effort to come to a unanimous decision, but if it cannot, it must move forward and act on the majority decision or delay the decision if time is not critical. Sometimes delay can cool off emotions or allow ideas to be digested, causing members to be more willing to support the proposed solution.

The principle of sacrifice is important to the team. Once we have been heard and our ideas considered, we must be willing to sacrifice those ideas to the team. They do not belong to us anymore. We give them up to the group. The group shapes, molds, adds to, subtracts from, and forms our idea. This is the consensus process.

Even if the decision is not our personal preference, unless the decision violates a personal ethic or principle we must for the sake of team unity and performance be willing to give up a bit of our personal ego and needs. Once a decision is made and we leave the room, we accept the team's decision as our own. If we do not, if members leave the room and fail to support the decision, consensus has not been reached and the decision will likely fail.

Some of the keys to reaching consensus are these:

Team members have a common goal, understand their customers, and understand their own performance.

They have a common understanding of the importance of a problem.

All team members have the same data or information. When teams study their data together and have the same understanding of its meaning, they are likely to reach consensus on appropriate actions.

Team members are flexible and willing to listen, collaborate, and respect each other's opinions.

Facilitation or leadership helps others voice their view comfortably and avoids power and personality conflicts.

Thorough discussion of problems and possible solutions takes place.

The causes of the problem are examined in a systematic manner.

The criteria for a solution are agreed on before the solution is selected.

Exercise:

Think of a group that you participated in that reached agreement on the solution to a problem. What led to reaching consensus successfully?

Steps to Reaching Consensus

When you have decided that consensus is the appropriate style for your decision, you may find reaching it easy simply through free and open discussion. However if you have many ideas gathered through brainstorming, you may need a more systematic process. If so, try the following steps to reach consensus.

1. Clean up the list of ideas.

Can some be combined? You will often have suggestions/ideas that are very close to each other and can be reworded to form one thought. The facilitator should not do this alone. He should invite the team to combine ideas. The facilitator may act as a member of the team and offer suggestions as well. Primarily the facilitator should be asking questions such as, "How do you feel about this....?" "How would you like to restate this....?"

2. Make a new list of the combined ideas so people can clearly see what they are considering.

Often you have to rewrite the list for clarity and readability. People will then be able to determine their preferences.

3. Do a pareto vote.

Apply the 80/20 rule and ask members to choose 20% of the solutions that they feel would have the most impact (that solves 80% of the problems). So, for example, if you had twenty proposed solutions, everyone would get four votes (20% of 20). Based on these votes, you will find some of the recommendations get few or no votes. If someone feels strongly about one that did not make the original vote, leave it on the list. It may be a great idea that others didn't understand. Ask the team members how they feel about dropping those. If there are any that someone feels strongly about keeping, leave them on the list. You will now have a list of a few, perhaps five to ten, possible ideas that the entire team understands.

4. Discuss pros and cons.

Up to this point you have not made arguments for or against one suggestion over another. Now is the time to campaign. Members should be invited to explain why they feel that one suggestion is the best idea. Other members should ask questions about how the solution would work. This is the time to get practical.

This discussion should be carried on in a positive spirit. Ideas should not be discredited, but practical difficulties should be discussed calmly and objectively. Frank questions should be asked in the spirit of exploring the possibilities of a solution. All of the members of the team have a responsibility to be open to considering each solution on its own merits. Every member should act as a responsible decision-maker, carefully listening and weighing the pros and cons.

It may be helpful at this point to take another flip chart page and make a pros and cons list for each possible solution. Ask the team members what they think would be the advantages and disadvantages of each. This will help the team come to a consensus.

One technique you might try is to have people defend ideas that are not their own. This forces them to explore other people's suggestions more fully.

5. Define criteria.

Another discussion the facilitator may wish to lead at this point is a **definition of criteria for the best solution.** For example are there funds available? If not, a low-cost solution may be a criteria. How much time will be required? Can the team implement the decision themselves, or will they require outside assistance? This, too, may be a criteria.

6. Ask the team members how they feel about the suggestions as they are now stated.

Is there any way to improve the clarity of the recommendations? The pros and cons discussion or the criteria discussion may have brought forth issues that can be incorporated into the final list.

There also may be some new ideas generated from discussion or ways to combine ideas in new ways.

7. Ask the team if there are still as many viable solutions.

It may now be apparent that only one or two of the solutions are truly viable, based on the criteria established. It may be that there is only one. If so, you have reached consensus.

8. If there are still equally viable alternatives, you should not vote.

Remember that it is often possible to act on more than one idea. If it is practical, there is nothing wrong with implementing two or three solutions to a problem. Problems often have more than one cause and require more than one solution. However if only one is possible, the majority view probably should be adopted by the team.

9. Check it out!

Ask each team member if he can support the solution(s) selected. This provides an opportunity to make a verbal commitment of support or to surface any resistance.

Exercise:

Choose a decision that the team feels is appropriate for the consensus style. Practice using the steps outlined in the text for reaching consensus.

Alternatively there are many exercises in trainer's guides for consensus-reaching that may be fun for learning the consensus process (e.g. *The Desert Survival Situation* or *Jungle Survival Situation* both by Human Synergistics).

Action Assignment

Identify some decisions that impact your team on a regular basis, and identify the current style for making that decision and the advantages or disadvantages of that style. Think about whether the current style is the most appropriate given the typical situation. What is an alternative style to the current one being used which might encourage ownership?

Decision	Current Style	Advantages Disadvantages	Alternate Style

Implementation Tips

1. Increasing team participation in decision making is one of the easiest ways to get early involvement in the work. Do it quickly but be clear about the boundaries.

2. Sometimes teams mistakenly believe they should be involved in all decisions equally. This is why the team leader should clarify which style he or she is using at each discussion juncture.

3. The team leader should discuss with the team where they want to be involved. Sometimes leaders over react and slow down decisions unnecessarily by trying to involve teams in everything.

4. Some team leaders and members confuse employee involvement with consensus decision making. Not every decision is made by consensus and employees can participate in many different ways. Don't let the meeting get bogged down in "committee-itis" due to this mistaken assumption.

5. Be patient with team decision-making. Like any other new skill it requires practice. The early team decisions will probably not be qualitatively any better than one the leader could have decided alone. However as the team learns to work together the "collective wisdom" of the group should surface.

6. Use the help of the coach to work on team dynamics during decision-making. This should help the group move faster through learning to deal with each other with candor and respect.

Chapter Nine

Solving Problems in Teams

The team will develop both the philosophy and the skills that lead to effective problem solving.

Objectives

1. To learn the five-step problem-solving model.

2. To learn problem-solving tools.

3. To learn how to apply the skills in team problem solving.

The Purpose of Problem Solving

In order to improve performance, whether financial or customer satisfaction, teams will need to solve problems as a group. Working together to both elicit creativity as well as to apply empirical analysis to problems can cause confusion through mixed signals and competing interests. Therefore, having a model to follow can lend the necessary structure to a group to allow both creativity and empirical analysis.

In this chapter you will learn a method of problem solving that will free the group from potential chaos and help achieve the satisfaction of effective problem solving.

One of the most important activities that teams engage in is problem solving. Continuous improvement is the result of the team members continuously studying their performance and then finding ways to solve problems within their process.

Teams solve problems when their team performance measures indicate that critical areas of performance are below the desired level, when the production process is "out of control," when quality of work life problems arise in the work area, or when they see any opportunity for improvement.

However when a group of people get together and attempt to solve a problem, they are likely to have difficulty because members may be using different approaches to solving the problem. It is like a group of people attempting to dance together, each listening to a different tune. For this reason it is helpful to agree on a step-by-step process for solving problems.

TEAMS SOLVE PROBLEMS

WHEN...
Their Performance Drops
Their Process Is "Out of Control"
Conflict Occurs
There Are Opportunities
    for Improvement

NOW!!!

Exercise:

Think about a successful problem-solving session in which you participated. Identify some of the characteristics of this meeting that made it successful.

_____

_____

_____

_____

_____

_____

_____

_____

_____

_____

A Philosophy of Problem Solving

Before we discuss the steps in the problem-solving process, it is important to have a healthy philosophy of problem solving.

Excellent companies have a healthy philosophy of problem solving. This philosophy recognizes that every problem is an opportunity for improvement and is a learning experience. This causes them to look for problems and continuously ask, "How can we improve?" Problems are a positive, not a negative, experience. People are not punished for having problems. They are encouraged to define and pursue opportunities for improvement.

Companies that have adequate to good performance are often more complacent about problems. They often say, "We're doing pretty well." Creating a philosophy of continuous improvement through "creative dissatisfaction" is one of the objectives of the team process. Cre-

A Problem-Solving Philosophy

Problems Are...

Opportunities to Learn.

Opportunities to Continuously Improve.

Best Solved Now!

Solved Without Blaming.

Normal.

Best Solved in Groups.

ative dissatisfaction is the awareness of the gap between where we are today and where we could be in the future. We realize that we must be creative to close this gap.

Creative dissatisfaction begins with a clear philosophy of problem solving. Following are some principles which we feel are part of that philosophy:

The Continuous Pursuit of Improvement

Excellence comes through the ardent pursuit of continuous improvement. Any world class athlete could have stopped pursuing improvement at many lower levels of achievement and been regarded as successful. For example, a collegiate pole-vaulter who is able to clear sixteen feet will place high in the NCAA track and field finals and will be regarded as highly accomplished by his peers, family, and coaches. This level of achievement, however, will not win one a place on the USA Olympic team. Becoming world class is a result of setting the bar at the next higher level. Satisfaction comes as much from the quest as it does from the accomplishment.

Solve It Now

Problems are best solved as soon as possible. The longer a problem continues, the more the people get used to it and no longer see it as a problem. It then becomes worse and increasingly resistant to change. Problems solved quickly are solved more easily.

No "Other-Guys"

Superior problem solvers have a strong sense of "internal locus of control." This is an acceptance of responsibility, a feeling of control over the events in one's life. Losers in life, poor performers, and organizations tend to blame the "other guys." This is an example of "external locus of control." People who believe they can exert control do not blame problems on the other guys but rather feel responsibility and ownership for problems and take action to find solutions.

Problems Are Normal

Life is not perfect. Problems occur in every organization. The difference is that in excellent companies, people constantly work on solving problems as they occur. Problems are opportunities to make things better.

Be Hard On Problems, Soft On People

Avoid blaming others and personalizing the problem. The team should focus on solving the problem, not on whose fault the problem is. Many managers consider themselves "tough managers," but when you examine the facts, you often find that these managers are neither tough on their real competition nor on problems. They are tough only on their own people. Great leaders like Alexander the Great and Lord Nelson were incredibly tough on their competition but displayed great affection and warmth for their people.

Teams Address Problems They Can Control

Team members should accept ownership for trying to solve problems in their area of responsibility even if they did not directly cause them. The key question is, "What can we do about the problems in our area where we are the experts?" This is our responsibility.

Problems Are Best Solved By Groups

"Two heads (or three, or four, or more) are better than one" if the people involved work well together. A group will have more ideas than one person and will be better able to implement a solution. There has been a great deal of research comparing the decision-making and problem solving ability of individuals versus groups. Individuals may make better decisions when immediacy is the priority, but when commitment and complexity are involved, groups win every time.

No Lone Rangers

By watching television - particularly shows like the Lone Ranger in which the hero rides in from out of town, quickly solves the problem, and then gets out of town - we learn to depend on others for solutions to problems. While experts can be called in and provide helpful input, the team members should learn to take the initiative and solve problems on their own. This way when they recur, the team will have more experience and self-confidence to find the solution themselves.

Where Do Problems Come From?

Teams, like managers, always have problems.

While this may sound depressing, it is true and should be accepted by all team members. The team members are managing their performance to their customer's requirements. The job of management is first to be informed, second to measure performance, third to continuously seek improvement in performance, and fourth to successfully implement improvement.

At every team meeting the team members should look at their score and assess their data as to quality performance, both the immediate performance and trends over time. Improving this performance is always a problem! As the team studies its process, they will identify opportunities to improve cycle time, eliminate quality variances, or reduce costs.

Problems also arise in the maintenance of current levels of performance. Machinery starts to break down, schedules between office workers conflict, people are preparing for a big meeting at the last minute, and everyone wants to use a printer in the word processing department at the same time. All of these are problems waiting to be solved.

People, directly or indirectly, are almost always involved in the problem. This is because the work process is controlled by people, directly or indirectly. For this reason, it is critical that the team approach problems without focusing on the "fault" of people but on how to be helpful in improvement.

The ability of your team to develop and implement solutions to problems will be the key to your success. Successful teams are teams that produce results through continuous improvement and problem solving.

The Five-Step Problem-Solving Model

Why use a problem-solving model?

To make problem solving efficient.

To order our thinking so everyone is "reading from the same page."

To help everyone pull together in a common direction.

To bring logic to problem solving.

To help team members avoid jumping to solutions before the facts are known.

To free people to think creatively about a problem.

Once the team has selected a problem to work on, the next step is to use a problem-solving process to solve the problem. Hundreds of different problem-solving processes have been studied and designed for groups to use when trying to arrive at a course of action together. Many of these are unnecessarily complicated, particularly for the majority of day-to-day problems with which teams are confronted. A simple and effective problem-solving model includes the following five steps. These five steps should be adequate to solve most of the problems that your team will confront.

Step One: Define the Problem

Describe the problem in terms that are measurable and observable; this is called pinpointing. For example if a series of jobs were improperly coded, include in the statement of the problem the job numbers involved and the coding errors. Pinpointing enables everyone on the team to have the same understanding of the problem as well as makes it easier to graph and track progress. It also sets the stage for working on

The *FIVE-STEP* Problem-Solving Model

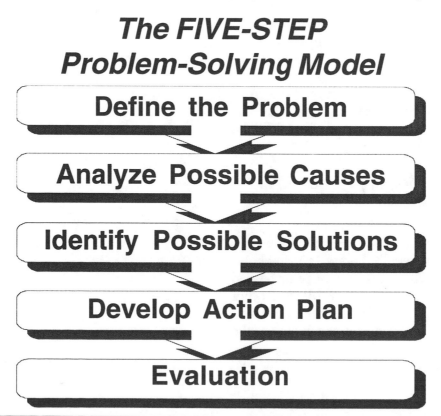

Define the Problem

Analyze Possible Causes

Identify Possible Solutions

Develop Action Plan

Evaluation

data-based analysis and solutions. Without pinpointing the problem in a measurable way, teams tend to meander through opinion and supposition instead of looking at the unbiased facts.

Describe the impact of the problem on others including service to customers, or employee satisfaction. This step is to ensure that the problem is significant enough to take up the team's meeting time. Based on this data analysis, the team can decide if it has a problem to solve and can move on to the next step.

Step Two: Analyze Possible Causes

What are the possible contributing factors? Present all the things that may be causing the problem. Include factors out of the team's control such as the customer changing his order and factors under the team's control such as poor performance, machine problems, and work methods. Team members should contribute all of their thoughts on possible causes. It is important that this step focuses on objective causes rather than on faultfinding.

The intent of this step is to get to the root cause or causes of the problem instead of addressing symptoms of the problem. Sometimes it is necessary to continue asking the question "why" to get the most basic causes of the problem before the team begins to look for solutions. (Try five "whys.") The cause and effect fishbone is also a useful tool at this step.

Step Three: Identify Possible Solutions

Once the root cause(s) has been established, the team should generate as many solutions as possible without judgment being passed by the person presenting the problem or other members of the group. This should maximize the quantity of alternatives and the quality of the

final solution. To do this, use the brainstorming process described later in this chapter. After you have generated a list of possible solutions, you should use the consensus process to select the solution(s) that are likely to have the most impact.

Step Four: Develop Action Plan

Nothing is worse than a meeting that ends with no action. Action is the payoff. Successful teams manage themselves in a way that creates reliable and predictable action toward the problem solution. Action steps should be clearly defined, volunteers requested for each step, and time frames agreed upon for completing each step.

Step Five: Evaluation

Your team's implementation plan to solve the problem should be reviewed at each team meeting. Also the performance area you are trying to impact should be tracked and reviewed to assess whether your team's solutions are having the desired impact.

Tools and Techniques for Successful Problem Solving

There are dozens of tools to help your team do effective problem solving. The following are eight of the most frequently used tools and tips on how to apply them at each step of the problem-solving model. The tools and techniques covered in this chapter are:

Pinpointing

Brainstorming

Consensus Reaching

Check Sheets for Data Gathering

Pareto Diagrams

Run Charts

Control Charts

Action Planning

Gantt & Pert Charts

Pinpointing

Pinpoint the Problem

The most important aspect of problem definition is to state the problem in such a way that everyone has the same understanding, and specific enough so that the group knows what to look for in order to find a solution.

Imagine that a problem is stated as, "People just don't seem to have a good attitude about their work." This is not a good statement of a problem. It may be accepted as a beginning point, but it must be better defined.

How do you know when people do not have a good attitude? Does this mean that people are not arriving to work on time? Does this mean that people are not friendly and smiling? Does this mean that employees are not as creative as they used to be and are not thinking of improvements? Or does it mean that the performance measures are going in the wrong direction? It could mean any or all of these things.

Without a more specific, pinpointed definition each team member will assume his own definition. Each member will be working to solve a different problem than the other team members. This will lead only to frustration and failure to implement a solution.

Be Data Oriented

It is always best, whenever possible, to pinpoint the problem in terms of hard data. Data is objective. Compare the following two problem statements: "Our average on-time shipment performance over the past six months was 95.6%. Last month it was 88%. I feel that we need to problem solve this." versus, "We surely haven't been doing a good job! In fact, we are doing terribly. Frankly our performance stinks, and we are going to really be on the hot seat if we don't get our act together."

The situation may be exactly the same in both of the above descriptions. The first does not include a lot of editorial judgments but simply presents the facts in a way that is objective. The second presents no facts and only editorial judgments. We would all react better to the first. This would lead to a more constructive problem-solving process.

To better pinpoint problems try asking questions such as:

- Where is this (is this not) a problem?
- When does it occur and how frequently?
- How long has it been a problem/when did it start?
- How can it best be measured?

When to Use Pinpointing

Select a problem that will help you improve one of the key measures of your team's performance. Focus on an area the team can impact to improve quality and use pinpointing in step one to clearly define the problem.

Exercise:

Look at each of the following "presenting" problems. Develop a pinpointed definition (a pinpointed behavior is performance which can be observed, measured, and recorded) that describes the exact performance or behavior and the gap between current and desired performance.

Presenting Problem	Possible Pinpointed Definitions	How could you measure progress?
There is a lack of trust among the employees.		
Our efficiency is terrible.		
There is a lack of cooperation between departments.		
We have a quality problem.		

Brainstorming

Brainstorming is a process by which people generate as many ideas as possible without evaluation by others. The key to brainstorming is the separation of idea generation and evaluation or judging the ideas that are generated.

There has been a great deal of research on creativity and problem solving. All of this research has supported the idea that the process of brainstorming leads to greater creativity, better solutions to problems, and commitment on the part of the group.

Brainstorming Guidelines

There are specific guidelines to be followed when brainstorming.

The objective of brainstorming is to **generate as many ideas as possible**. The group should strive for quantity, not quality.

Brainstorming means that free thinking is encouraged. Therefore it is important that there be **no criticizing or judging of ideas** during brainstorming. There will be time for evaluation later. Try not to evaluate or edit your own thoughts before offering an idea. The best thinking comes from groups that generate as many ideas as they can.

Everyone should be encouraged but not pressured to participate.

The group should be encouraged to **build on or combine ideas.**

Encourage free thinking. The benefit of wild ideas is that they often stimulate a new thought. They are also sometimes humorous, and **humor seems to be one of the ingredients for creative thinking**. Remember if the leader does not offer a "wild" idea, chances are no one else will.

Follow the rules throughout brainstorming. Brainstorming is a combination of wild thinking and a structured process. The best thinking comes when you follow the guidelines.

Always use a flip chart to display ideas so that everyone can see them. This will stimulate thinking. As flip chart pages get filled up, do not flip them over so they cannot be seen. Tear them off and tape them onto the wall so the group can continue to see them.

Types of Brainstorming Methods

There are several methods of brainstorming. Different methods have different advantages. You may want to experiment with your group to see which is most effective with your team.

Freewheeling

In the *"freewheeling"* method everyone contributes ideas spontaneously. The advantage of this method is that it encourages creativity as people build on each other's ideas. The disadvantage is that quiet members of the group may not speak up. You may miss some people's ideas.

Round Robin

In a *"round robin"* people take turns presenting their ideas one at a time. The advantage of this method is that all people get equal chances to speak up, and quiet people are more likely to contribute. The disadvantage is that it stifles spontaneity, and sometimes members forget their idea by the time their turn arrives. In this process members should be allowed to "pass" if they have no suggestions.

Slip Method

In this method everyone puts ideas on a slip of paper and passes it in to the leader or facilitator. This method's advantage is that some people may be more candid and creative with their anonymity preserved. The disadvantage is not hearing another member's ideas which often trigger add-on creativity.

These three forms of brainstorming are applicable for steps two and three: analyzing causes and identifying solutions. It is most important to remember "generate before you evaluate." Another form of brainstorming that is unique to identifying causes is the cause and effect diagram.

Cause and Effect Diagram (Fishbone)

Cause and effect diagrams can be used for any problem including manufacturing, safety, work, attendance, or interdepartmental problems. They are used when trying to identify root causes to a problem.

How do we construct a cause and effect diagram?

1. Pinpoint the quality variance you want to improve. This is the problem you are trying to solve.

2. Write the variance or problem on the right hand side, and draw a horizontal line to the left.

3. Select the main categories which may be causing variation in the quality characteristic. For manufacturing processes it is helpful to think in terms of Shewhart's concept of a process (machinery, methods, materials, measurement, and people). Each main factor forms a branch off the horizontal line.

4. Brainstorm specific causes for each category. These causes are written on branches off the main factors.

Imagine that we are a mail-order company that sells personal computers and related software and equipment such as monitors, add-on boards, memory boards, software, and related items. A personal computer magazine conducted a reader survey to judge mail-order houses on their customer service. Our ratings were not disastrous, but they were not good. The survey did not specify what the sources of dissatisfaction were. So we have got to figure it out.

Using the cause and effect diagram, a team of telephone sales reps brainstorm possible causes of customer dissatisfaction. You can see some of their ideas below.

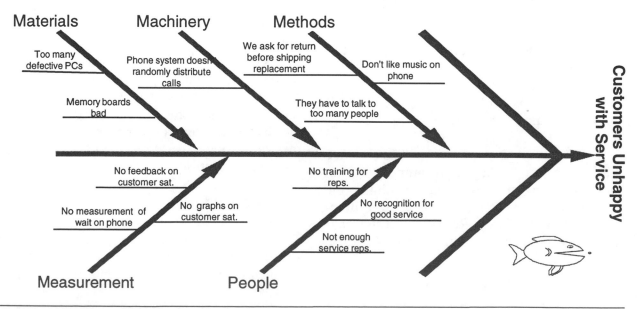

Exercise:

Use the blank fishbone diagram below and brainstorm all of the possible causes of a child not completing his homework. Use the main causes of **Methods, Materials, Machinery, Measurement** and **People.** You may do this with your team or individually and then discuss it with your training group.

(Note: Other labels can be used for the "bones", such as process, rewards, training, transportation, etc.)

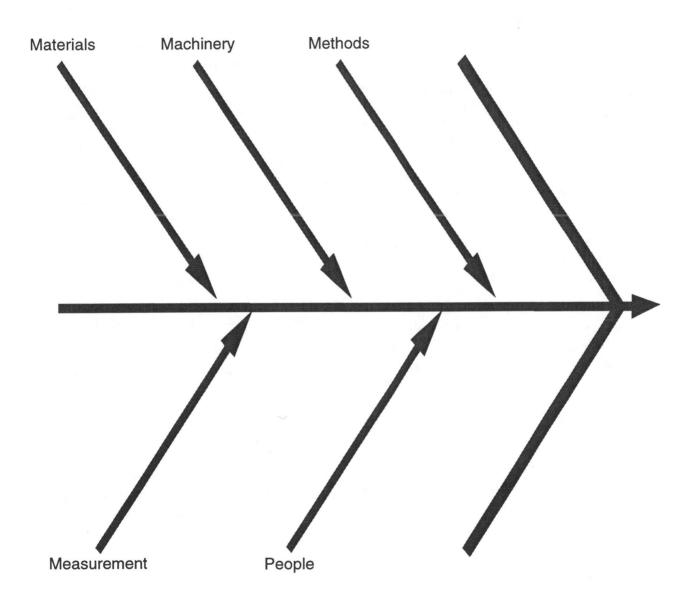

Reaching Consensus

The consensus reaching process was described in Chapter Eight. In this chapter, we will apply the technique to choose the most likely causes to the problem we want to solve.

After the brainstorming has been completed, you are ready to discuss and analyze the ideas. If you were brainstorming causes to the problem, you may want to prioritize the major causes where corrective action can be taken. The decision-making process requires that the team leader guide the team through a discussion and evaluation of each of the brainstormed ideas.

This discussion involves identifying the advantages and disadvantages of each idea. It may also involve combining parts of different suggestions. Rarely is a final choice only one person's idea. It is most often a combination of several suggestions which have been molded into one "best" choice as the team members discuss their opinions.

The team should follow these steps to reach a consensus on the causes that are most critical and that should be analyzed:

1. Restate the original problem to remind everyone what the team is trying to resolve. When reaching consensus on possible causes of a problem, team members do not have to agree on only one. You may analyze three to five different causes. Therefore it is okay if members have different opinions about the causes of the problem.

2. Review the ideas generated during brainstorming. Ask team members to note any item that they do not understand. Solicit clarification from the contributors.

3. Combine duplicate ideas. This will narrow the list somewhat. If there is disagreement about whether or not to combine, it is better to leave the items separate at this point.

Do not combine all the ideas into over-generalized categories.

4. Have members vote for the causes that they feel are most probable and have the greatest impact on the problem. At this point team members can explain the reason for their choices as they indicate their votes. It is often good to apply the 80/20 rule. Select the 20% of causes that impact 80% of the problem.

5. Narrow the list. Ask the group if it is okay to drop from consideration items for which there were no votes. After the vote each team member can explain why he voted for a particular idea and actively try to sell the team on the choice(s).

6. Decide and determine the criteria for causes and the resource limitations facing your team. For example, one criteria for causes may be that the causes must be controlled by the team or that there may be budget limitations to replacing equipment. However the team may decide they want to address all issues and not limit their parameters.

Continue to narrow the list, and test for possible consensus. Check to see if it makes sense to investigate all of the causes remaining. If you are unable to reach consensus, move on to the next step.

7. On the narrowed-down list discuss advantages and disadvantages of addressing each cause. What is the evidence that this cause is most frequent, intense, or significant to the problem? This is the time to argue and persuade. A good way to handle this discussion is to use an easel sheet for each cause, writing the pros in one column and the cons in another. Hang the sheets on the wall for further consideration.

8. Reach final consensus. Based on the advantages/disadvantages of the discussion, reach final agreement on the causes that the team will either investigate or implement. Again vote on those causes that are most probable.

Data Gathering

In the next step, after you have selected causes to investigate, there needs to be some method for determining which causes are, in fact, the most significant.

In order to do that, some method of data collection needs to be employed to determine which causes occur at the highest frequency or cause the greatest impact.

One tool to use is to collect the data collection on a check sheet.

Check Sheets

A check sheet is a piece of paper divided into spaces for different time units, types of defects, or events. It is called a check sheet because the person gathering the data will place a check in the appropriate space for each defect or event as it occurs. This data will then be transferred to a graph, chart, or other analysis tool.

The following is an example of the use of check sheets.

Improving Customer Service in a Mail-Order Business

This company sells personal computers and related products. They have received poor ratings for customer service by a leading PC magazine. They have decided to gather the facts. These three check sheets are all used by the service reps who answer the phones. They first decided they needed to know when the calls were coming in to reduce the time customers waited on the phone. You can see that the number of calls is not evenly distributed through the day. There are peak times when they could increase capacity.

They also decided to pinpoint which type of products were the greatest source of complaints so they could focus their energy on solving problems related to those products or even drop those products if they caused too much dissatisfaction. They began this process by keeping check sheets with the general categories of products. You can see very clearly that software and memory boards were the greatest sources of complaints.

They then decided to gather data on which types of customers the complaints were coming from. Again just from looking at the check sheet, you can see that home users make more calls with complaints than small businesses or larger corporations.

From these examples you can see that check sheets are a simple way of gathering data and the first step in analyzing the problem. This tool could be used in either step one, Problem Definition, or step two, Cause Analysis.

When Do Customers Call? Calls per hour beginning at...

8AM	9AM	10AM	11AM	12PM
✓✓ ✓	✓✓✓ ✓✓✓	✓✓✓ ✓✓✓	✓ ✓	✓✓ ✓

1PM	2PM	3PM	4PM	5PM
✓✓ ✓	✓ ✓	✓ ✓	✓✓ ✓	✓✓✓ ✓✓✓ ✓✓✓

What Are Their Concerns? Problems by product /one day.

PCs	Monitors	Memory boards
✓✓✓ ✓✓✓ ✓✓	✓ ✓✓	✓✓✓✓ ✓✓✓✓ ✓

Modems	Software	Other
✓ ✓✓	✓✓✓✓✓ ✓✓✓✓✓ ✓✓✓✓	✓✓ ✓

Types of Customers with Problems.

Home Users	Small Business	Corporate Accts
✓✓✓✓ ✓✓✓✓ ✓✓✓✓ ✓✓✓✓ ✓✓✓	✓✓✓ ✓✓ ✓✓✓	✓✓✓ ✓✓

Pareto Diagrams

Vilfredo Pareto was an Italian economist who defined the 80/20 rule. He said that 80% of trouble comes from 20% of problems. If we can identify those 20% of the problems that are causing 80% of the trouble, we can make better use of our time.

A Pareto diagram is a special type of a bar chart used to determine which problem to work on first. The problems or causes are listed on the X (horizontal) axis. The frequency or cost associated with each problem is plotted on the Y (vertical) axis.

Imagine that the team members responsible for improving customer service in our computer sales organization gathered data on their check sheets for ten days. Then they added up all of the complaints in each category. They then computed the percent that each category represented of the total number of complaints. This is illustrated on the Pareto chart at the bottom of this page.

Why do we use a Pareto diagram?

The Pareto diagram allows us to determine what the major problems are, i.e., those that happen with the greatest frequency. The Pareto diagram allows us to separate the "vital few" from the "trivial many." This permits us to focus our time and attention where it will have the most benefit in solving a problem.

When can we use a Pareto diagram?

A Pareto diagram can be used in many situations. In real life it can be used to determine the major causes of why marriages fail or survive, what kind of gardening techniques are most successful, or why people are watching less commercial television than they did previously. In the business environment Pareto diagrams can be used to determine the major causes of injuries, waivers, delayed shipments, invoice errors, etc.

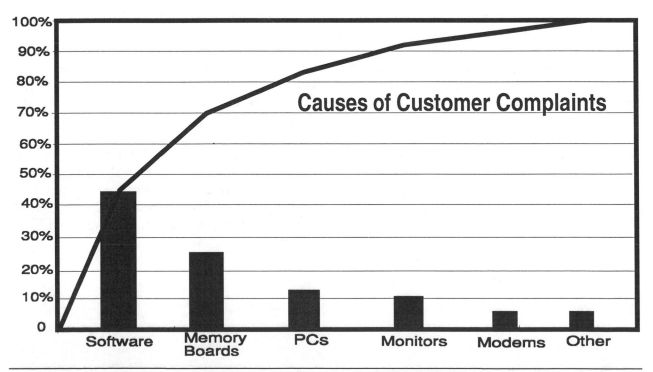

Causes of Customer Complaints

A Pareto diagram is the first step in making improvements to a process. It points out the major problems and provides a method of obtaining consensus on what are the major problems. It permits you to concentrate limited resources on key areas.

It is important to use common sense when you interpret Pareto diagrams. For example a Pareto diagram on types of injuries does not take into account the severity of the injuries. Hand cuts may have the greatest frequency, but you may want to work on eye injuries first.

How do we construct a Pareto diagram?

1. Define the problem.

2. Brainstorm causes, and select which ones to use on diagram.

3. Select the time period to be covered on the diagram.

4. Collect data on the frequency of occurrence for each cause during the time period.

5. Draw the X and Y axis, putting the proper label and units of measure on the Y axis.

6. Under the X axis write in the cause that occurred with the greatest frequency first, then the next most frequently occurring cause, etc.

7. Draw in the bars. The height of the bar will correspond to the value on the vertical axis.

8. Plot the cumulative frequency to determine if you have 100% of the problem accounted for in your analysis.

9. Title the graph, and include other important information such as the data collection period.

Exercise: Designing a Pareto Diagram

You work in the mail room. Employees have started complaining about delays in getting their mail delivered. This problem has caused other serious problems since some important documents have not been delivered on time. The problem has been given to the mail room's natural work unit team to solve. You are a member of this work team. The team does not know why the problem is occurring. The first step is to determine the major causes for the mail not being delivered or received on time.

Step 1. Determine the causes to be used on the diagram. This can be done by brainstorming. After brainstorming all potential causes, the team selected the following major causes:

- Mail had insufficient postage.
- Mail was torn in postage metering machine.
- Mail had incomplete address.
- Mail was delivered to wrong internal office.
- Mail had no return address.

Step 2. Select the time period to be covered on the diagram. The team decided to collect data over a two-week period. They felt that this would be sufficient to determine what the major causes were.

Step 3. Total the frequency of occurrences for each cause during the time period. After collecting the data for two weeks, the team totaled the frequency of occurrence for each of the causes listed in Step 1. The results are as follows:

- 25 letters had insufficient postage.
- 15 letters were torn in the postage metering machine.
- 45 letters had incomplete addresses.
- 12 letters were delivered to the wrong internal office.
- 3 letters had no return address.

Step 4. Draw the X and Y axis, putting the proper label and units of measure on the Y axis.

Step 5. Under the X axis write in the cause that occurred most frequently first, then the next most frequently occurring cause, etc.

Step 6. Draw in the bars. The height of the bar will correspond to the value on the vertical axis.

Step 7. Title the graph, and include other important information.

It is evident that the major cause of poor mail delivery is letters with incomplete addresses. This cause is the one that should be worked on first to improve the mail delivery.

The same principle can be applied in Pareto Voting. This is a method of narrowing down a long list of brainstormed ideas to a critical few. In steps two and three you can ask your team to take a 'Pareto Vote'; everyone has a chance to vote on the 20% of the ideas that he believes will address 80% of the solution. This can be the first step towards reaching consensus.

Causes

Run Charts

Most of the graphs and charts that you have seen are probably run charts. If you look in the financial section of the newspaper, you will often see run charts of economic indicators such as inflation or stock prices charted over time. In the workplace you may see run charts of company orders, orders sent out on time, attendance, and other performance measures.

By looking at a run chart, you can immediately gain an understanding of the essential characteristics of that performance. Is it going up or down? Have there been periodic changes such as seasonal changes? Does it vary greatly or slightly? All of these questions can be answered almost immediately by looking at a run chart. The two most common uses of run charts in problem solving are a) to diagnose a problem and b) to determine if your intervention has worked.

A run chart:

1. Is a graph that visually represents performance over time.

2. Lets us track how the environment is affecting performance to date by analyzing the effect in the data.

3. Shows us baseline performance.

4. Shows us the trends, variability, and cycles of performance.

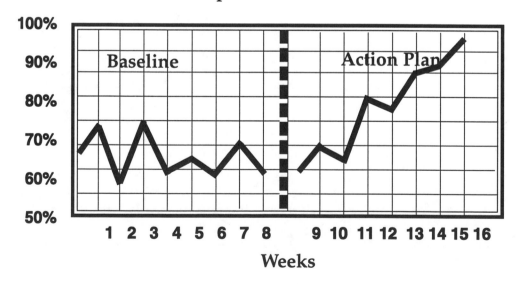

Shipments Sent on Time

Analyzing Trends

Look at the following graphs. What can you conclude from them, and what action would you recommend? Assume that each graph represents the percent of first quality, defect-free widgets. The top of the graph indicates 100%; the bottom of the graph indicates 75%.

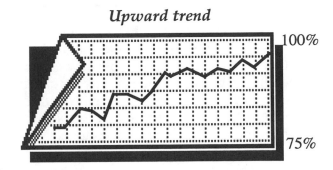

Upward trend

100%

75%

You can see that any trend indicates that the performance is not stable. Something is currently having an impact on performance and creating change. If the trend is upward, you would be well advised to continue observing the trend and wait until the performance is stable. If you make a change now, you will not be able to tell if the change you made caused the performance to improve or if it caused it to stop improving. Remember that no single change causes performance to improve forever. Sooner or later it will level off.

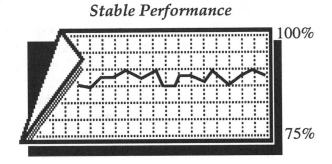

Stable Performance

100%

75%

If performance is stable your process may be functioning smoothly at it's current capacity. You may want to consider an intervention that causes some breakthrough performance change!

If performance is trending downward slightly, you may wish to wait until a stable state is achieved. However if the cost of this decline is great, or if it is declining rapidly, you may wish to brainstorm possible causes and make a change hoping to reverse the trend. You may sacrifice some of the scientific methods for the sake of better serving your customers. Control limits are helpful in determining when to take corrective action.

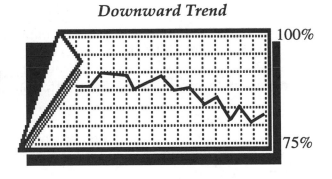

Downward Trend

100%

75%

Trend charts are helpful in determining a problem definition, analyzing causes, and evaluating whether your action plan is working. They may be a precursor to control charting or often used as a tool by themselves when the data being collected doesn't lend itself to a control chart.

Statistical Process Control and Control Charts

Analyzing problems will usually mean gathering data and trying to understand what those numbers mean. If there is one key to Japanese quality, it has been their ability to understand performance statistics and to analyze those statistics. Dr. W. Edward Deming, a statistician, is given much of the credit for establishing a culture focused on quality in Japan. He taught statistical concepts that are one of the keys to quality.

Many manufacturing and office environments now use statistical process control (SPC). SPC allows both individuals and teams to gain a better understanding of their own performance and provides a basis for problem analysis. *It is not our purpose here to teach SPC thoroughly.* However a few of the concepts will be helpful.

All managers and employee teams manage a **system** which is comprised of essentially three parts: **Inputs,** the **Process,** and **Outputs.**

An example of a system would be the operation of a handgun, rifle, or even a battle tank. There are inputs into the system including the bullets that are fired. There are outputs, also bullets, but which now look very different.

The bullets have been transformed by the system. All work systems are transformational processes that change or add value between input and output.

The performance of any system can be analyzed by gaining knowledge of the output. To know how the system is performing, we want to know exactly where the bullets are falling. Will all of the bullets fall in the same place? Never! No system has the capability to produce a straight line or have perfectly consistent performance.

Zero defects would take place when every bullet falls exactly in the center of the target. The only way this can be achieved is to place the barrel of the gun right in front of the target. This only makes you ignorant of the actual performance of the gun. If the gun is placed back at a reasonable distance and we examine where the bullets fall, we will see that there is variability within the performance of this system. Bullets fall around a mean or average. In this case the average is about in the center of the target. There is a standard of deviation from the mean. In other words it is normal for bullets to fall a certain distance from the mean or center. This is called system capability.

The terms *variability, mean,* and *standard deviation* are all statistical terms that describe the characteristics of the performance of a system. It is useful to know the variability, mean, and standard deviation of performance in your own system. Your team may want to discuss how these concepts apply to your own performance and how to calculate these numbers.

When examining the pattern of bullets, we can see that no person is to blame for a slight deviation from the center of the target. It is normal system performance. The only explanation is that bullets fall at random within this pattern. Therefore there is no reason to blame the operator or change the way you shoot the gun or buy a new gun.

In order to improve the performance of the system (reduce the variation and bring the pattern closer together), we will have to redesign the system. For example adding six inches onto the barrel of the gun would be a system redesign. This cannot be accomplished by the operator alone. It will require team effort and managerial approval.

If, however, a bullet falls well beyond the normal pattern, we can quickly conclude that this is not a variation within the system. It is the result of something outside of the system. It is a "special cause."

There are two types of quality problems that your team should address in their problem solving activities:

1. A Variance from System Performance

If you buy a car and it is a "lemon," e.g. the electrical system cannot be made to work properly, you have bought a variance from system performance. This problem is not the result (let us assume) of the way the car was designed but the way someone installed the wiring in the car. It is a special cause, a bullet that has missed the target altogether.

2. A Variance from Customer Requirements

In this case the car you bought does not handle very well. You are not comfortable with the soft steering and lack of precision. You are a dissatisfied customer. However every car of this type performs in exactly the same way. There is nothing wrong or deviant about this particular car. This problem is not a special cause. It is a common cause. The problem is within the system; it is a matter of how the system was designed. There is not a worker, mechanic, or operator who can be blamed for this concern. There is no bad piece of equipment or other "failure" that can be blamed. The car is performing as it was designed. The system itself determines this performance, and the problem is that the entire system is not designed to meet this customer's requirements. This system can be considered to include the automotive design process, engineering process, etc. It is obvious that system problems require entirely different solutions from true defects which indicate that there is something out-of-control within the system.

Inputs	**The Process**	**Outputs**
(From Suppliers)	(The Team's Work)	(To Customers)

Control Charts

Below you can see a statistical control chart. A control chart plots the data over time and indicates a mean for that set of data. For example the number of bad parts per day, week, or month or the number of typing errors per page can all be plotted with the mean indicated. A quick glance at a control chart can tell you a great deal. You can see the normal range within which the data points fall. Within three standard deviations is generally performance within the system's capability. The upper (UCL) and lower (LCL) control limits are plotted so that you can quickly see if a data point is outside of the range which can be considered normal system performance.

If performance is occurring outside of the control limits, we can say that the system is out-of-control, and there is a problem that must be solved. If the system is in control, we can then ask how the system performance can be improved, either by reducing the variability, or by increasing the overall level of performance.

Developing an Action Plan

Developing an action plan is neither difficult nor complicated. It is, however, the most important step in the problem-solving process. Have you ever been in a meeting where there was great discussion, lots of ideas shared, but somehow nothing was ever decided? This is very frustrating. It is also very common. Remember, people want something to happen as a consequence of this meeting. Action plans are one way of ensuring this.

The value of the team's effort is in its actions, not its words. The action plan is like the paycheck at the end of the week. It is the result of a lot of effort. It is a simple thing, but it is important. Be sure that you never leave a team meeting without being certain of what action steps have been agreed upon by the team, who will do them, and by what date.

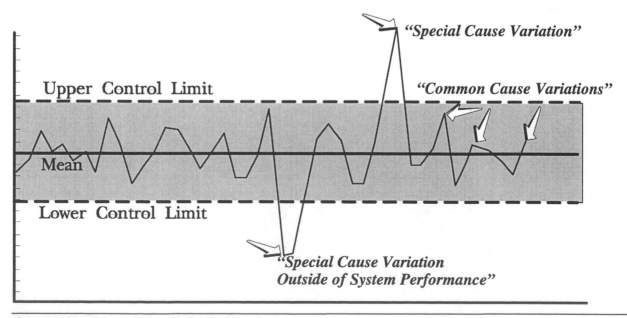

To develop an action plan for your problem solution, follow these steps:

1. Define *What* needs to be done.

2. Agree on *When* it needs to be done.

3. Agree on *Who* will do it.

4. Develop a visual plan, a PERT, or GANTT chart if the plan will take a long time to implement.

5. Periodically review the plan.

1. What?

The solution to a problem is always a "what." You may have agreed that in order to solve a problem, you need to rearrange equipment, buy a new software program, provide additional training, or work more closely with your supplier to help him meet your specifications.

In order to have a successful action plan, you need to break "what's" down into discrete steps. It is the basic nature of all planning that you begin with a large or general action, and you then define the steps or smaller actions that will lead you to the larger accomplishment. For example you may say that you want to have a social event, a picnic for your team. A social event is a general "what," but in order for that to become a reality, many smaller actions must be defined. Where will it be held? When? What will we eat? What will we do when we get there? What invitations will be sent out?, etc. All good planning, whether planning a picnic or planning the design and construction of a new aircraft, is based on the process of going from the larger or general to the smaller or specific.

When team members are developing an action plan, they will want to discuss how much detail they should plan as a team versus how much planning or decision making they want to leave to an individual. For example in planning a picnic, you could decide as a team who plans the menu, where the food will be bought, who will

buy it, how it will be cooked, whether it will be cooked well-done or medium-rare, and how much salt and pepper to shake on. Obviously this would be ridiculous!

Do not feel that you must plan every action. You must use judgment and plan to a point and then delegate the decisions and planning to an individual or a group.

2. When?

Often teams decide that some action must be taken, but they fail to agree on when it needs to be taken. The problem is that every member of the team has some expectation about time. One member may feel that this action is urgent and should be taken today. Another feels that anytime within the next six months would be OK. Obviously this is likely to lead to conflict or frustration among the members.

The issue of specificity may again come up. The team does not have to decide on the exact hour that something must be done. However some approximate date should be identified.

3. By Whom?

When developing an action plan, ask for volunteers for each action step. Sometimes the team leader may need to encourage volunteering with the question, "John, how would you feel about taking responsibility for...?" Or another team member might help by suggesting that, "John has a lot of knowledge about that subject; I think he would be very successful."

When deciding whom you will want to take responsibility, take into consideration the availability of time the individual has, his skills and his motivation. It is often the case that the busiest people are the ones who most often volunteer or who are often asked to take on additional responsibility. This is a natural process. As someone proves that he is reliable and successfully gets things done, he is asked more often, and eventually he is over burdened. The team should consider sharing responsibilities to help all members grow.

The assignment of tasks and responsibilities should also take into account developmental needs. For example the task may be to go and meet with a customer or supplier and discuss his requirements or problems. Several team members may already have met with customers and suppliers. Another team member has not. Of course those who have already interviewed other customers or suppliers successfully may be the most qualified to do it again. However if the same people are always asked, others do not get this opportunity and their perspective is limited. A good solution would be for one experienced and one inexperienced member to share this task.

4. Visualize the Plan

Just as graphs are helpful for understanding performance, GANTT and PERT charts are helpful for understanding the actions to be taken and managing the action plan. These tools are essential to managing complex projects. They may not be necessary for the simple task of planning a picnic, but if the plan to improve performance requires more than ten different activities and a number of people over more than one month, these tools will be helpful.

You have probably seen a GANTT chart. It simply defines the activities on the left side down the page and a time line across the top from left to right. With this simple device posted in a common area for all team members to see, everyone will know where the team is, what is happening now, and when to expect the activity to be completed. This also serves as a form of motivation to team members to continue making progress on their action plan.

A PERT chart illustrates the relationships between different tasks in a project or action plan. It illustrates the predecessor and successor tasks, the dependent relationships between tasks. The illustration on the next page is a PERT chart of the same training plan that is illustrated on the GANTT chart. The numbers for each task correspond.

You will see that the second and third tasks, deciding on the content outline and researching possible trainers, are dependent on

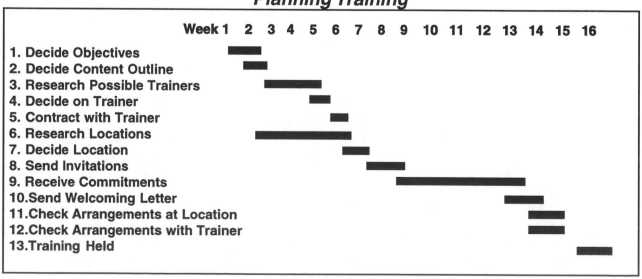

GANTT CHART
Planning Training

Week 1 2 3 4 5 6 7 8 9 10 11 12 13 14 15 16

1. Decide Objectives
2. Decide Content Outline
3. Research Possible Trainers
4. Decide on Trainer
5. Contract with Trainer
6. Research Locations
7. Decide Location
8. Send Invitations
9. Receive Commitments
10. Send Welcoming Letter
11. Check Arrangements at Location
12. Check Arrangements with Trainer
13. Training Held

the first task, determining the objectives. Deciding the trainer, task four, is dependent on task three but not two. You can also see that task six, researching locations, is not dependent on any of the previous steps other than deciding on the objectives for the course. You can think of a PERT chart as a map of the activities in an action plan.

The PERT chart can also be made with different information in the activity blocks. For example the chart may show the names of the people who are responsible for each task, the number of hours, days, or weeks required for the completion of each activity, or the actual data on which a task will begin and end. There are personal computer software programs that will automatically create both PERT and GANTT charts by inputting the information on one activity report. The information can then be printed out in many different formats. If you are managing complex projects with many different activities, you will find these software programs very helpful.

It is very helpful for a team to see both the GANTT and PERT charts at the same time as they plan their action plan and as they review their progress.

5. Review the Plan

It is surprising how many good plans are developed but never implemented. The next problem or crisis takes over the energy of the team, and they forget what they have already decided to do. Every team meeting should include a review of action plans and their progress.

Some member of the team should act as secretary or recorder and bring all of the commitments to action to the team meeting. The team should always consider altering the plan if members are having difficulty meeting their agreements. The action plan is a working document, and it is normal to adjust the plan as the team works on its implementation.

PERT CHART
Planning Training

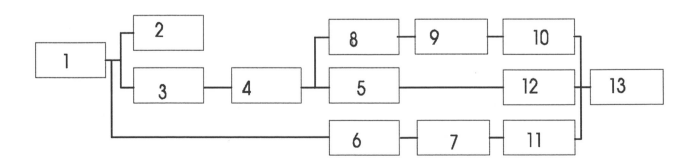

Exercise:

Assume you are planning a celebration event with your team. Use the Team Action Plan on the next page to devise steps necessary to make the party fun and successful.

Team Action Plan		
Team: **Date:** **Target Performance or Problem:**		
What Action?	**When?**	**By Whom?**

Action Assignment

1. Review the Five-Step Problem-Solving Model, and discuss the philosophy of problem solving.

2. Post the model on the wall.

3. Select a problem, and brainstorm a list of possible causes to the problem.

4. Brainstorm solutions to one of the following situations:

   a. Ways that your team can improve quality.
   b. Ways that good performance can be rewarded.
   c. Ways that your team can make the weekly team meeting more efficient and effective.

5. Ask for a volunteer to facilitate the group in reaching consensus on the best solution(s).

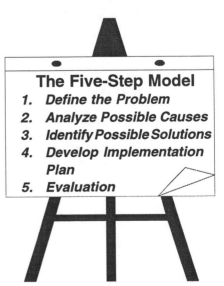

The Five-Step Model
1. *Define the Problem*
2. *Analyze Possible Causes*
3. *Identify Possible Solutions*
4. *Develop Implementation Plan*
5. *Evaluation*

Implementation Tips

1. Teams tend to resist a systematic approach to solving a problem because the disciplined step-by-step approach slows them down. Start your teams off with relatively uncomplicated problems to learn to use the model.

2. Not all of the team's problems will require this approach. Don't force some of the easy, "quick-fixes" through this process if solutions are readily apparent.

3. With more complex problems, the team will only be able to get to step two in one session. Then they need to collect some data on frequency of causes to determine the most critical to solve.

4. Don't let the team jump to solutions before they have analyzed causes. This often results in putting on a band-aid but not solving the root cause.

5. Initially it is helpful to have a team coach lead you through the steps until people understand the model better.

6. Remind the team frequently that in a culture of continuous improvement, we <u>welcome</u> problems!

7. It is acceptable to have some subset of your team do some work on analyzing the problem and return to present alternatives to the larger group. However, if you are delegating steps, don't make them rework the process with the entire group again.

8. Be aware of "groupthink" if you have a mature team or homogeneous group. This is when everyone starts to think alike and decisions lose the necessary critical analysis or creative thinking to come up with innovative ideas.

9. If you have a diverse group, encourage participation by everyone but don't force quiet people to talk a lot. They may need time to think through a problem and prefer not to speak their opinions until they have thought through their options. This is particularly an issue to address during brainstorming and consensus reaching.

Chapter Ten

Renewal: The Continuous Improvement of Team Systems

The team-based organization should continue to evolve and improve to stay ahead of the customer's needs. This requires a flexible attitude of both manager and worker and the development of comfort with continuous learning and change as a constant way of life.

Objectives

1. To understand why organizations must continue to learn in order to prosper and thrive in a changing environment.

2. To learn the tools and techniques to help people manage in a changing environment including creating high performance work teams, motivating teams, and understanding the systemic approach to managing human performance.

3. To understand how the role of the manager changes in a team-based organization.

Becoming a High-Performance Team

When a team reaches maturity, it has achieved a state of interdependent relationships among team members, with customers, and with other teams. It is now self-managing, and the team members make decisions about their own performance, plans, and activities.

To be self-managing is a privilege. This privilege must be earned. How does a team earn this privilege? The major way is by demonstrating that it will act responsibly in a manner consistent with the objectives of the larger organization and with those of its customers. It has demonstrated its success in managing its own performance.

In previous sessions we have discussed many aspects of managing performance. We have discussed the importance of focusing on your customer. We have discussed the importance of studying and improving the work process, keeping score, and solving problems. These are all part of managing performance.

There is another aspect to managing performance as an ongoing business team. While there may be performance problems caused by supplies, materials, machinery, methods, and measurement, people may also contribute to the problem. Managing people, their skills, and motivation is critical to the long-term sustained success of your team.

On the next page you will see a cause and effect diagram illustrating the influences on human performance. There are many models that can help define the causes of human performance. Many of them are very complex, theoretical, and not that helpful. The influences that you can do something about are not that complex, and the model on the next page represents the forces that you can influence as team members and leaders.

Just as machines have a capability to perform, so do people. Few are capable of running a four-minute mile or lifting 500 pounds. I am sure that we could improve our performance with training and practice, but nature has endowed each of us with some basic level of capability for development. You may be able to tune a car to run a few miles an hour faster, but you will never be able to tune a 1960 VW Beetle to compete with a Ferrari Testa Rossa no matter how hard you work.

Every employee coming into the workplace has a measure of both physical and mental capability. That capability is then developed. It can become somewhat more or less, depending on the elements of the *work system* and the *social system.*

If the *work system* defines the individual's work as only doing a single repetitive task, this will do little to develop the capability of the individual. Because of the requirements of that job, the individual will not have the opportunity or encouragement to develop other skills. On the other hand if the job is defined as accepting responsibility for an entire work process and managing a team's own performance, all the individuals are far more likely to develop new capabilities.

The *social system* affects both capability and motivation. The availability of training is part of the social system. Feedback and reinforcement also help increase learning and capability.

Motivation is different than capability. Two football players may have equal capabilities, but that fact does not mean they will perform the same. One may have a passionate desire to win and excel, and he may read his play book every night and work out every day during the off-season. The second may feel that he is so talented that he does not need to work hard, and winning or excelling is not very important to him. It is very unlikely that the second player

---

will match the performance of the first. The first player is obviously more motivated than the second.

Team members and team leaders influence each other's motivation. Motivation is affected by many forces including many outside of the workplace. While the team members cannot control motivation completely, they can increase the probability that each team member will try to contribute to the extent of his capability.

To become a high-performance team, you must evaluate the "social systems" for your team to see if it contains the critical ingredients. They are 1) a clear sense of purpose, 2) goals and objectives, 3) team member skill and competence, 4) feedback and accountability, and 5) reward and recognition.

A Clear Sense of Purpose

For a group truly to reach the level of a high-performance team, it needs to have a clear sense of purpose. Purpose answers the questions, 'What is our output as a team, and what do we want to accomplish?' Having a demanding performance challenge cements teams more than any other single ingredient. A group of people excited about accomplishing something becomes a team very quickly.

Becoming a High-Performance Team

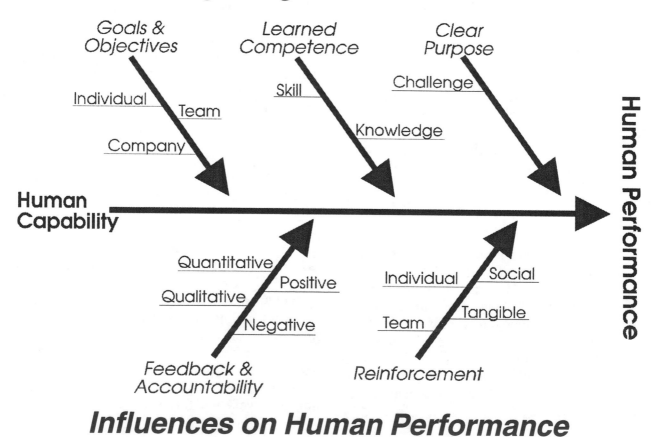

Influences on Human Performance

Setting Goals and Expectations

Teams should have clear and attainable yet challenging goals. Typically self-managing teams set more rigorous goals for themselves than would have been set by their managers. Quality goals should reflect the balance between the needs of the customer and the health of the business.

When employees feel responsible for their work and have control over their work process, they will want to set goals and expectations. If you play golf, it is natural to set a goal for how many shots will be required to complete the eighteen holes as you teeoff. If you are a runner, you probably set goals and track your performance in terms of the number of miles per week, minutes per mile, or days per month on which you run.

This goal setting establishes the basis upon which we feel self-satisfaction. Meeting goals is a reinforcing experience. We believe that the most useful objectives are those set by those who must perform.

When developing a goal-setting process, you should review the scorekeeping system you developed during the previous chapters. Each of these measures can be a subject of goal setting.

Goals can be set on many different levels in an organization. You may be aware of *company goals* for achieving market-share levels, revenue levels, quality performance and recognition, or creating new products or services. The company establishes an annual plan as well as a strategic plan. The annual plan represents the company's plan for the next year, and the strategic plan represents the company's goals for three, five, or ten years. Both are useful for establishing the company's direction and coordination efforts toward a common purpose.

Team goals fulfill the same purpose. *Team goals* may be short term, months or weeks, or they may be more strategic for a period of a year or more. Obviously in a large company you have little control over the company goals. However you can have a great deal of impact on your team's goals.

Highly successful people are most often individuals who set their own *personal goals.* These may be goals for further education, learning new skills, achieving financial objectives, or other events important to the individual. Personal goals are an important aspect of individual continuous improvement. There is always a gap between who we are today, and what we can do today and who we could be tomorrow or what we could do tomorrow. Personal excellence is the personal pursuit of continuous improvement.

Setting goals is one of the oldest, well-proven methods of improving and managing performance. This does not contradict the concept of continuous improvement; it simply fills a human need of satisfaction for reaching some specific point.

241

Learned Competence

Performance requires competence. You can have the world's best computer and software, but if you do not know how to use them, they are worthless. High-performance teams require the ongoing development of competence.

The traditional work system in which individuals were assigned to narrowly-defined jobs and closely supervised inhibited the development of competence. The new work system requires higher levels of competence. It is often the case that when self-managing teams are implemented, the employees spend a great deal of their time during the first year simply gaining knowledge and understanding of the operation of the larger system. They also become cross-trained so that they can assist each other, move easily from one assignment to another, and help each other solve problems. It is also important that team members gain a greater understanding of the business they are in and of how their performance impacts the bottom line of the company. Anyone who has ever managed his own business understands that it is a constant balancing act which requires an understanding of the financial impact of all decisions. Teams need to have the same grasp.

The team, with help from its manager, should plan for the development of skills and knowledge needed for their team to manage its processes and serve its customers.

On the next pages are two forms which can help you and your team develop a plan for increasing competence. The first form can be used by the team to define those skills that are required by the team to enhance their performance. The second form is one which you might use to plan the development of your own competence.

While the company and the team share responsibility for assisting in your development, each individual can also take the initiative to develop his own plan for personal improvement. You may want to think about which skills you currently possess and which skills you would like to develop in both the short and long term. How will you develop these? When?

Make your own plan for the development of your own personal competencies.

Team Member Skills

Priority	Technical Skills	Interpersonal Skills	Business Skills
A. Basic Requirements To Be Team Member			
B. All Members Should Develop			
C. Most Members Should Develop			
D. Some Members Should Develop			
E. Would Be Helpful To Optimize Team Performance			

Personal Goal Plan

Short-Term Goals	Actions Necessary to Achieve	Date
A. Technical Skills		
B. Interpersonal Skills		
C. Business Skills		

Long-Term Goals	Actions Necessary to Achieve	Date
A. Technical Skills		
B. Interpersonal Skills		
C. Business Skills		

Feedback and Accountability

To become a high-performance team, each member must feel committed to the team's goals and know what his or her responsibility is to attain those goals.

It is essential that the team have full knowledge of its performance at all times. If a team is to function like a small business with regard to its job responsibilities, it must establish a feedback system to provide itself with timely, measurable, and useful performance feedback.

Feedback can be delivered to teams in many ways. A team may create a display of numerical, data-based feedback. This display may be in graph, chart, or narrative form. A manager may write a memo and send it to those involved, post it on the bulletin board, or read it in a team meeting.

In many high-performance teams, performance feedback is delivered by teammates to their peers. The more comfortable and knowledgeable each member is about his or her peer's skills, the easier it will be to share knowledge and support each other. A good sign of a self-directed team is when members feel free to give each other feedback, both positive and negative.

Reinforcement

Understanding and providing positive reinforcement is the key to motivation. Over the last fifty years scientists have been studying the forces in the environment that increase or decrease performance. It is an indisputable fact that when desirable consequences follow a behavior, that behavior will tend to increase or strengthen. Behavior is learned through the process of reinforcement.

When children are praised for cleaning their room, they are more likely to clean their room in the future. If they clean their room and their parents pay no attention, this performance will weaken. The behavior will not be learned.

When executives are shown appreciation for giving their time to a project, they are more likely to volunteer again. Whether child or adult, we all respond to the power of positive reinforcement.

It is a common reaction to the idea of positive reinforcement to say, "It is their job; they ought to want to perform well without my having to say anything." It may also be theoretically true that every child "oughta wanna" do his homework, clean his room, and behave in the most polite manner. Unfortunately if the parents have not taught these behaviors and reinforced their performance, they will not occur with any regularity. It can also be said that every person "oughta wanna" work hard, contribute to his community, and serve his country without any reinforcement. Unfortunately we must live in the world of reality, not the world of "oughta wanna."

To achieve a high performance work team, you must have positive recognition as a critical ingredient.

Positive reinforcement need not be formal or structured. In fact it can be casual, even fun! The division president of a major high technology firm bought congratulatory ice cream cones for his colleagues from an ice cream stand on a Washington street corner immediately after they had successfully closed a key government contract. Ice cream cones became badges of honor for the countless hours worked to complete the proposal. Photographs of the entire project team holding ice cream cones now adorn offices, creating never-ending opportunities to retell the story.

At a Rocky Mountain oil refinery a maintenance team earned special jackets in recognition of their excellent safety record. The team requested that they be allowed to decline the jackets and donate the cash equivalent, matched by the refinery, to a local charity of their choice.

At a textile manufacturing plant in the Southeast, hourly employees designed a plan to increase their own recognition of peers. Every employee has five points to "spend" each week.

When one employee notices another being particularly productive or helpful, he or she transfers a point to the deserving individual. The employee with the most points at the end of the week is recognized in a team meeting and gets a token of appreciation such as free coffee.

In a discussion group about management style at a large office products company, a service technician complained, "You can get a monetary reward from a manager for good performance, but you never hear 'Good job!'"

Sometimes companies have pay, profit sharing, or bonus money tied to team performance. While this is a desirable end state, typically most high-performance teams value the quality of their output and the appreciation of their teammates above all else.

Why Celebrate Improvement With Positive Reinforcement?

✔ It increases self-motivation & self-management.

✔ It emphasizes "winning," "fun."

✔ It reduces reliance on punishment.

✔ Intrinsic reinforcement is not enough.

Putting It All Together

To incorporate all the influences on human performance into a specific game plan for changing human behavior, you may want to consider the P.R.I.C.E. Model. This model is applicable to an individual or team plan to improve human performance. To become a high performance team, every member of that team needs to be working at his individual level of excellence. Try using the P.R.I.C.E. model to achieve that level of team excellence.

For example if a team member realizes that his low skill in computer literacy is hurting both his work and his contribution to the team, he might use the P.R.I.C.E. Model to help address the problem. The model is applied as follows:

Pinpoint: Define which software program he needs to learn and to what level of expertise.

Record: Take baseline data on how many software programs he is currently competent in running now.

Intervene: Using the A-B-C Model, assess what consequences are currently interfering with him learning these programs and having time to practice his skill. Set specific goals for what the learning acquisition will be and when he will be evaluated.

Change Consequences: Establish a reinforcement program to reward successful steps to goal attainment. Try to eliminate those things that are encouraging the avoidance of practicing on the computer.

Evaluate: After an appropriate period of time (two-four weeks) assess progress and determine if any changes in the plan need to be made.

THE *PRICE* MODEL FOR BEHAVIOR CHANGE:

PINPOINT

RECORD

INTERVENE

CHANGE **C**ONSEQUENCES

EVALUATE

The Role of the Manager in a High-Performance Team

As all these organizational systems are shifting to support a team's structure, so will the role of the manager. The successful manager in the new organization will require new and different skills.

The shift in the nature of work, organization, and management is global and eventually will affect every organization and job. There can be no going back. There may be hesitation and momentary setbacks, but it will never be the same. The manager's role is changing forever.

The team process requires a redefinition of management responsibility. The supervisor of old - checking up on the performance of his workers, making all of the decisions regarding the work group - will be out of place in the new systems.

The requirement for change on the part of management raises fears about job security and the new role managers are to play. There will always be a need for managers. While teams may become increasingly self-managing, they will still require coordination, leadership, and technical expertise.

One way to understand the new role of managers is to consider the shift from non value-adding effort to value-adding effort. If the supervisor is simply observing the work of others, he is not adding value to the work. On the other hand if he is working on improving a technical process that can make the team's work more effective, he is adding value. By the account of supervisors themselves, as much as fifty percent of their time is spent in activities that add no value to the customer or the product.

Our supervisors and managers are obviously considered to be competent, capable, and motivated individuals in the organization and that is why they were promoted to these positions. It is a waste to employ them in ways that are not value-adding. There is nothing wrong with the motivation of these individuals. There is something wrong with the system.

The role of the manager must be that of developing people, encouraging innovation, reinforcing improvement, helping to adapt to change, and managing boundaries between teams of individuals.

The system, the designed function of jobs, must be reconsidered and all jobs defined in a way that utilizes the resource, the talent of the individuals, in a value-adding manner.

The following diagrams illustrate the various relationships and roles a manager may play as the team evolves.

Stage 1: The Newly-Formed Team

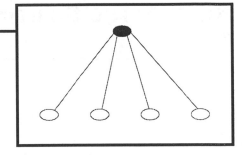

TEAM LEADER

Leader is very directive.
Leader reviews all results.
Leader is responsible for follow-up on individual performances.
Leader manages staff one-on-one.
Leader conducts meetings.

TEAM MEMBERS

Members do not know all the measures of team outputs.
Members work primarily as individual specialists.
Members are primarily concerned with their individual needs and performance.
Members are developing technical competence.
Members are just beginning to learn about team skills.

Stage 2: The Manager-Centered Team

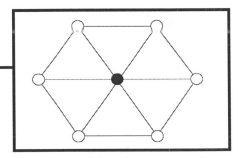

TEAM LEADER

Leader is modeling/explaining "This way is why."
Performance results are reviewed as a team.
Leader encourages members to participate in finding solutions to team's performance gaps.
Leader solicits input to goal setting.
Leader still schedules most work.
Leader seeks customer feedback.
Leader is teaching team members the "business" side of their performance.
Leader ensures the team scorecard is integrated with rest of organization.

TEAM MEMBERS

Members are asked to provide input on how to improve production, quality, etc.
Members meet together with leader on a regular basis for reviews of team results.
Members have developed individual technical competence.
Members understand outcome goals.
Members maybe getting cross-trained.
Members help in developing standards and goals.
Members are beginning to solicit input from each other.
Members are beginning to view their work with a more "macro" perspective.

Stage 3: The Shared-Leadership Team

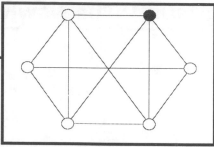

TEAM LEADER

Team leader role is rotated.

Leader supports team members in addressing performance gaps.

Leader leads peer-performance review session.

Leader assists with the training needs.

Leader assists team in budget decisions/equipment purchases, etc.

Leader participates in a "360° appraisal."

TEAM MEMBERS

Team is learning to achieve consistent results as a team using a balanced scorecard.

Team is taking on more of the administrative and managerial responsibilities.

Team meets regularly to review results.

Team still relies on leader's expertise in business review and meetings.

Team is taking over more of the day-to-day operations.

Team members are holding each other accountable for results.

Stage 4: The High-Performance and Self-Directed Team

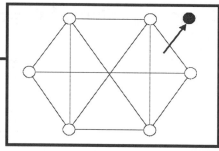

TEAM LEADER

Leader becomes a coach to team.

Leader provides support on analysis and design of changes.

Leader helps with boundary issues with other departments and headquarters.

Leader looks to outside environment for strategic opportunities.

Leader provides continued training and mentoring for technical and interpersonal growth.

Leader is a "broker" for new job opportunities, positions, and projects in the organization.

TEAM MEMBERS

Team requires little or no support from leader to manage their business.

Team begins to manage across department lines to meet results.

Team spends more time learning to enhance and improve products and processes.

Team works together well and finds creative ways to align individual needs with customer and organizational needs.

Team develops budget and business criteria for success.

Team is capable of both continuous improvement and inventing new products and services.

The New Roles of Future Managers

In the team-based organization managers will not be viewed as one type. Rather, different functions will be assigned to different managers depending on their particular skills. Some managers are better at solving technical problems, and others are better at coaching in people skills. Some management positions will include a number of different types of functions.

The following are some of the roles and responsibilities of the new manager:

The Manager as Leader

Leadership will never go out of style. People will always need inspiration, role models, and a vision of the future. Leadership is even more necessary in an organization in which individuals are expected to accept responsibility for managing themselves. People will take responsibility when they have an understanding of the direction, hopes, and aspirations of the organization and feel they have a stake in its success.

Leadership is not cheerleading. Cheerleaders stand on the sidelines; leaders are on the field, playing the game! Leaders are an encouragement to others because they are willing to step forward, take risks, and create new paths to follow.

Many managers want to be leaders, but they want to lead on their own terms. They want to lead without making changes within themselves. They want to lead without taking risks. They want to lead without veering from the tried and true. They want to lead without stepping out of their own area of comfort.

American corporations are overmanaged and underled. We need less control, less structure, and less procedures. We need more vision, more innovation, and more leadership.

The Manager as Technical Advisor

Many managers, perhaps most, have specific technical expertise that is vital to the success of their organization. Most were promoted because they had demonstrated this individual competence.

The organization of the future will define its core competencies. The core competencies represent the strategic competitive advantage, the source of innovation, the knowledge base upon which the future of the organization will be built. A manufacturing company must strive to possess the world's greatest experts in their manufacturing process. A sales organization must strive to possess the greatest competence in sales and marketing. Research organizations must strive for the world's most competent researchers.

The only way an organization can possess competence is to recognize and reward competent people. However this does not mean that the most competent technical people should be supervising employees. They should be coaching, advising, training, and developing their technical competence. Unfortunately we have structured our organizations so that the only way a technically competent person can be recognized is to move into a supervisory job for which she may be ill-suited. It is much like making the best brain surgeon in a hospital an administrator. The administrator spends his time with budgets, plans, and other things that have nothing to do with brain surgery. This would be an obvious waste of competence.

Similarly in business organizations we do the same thing. On the following page you will see a set of possible organization charts. The one most likely to resemble the current organization is on the left side. This is the normal chain of command structure with individuals reporting to individuals. The others are alternatives. They are more typical of the team-based organization. You see small groups reporting to a manager with groups of technical advisors. There may be technical subject matter experts on the team who participate on an expert team led by an expert advisor.

Employee teams will need to seek expert advice. The greater the expert advice available and the more fluid the communication between teams and experts, the more successful the entire organization.

The Manager as Facilitator

In the past the manager made the decisions. In the future the manager will be judged by how well he assists others to reach the best possible decisions.

The team facilitator may be the manager. He may lead the meetings. Of course a team member may also serve as the facilitator. In either case there will be a manager who can assist the team in its functioning. There will be a need to have a manager to whom the team can appeal if it is unable to solve a conflict or make a decision. There is often a need for a manager to evaluate the functioning of the team, to oversee the performance of the team, and to provide help when necessary.

This manager should have the skills to facilitate and to help the group reach decisions in a mutually beneficial manner.

The Boundary Manager

The team is not an island unto itself. It lives within an integrated structure. There are boundaries between the team and other teams. There are boundaries that define the decisions which may be made by the teams and which must be made elsewhere. Also there are boundaries on the behavior that the team members may judge for themselves and the behavior which is required by the larger organization. Someone must manage these boundaries.

The team exists within a chain of customer/supplier relationships. Work flows to the team from suppliers and from the team to customers. Under normal circumstances the team may manage the flow in and out by itself. But what happens when the team decides to do some work itself that was formerly done by an internal team that was a supplier? Or what if the team wants to outsource some work? Is this permis-

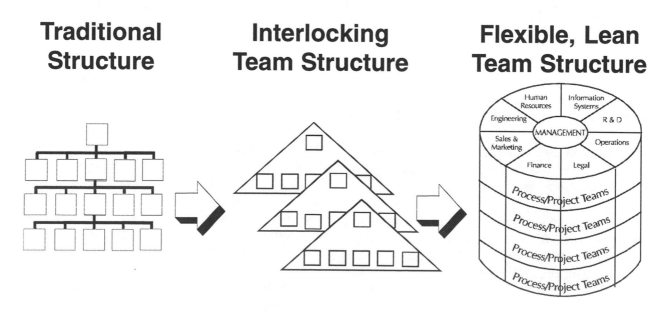

Traditional Structure

Interlocking Team Structure

Flexible, Lean Team Structure

sible? These are boundary questions, and there must be a manager who either can make this decision or facilitate a mutual decision.

Teams will test boundaries to find the limits of their decision-making authority. There is a natural learning curve when teams are formed. At first they may not believe they can make many decisions at all. Then as they discover their new freedom, they will test its limits.

There are limits to team decision-making. Can they decide to buy a new piece of equipment? Can they decide to change their schedule? If so, by how much can they make the change? Dozens of decision boundary questions will arise. All of these must be answered. When teams are first formed, the new manager will attempt to define the decision-making boundaries. However it is virtually impossible to anticipate fully all of the possible questions that will arise. There must be a manager available to help define these boundaries.

Teams will generally do a good job of defining acceptable and unacceptable behavior within the team. Generally as they mature they will be able to give each other feedback to correct misbehavior. However there will be exceptions. There will be the unfortunate case when a team is intimidated by the individual or does not have the strength to give the misbehaving individual feedback. Again there will be a need for a manager to whom the team or individuals can appeal.

The Manager as a Coach

As the team evolves, they may want to run their own meetings and select a peer to lead the team. If the manager and team members agree the team is ready, this is a good time for the manager to step out on the sidelines and become a coach. The coach's role would then become to observe, give feedback, advice and instruction, but he would not participate in the decision-making of the team except as an "outside expert." For the manager truly to become a coach, the team needs to be very well-functioning.

The Manager as a System Integrator

The team process is a whole system, based on values and vision. The team process is a culture, a normal way of life in the organization. The structure of teams does not stand on its own. It requires both technical and social skills. It requires systems, including those of information flow, feedback, compensation, and decision-making. It requires a style of communication and a style of leadership on the part of managers. It is helped by symbols that support the ideas behind the team process.

Dr. W. Edwards Deming said that managers are responsible for the system. This includes both work and human resource systems. Through the team process, employees at all levels share in the responsibility for improving the systems. However there are certain systems that are likely to remain controlled by managers. Who will determine which information is shared? Will financial information be shared? Which financial information will be shared and with whom will it be shared? Who will conduct appraisals? Who would select new team members? Who will discipline poor performers?

These are only a few of the many questions that will arise as the teams that will require an examination of the current systems mature. It is the responsibility of the managers to articulate values and vision and then create alignment between these and the systems, structure, skills, style, and symbols. This will be an ongoing process, but it will become increasingly critical as the teams begin to explore their boundaries. Some of these decisions can be made by individual managers as their teams evolve, but others will require "going to bat" with staff groups at the corporate level who are keepers of the systems. Managers need to be prepared to be trail blazers, for systems change.

The Manager as Mentor

There is no more important function in the organization than the development of people. People are the future of the organization. While there may be a training department who will contribute to this development, they cannot accomplish the task alone. While teams through their problem-solving and improvement efforts will be a forum for human development, they cannot accomplish the task alone.

We learn from other people. We learn skills from those who are competent in particular areas. We learn from other people who take the time to coach us, to encourage us, and to demonstrate their interest.

It is a very common experience that those who have risen to leadership positions in the organization have had the good fortune to have the encouragement of a mentor, an individual who took the time to develop a personal relationship and provide individualized feedback. Whether you are a technical expert or a leader/facilitator, you can make a great contribution to the life of another human being by developing a mentoring relationship to help the other person on his path of development.

The Manager as a Process Champion

In most organizations undergoing changes, there are lots of great ideas on what needs to be done differently but too few people dedicated to getting these ideas implemented. One excellent use of managerial resource is as a process champion. A process champion is a person who is dedicated (often as a full-time job) to getting a particular process implemented. Whether this is a reengineering exercise, a new product being developed, or a cultural change such as diversity or flexible working hours, someone with "political weight" and good facilitation skills needs to lead the team working on this process implementation and see it through to completion.

Managing Renewal

It is important to understand that maintaining a spirit of renewal or continuous improvement requires both managing the tactical interventions to stimulate learning and growth as well as stimulating a vision and triggering the hearts and imagination of the people. Think of the following twelve "paradigm shifts" when you think of the future. These will help to keep your teams focused on where they are trying to go.

Control Management to Commitment Management

The culture of our organizations is changing because the nature of work and workers is changing. In the past work was controllable. On the assembly line jobs were repetitive and required little thought. Performance could be measured simply and reward and punishment administered to provide control. The manager was the person who counted, controlled, and determined reward and punishment.

Today the critical performance is thinking about better ways to get the job done, initiating action to improve, and creating new products, services, or methods. These are not so easily "controlled." They require innovative thinking, risk-taking, and autonomy.

The manager must give up control to those who have their hands on the work. High control increases fear and reduces risk-taking, initiative, and creativity and destroys the very performance that is key to today's success. High control requires high management overhead costs. Eliminating fear and unnecessary control increases commitment, creativity, and other discretionary effort.

Managers create commitment by sharing vision and values, involving employees in decision-making, facilitating knowledge of customers and performance, and helping to improve the process.

Task Focus to Process and Customer Focus

In the past managers were responsible for defining employee responsibility in terms of specific tasks. Industrial engineers measured each movement, and the manager's job was to cause employees to adhere to the task definition. In today's work environment the "right" task definition changes too frequently as methods and machinery are continuously improved. Highly specific definitions quickly become rigid and an obstacle to improvement.

To optimize quality, employees at all levels must understand who are their customers and what are their requirements. They must be involved in efforts to improve their process to meet customer needs. A quality organization is a customer-focused organization. A customer-focused organization defines work in terms of responsibility for complete processes that serve customer needs.

Managers must know who their customers are. Even the president of the company has customers. Among those customers are the employees, stockholders, end-use customers, internal customers, and the community. The manager's job is conditioned by his understanding of the needs of his customers.

Command to Participative Decision-Making

Command decision-making has been the dominate, male, decision-making model for most of mankind's existence. In Henry Ford's factory the workers were mostly uneducated and had little knowledge of the work process beyond their immediate station on the assembly line. Command decisions produced the conformity and uniformity that led to success in the highly repetitious work.

Things have changed. Rather than centralized command decision-making, we need commitment, involvement, and ownership which lead to creativity and acceptance of responsibility. Even the President of the United States must consult with other leaders. Corporate CEO's must consult with stockholders, analysts, and interest groups. The degree of system integration or interdependence between organizations and people dictates a consultative or consensus decision process.

Most managers are now struggling to find boundaries that define the appropriate style of decision-making. It is very difficult to switch styles. We develop habits of decision-making which are hard to change. It is normal to be somewhat confused and to have difficulty making this transition. If you are experiencing this difficulty, you may take some comfort in knowing that you have lots of company.

Individual Work to Teamwork

In the past managers assigned tasks to individuals and then rewarded or punished these individuals. This worked well as long as the tasks were simple and independent. Today tasks are increasingly complex and interdependent, requiring greater teamwork. Teamwork requires decision-making by the employee and among employees. Today in many team-based organizations employees are making their own decisions about which tasks will be completed by whom. They may take turns rotating tasks, or they may choose to specialize in tasks.

Now the manager helps the team make good decisions and assures that the process is functioning well.

Experts and Labor to Experts All!

Even in our laws we have enshrined the class distinction of labor and management, salaried and hourly, thinkers and doers. Perhaps this class distinction made sense on the farm or in the primitive factory. It does not make sense today!

Today "workers" may operate multimillion dollar pieces of complex, computer-controlled production machinery which in itself represents a whole production process. Most employees today are "knowledge" workers regardless of the color of their collar, whether they push paper or steel. Accepting and promoting all employees as experts in their process is critical to the thinking of a quality organization.

Managers may still be expert in a particular technical area. Increasingly the role of managers will be to advise and educate the team on technical matters and assist in the improvement of equipment and technical processes. However the team members are also an expert team. They are expert on their process, and it is the manager's role to assure their competence, to provide the training, coaching, and feedback that will allow them to succeed.

Punishment to Positive Reinforcement

On the sailing ships of the British navy Lord Nelson and the other captains ruled by leadership and punishment. Specifications detailed the punishments for any offense from flogging to the yardarm. The men expected and the captain relied upon strong punishment. The men were conscripts with few options and largely ignorant. The nature of the work and the workers was consistent with the use of punishment.

In the modern organization everything has changed. Little punishment is allowed, and everyone seeks and expects recognition and reward. Behavior is a function of its consequences.

You get back that which is rewarded. Performance must be made to matter with positive reinforcement.

Many managers have a great deal of difficulty providing positive recognition. Praising others is uncomfortable. For years they have seen their role as enforcing proper discipline, assuring that people are doing their assigned tasks, doing what they are "supposed" to do. If they are "supposed" to do it, they should not have to be praised for it! Right? Wrong!

Today it is the manager's responsibility to provide an environment in which employees are encouraged to make suggestions, think creatively, and become enthusiastic about their team's performance. This can be accomplished only if managers recognize good performance, are outspoken in their praise, and demonstrate that they truly value the initiative of their associates.

One Right Way to Continuous Learning

Products and services, requirements, and work processes changed slowly in the past. These change overnight today. By the time the "right way" is discovered, a new way is required. We must adopt the "racing spirit." Like continuous improvement of race cars on the track, we must constantly be looking for a better way.

In the past the manager was the authority on the right way to do things. If he did not know how it was supposed to be done, he was seen as weak. Therefore he often acted as if he knew the right answer even when he did not. Now the manager is liberated from this dehumanizing assumption.

Now it is assumed that the "right way" is constantly moving forward. The new, "best way" may come from the lowest-level employee who has his hands on the product. Now the manager is not judged by knowing the right way but by helping to facilitate continuous improvement.

Continuous improvement is possible only if everyone at every level and in every function is involved and accepts responsibility for improving performance. This includes the manager as well as the customers.

Record Keeping to Scorekeeping

In the past managers kept the numbers to keep track of others. Managers kept track of employees. Customers kept track of their suppliers. Accounting kept track of everybody. The assumption was that people fundamentally could not be trusted.

The manager in the team-based organization assumes that people can be trusted, given the correct system. A part of that system is numbers that allow people to keep their own score, set their own objectives, and experience the game of business. The manager today helps to provide the numbers to the team. The manager helps to provide numbers to suppliers so they can improve their work.

The manager in a team-based organization is a coach. What do coaches do? They provide feedback to their members. The best kind of feedback is facts, numbers, and scores on the performance of the team. The coach helps to interpret those numbers based on his own experience. The coach helps the team members by suggesting things they can do to improve the numbers. However when possible, the coach allows the team members to decide on their own actions.

Tall and Rigid Structure to Flat and Flexible Structure

As civilizations and companies rise, the buildings grow in height and have increasingly specialized rooms, complex patterns, and decorations. The organization chart and the patterns in our minds follow suit.

Bureaucracies have many layers and become rigid. Bureaucracies create fiefdoms within and internal warfare among competing departments. The wall grows, isolating people and slowing the work process. Improvement becomes increasingly difficult.

The team-based organization is in motion with experts working across functions or disciplines, taking responsibility for the entire process that serves customers. Because people are trusted and work in self-managing teams, rigid structure and layers of management are not necessary.

This has tremendous implications for the manager. In the past managers measured their success by their rank, by the number of rungs on the ladder they had climbed. In the future there will be fewer layers of rank. If managers continue to measure their success based on rank, they will find themselves disappointed.

In the future managers will measure their success based on genuine accomplishment: new products developed, new levels of performance achieved, new methods developed, and new customers served. These are the genuine accomplishments of business, not levels or ranks. Managers must be recognized and appreciated for these contributions. New systems of compensation and recognition must be developed to encourage managers to spend their time and energies on activities that add value to their true customers.

Unstated Values to Stated and Shared Values

In the past leaders were not accountable to those below and did not need to reveal their principles. They answered only to someone above. The United States *Constitution* established the pattern of an agreed-upon set of principles to which the governors and those governed would mutually adhere.

Likewise quality organizations have clearly-stated values that define desired behavior, ethics, and goals. When values are clearly stated and shared, they serve as a unifying force directing energy toward productive effort.

Stated and shared values create a problem for managers. They are expected not only to conform to these principles but to be an example. If the organization values teamwork, managers are expected to model teamwork. If the organization values customer focus, managers are expected to model customer focus. If the organization values continued learning, managers are expected to model continued learning. This is a heavy burden for managers to bear.

Tough on People to Tough on Competition

One of the greatest misconceptions about leadership in the past is that leaders were tough on their own people. The world's greatest military leaders (Alexander the Great, Lord Nelson, Napoleon, etc.) all demonstrated great affection and affiliation, even tenderness, toward their own people. They were hard on their competition. Many of our so-called "tough" bosses such as Frank Lorenzo at Eastern Airlines are tough on their own people and easy on their competition. Other airlines have thrived while Lorenzo has been "tough."

Wealth-Consuming to Wealth-Creating

The quality organization fulfills the fundamental role of a business organization in a free society by creating new products and services. This creates new jobs and adds to the collective wealth of the society.

Those of us in business organizations can feel good about our contribution to society. We fulfill a worthwhile and noble purpose. It is the business organization that creates jobs, goods, and services and determines the wealth of the society. In poor countries it is likely that the business institution is not fulfilling its purpose.

Within our organizations we have a responsibility to ensure that we spend our resources in a way that adds value and creates wealth. This can be accomplished only if managers see themselves as responsible for creating new products and services, improving products and services, making better use of all resources, and thereby creating new jobs. This is the wealth-creation process.

Exercise: Defining Role Changes

In small groups you may wish to discuss the implications of each of the twelve paradigm shifts in terms of how this shift might affect your job. For each paradigm shift identify some of the ways your job might change from its current functions to future functions.

How many of these changes can you make now? What would the new behavior or activity look like in the shift to the new paradigm?

1. **Control to Commitment:**

2. **Task to Process and Customer Focused:**

3. **Command to Participative:**

4. **Individual Work to Teamwork:**

5. **Experts and Labor to Experts All:**

6. **Punishment to Positive Reinforcement:**

7. **One Right Way to Continuous Learning:**

8. **Record Keeping to Scorekeeping:**

9. **Tall and Rigid Structure to Flat and Flexible:**

10. **Unstated Values to Shared Values:**

11. **Tough on People to Tough on Competition:**

12. **Wealth-Consuming to Wealth-Creating:**

Organizational Redesign

As your company strives to improve performance and customer satisfaction through creating teams and culture change, it is important to be constantly evaluating the consistency of your systems. If there is misalignment, there will be ensuing confusion and doubt. Tampering with one piece of the organization without addressing the interdependent parts is like removing one piece of a watch. It quits working despite the fact you haven't touched anything else. The critical pieces of an organization fall into five S's: *S*tructure, *S*kills, *S*ystems, *S*tyle, and *S*ymbols.

Structure is how the organization is put together to get work done.

Skills are the technical and interpersonal competencies needed to get the job done.

Systems are the "glue" that impact the human behavior in the organization including such things as hiring, training, compensation, information, and promotions.

Style is the amorphous description of how people are managed and how they treat each other. It captures the behavioral component of the organizational culture.

Symbols are the components of the culture that are reflected in the trappings that distinguish one group of people from others. We look to symbols to signify the values of the organization.

While implementing teams in your organization, you will find that changing your organizational structure causes your other systems to be out of alignment. It may be that your organization can evolve through various iterations to a good fit, or you may decide you need a formal redesign effort. To pursue this line of thought, please see our *Whole Systems Architecture* manual.

Action Assignment

Assess how close your team system is to creating a culture of high performance teams using the five S's model (*S*tructure, *S*kills, *S*tyle, *S*ystems, and *S*ymbols). Looking at those things over which you exert some control, what influences could you change to make your team move closer to a "high-performance team?"

Implementation Tips

1. Always keep in perspective that becoming a quality organization requires a constant effort; it is not an end state to be achieved and then the organization breathes a "sigh of relief" and relaxes.

2. Help your teams see this process as a lifestyle change. Try correlating it with getting in physical shape. It takes many different techniques, a lot of motivation and team encouragement, and you cannot stop working at it.

3. Help teams avoid frustration by setting "mini-goals" to achieve and then celebrating their accomplishment. Too often teams look at their "ideal state" and feel they are failing until they reach it.

4. The degree to which a team can become "self-directed" is highly variable. Realistic goals should be set on this issue, and in some cases it may be unrealistic. Here are some issues to consider: How technical is the work? How interdependent are the team members? How much can they become cross-trained? How constant is membership and leadership of the team?

Chapter Eleven

Case Studies

Case studies exhibit examples of successful team systems from which we can learn and understand the connection between quality, competitive success, and teamwork.

A Note on How to Read Cases

There is no one "right way" to implement the principles and practice of quality management and teams. The reason to study cases is not to find a cookie cutter approach that you can apply to your organization. Rather the reason to study cases is to see how others have innovated and found methods that worked for them in their situation, and to expand your own experience.

Look for principles, not prototypes to imitate. One company may have had their meetings everyday and found this successful; another may have formed cross-functional teams; another may have started with management teams. However their situations are not identical to your own. What made it work for them? How are you similar, and how are you different? What would happen if you did it that way? Is there a better way? What was the principle they were applying, and how can you apply that same principle?

The purpose of cases is to help you think creatively.

Some use them to avoid thinking. The real meaning of team management is that you with your team are capable of becoming your own *"world's greatest experts."*

Team Management in a Textile Fibers Plant

By Jennifer Howard,
Miller Howard Consulting Group

Walking through this textile fibers plant in the Southeast, you would not hear people talking about "business as usual." A changing market place for their commodity products along with fierce international and domestic competition has put pressures on prices and demanded consistency of product quality. The traditional style of managing had proven to be no longer acceptable: it was incapable of meeting the demand for quality. The one thousand managers and employees in the plant recognized this and jointly engaged in the process of turning the business around. The team management system was one of the major vehicles through which this was accomplished.

The plant manager formed a steering committee with his department heads to design the change effort under the direction of a Miller Howard Consulting Group consultant. This team defined two types of objectives for the process: measurable "key result areas" which reflected the health of the operation plus some behavioral characteristics which reflected the culture of the organization. The key result areas were as follows:

Customer Satisfaction
Product Quality
First Grade Yield
Controllable Conversion Costs

The cultural traits they wished to create in the organization included the following ones:

Increased involvement in decision-making including pushing decision-making to the lowest possible level.

A customer-driven environment in which every individual felt it was his job to meet the needs of his internal or external customer.

A team philosophy which would turn the *they's* and *theirs* into *we's* and *ours*. They wanted to develop teams which would take ownership for problems and seek solutions to these problems.

An individual commitment to excellence in decision-making and performance. This cultural trait would be evidenced by individuals genuinely feeling that they can make a difference to the operation; a person taking action to correct what he sees as wrong; and individuals feeling that when they do a good job, it truly makes a difference to the team, the boss, and the organization.

Methods

The implementation of the team management process proceeded in the following manner:

1. The steering committee began by requiring team membership of every individual in the plant. Every employee became a member of a team with his boss and a leader of a team with his subordinates. This established an interlocking system of natural unit teams at all levels of the organization.

2. Five internal consultants were trained to help carry out the training and follow-up consulting necessary to help managers change their management style.

3. All managers received training in team management skills such as how to conduct effective meetings in performance management skills, how to set up feedback systems on critical business measures; and on group problem-solving skills such as how to brainstorm and reach consensus.

4. All hourly employees received an orientation on what the team system was and what it was expected to accomplish.

5. An integration plan for team management and quality management with its focus on the use of statistical process control was implemented.

6. All the teams began to meet weekly to review their performance data and to take appropriate action based on the data.

7. Cross-functional teams were formed on an as-needed basis to address problems confronting multiple teams.

8. Ongoing consulting continued to reinforce successful team meetings and to assist teams who were having difficulty.

9. After about eight months of meeting, the teams became more independent, and the consultants pulled out while handing over the follow-up to line management.

Results

There were many measurable gains made from this process as well as dramatic improvements in less tangible areas such as communications between shifts, increased decision-making at the hourly level, in-depth problem solving occurring by the people who would implement the solutions, and competition between groups being replaced by teamwork.

As of the writing of this paper, the most dramatic measurable results were realized in the plant's major product line. This product line had earnings for the first time in four years in the first quarter of 1987. In the second quarter those earnings were doubled. The plant's overall earnings increased by over nine million. Other data revealed an overall conversion cost per pound of product had decreased by ten percent, and waste had decreased by sixteen percent. One of their major customers agreed to a significant price increase due to the plant's improved product quality and reliability.

In the less measurable areas there is much evidence of teams working to be more cooperative, more productive, and more customer-oriented. There are hundreds of examples similar to the following ones:

One team began reviewing how well they had supplied ceramic yarn guides to their customers in the fibers' operating areas. This equipment supply hadn't been perceived as a major problem, but when it was evaluated, the team found there were over 150 stockouts of these guides each week. The group came up with eight ways to supply their customers more efficiently. The ultimate result is better service and a reduction in the quantity of the in-house guide stocks.

A general labor team decided to reduce the number of filter tow bales rejected due to dirt and oil contamination. They found a novel way to identify leaking hydraulic pipes for repair by maintenance. At the same time they examined their own procedure and found a number of ways to improve the quality of their services without any increase in cost or labor.

An example of the impact of team management on cross shift cooperation occurred in the packing department. The typical habit of the shift employees as the shift was ending was to pack their last crate, put their things away, and socialize until the end of shift. As a result of discussions during team meetings the shifts decided to use their last fifteen to twenty minutes to setup for the next shift. It was determined that it saved the department about thirty minutes of packing time per employee by having all the tools and packing equipment laid out prior to shift start-up.

Discussion

No one team or department has generated these results. Production areas have worked together with the lab, maintenance, and raw materials supplier teams to realize these gains. The structure of team meetings coupled with expertise in statistical process control, performance management, and problem solving has served to put this organization in the position of being able to manage performance in a consistent, organized, and well-communicated manner. Necessary communications now have a vehicle for moving quickly up and down the organization. In addition to tapping into the team structure itself, top level managers are often seen walking through the plant talking to operators about team meetings and their team's performance data.

At this time, there have been several people recognized for their contribution to the success of the project. The plant manager was promoted to head all of the textile operations of the corporation, and several supervisors have moved on to the other divisions as internal consultants to help in the implementation of the team management process throughout the company. This type of significant and public reward for making team management successful in an organization is a critical step in demonstrating the commitment of upper management to make the "new management culture" a way of life.

Team Management in the Oil Fields

By Jennifer Howard,
Miller Howard Consulting Group

Overview

This case study is of how Texaco, Eastern Exploration & Production Inc., rallied following the oil industry's difficult times in the mid- 1980's and Texaco's twenty percent downsizing in 1989. Rising to a challenge by Texaco Inc.'s CEO to apply for the Malcolm Baldrige Award by 1992 and along the way, "become the most admired" oil company, the East Region's management chose a plan for total quality by implementing total employee involvement through team management. With all 2600 employees on a team that meets regularly the team members and leaders learned successfully to identify and interview their internal and external customers, map the work flow of their primary processes, and look for improvements; create team scorecards that tracked customer satisfaction and business measures of the team; and analyze and solve problems through group problem-solving techniques. Each team was responsible for running its piece of the business, and many team members also worked on cross-functional teams dealing with more macro process improvements that cut across functional lines. To support this process, there were approximately twenty internal consultants working with each of the 300 teams.

The unique challenges facing this organization in implementing a total quality management effort were not only its large population, but also the geographical dispersion of the employees. The East region's territory encompasses the entire Gulf of Mexico plus roughly the eastern half of the continental U.S. from Texas to the East coast. Employees in outlying areas on both offshore and onshore drilling and pro-duction locations presented some challenging logistical issues. To further complicate implementing a team approach, the offshore platform employees met on a seven-day on, seven-day off shift rotation making regular team meetings with their supervisors (who had different shift rotations) very difficult.

After only a year and a half since implementation employees are energized by the changing culture, a true sense of ownership of their process, and the remarkably-improved communications they are experiencing. Their empowerment and problem-solving skills have led to a wealth of money-saving ideas particularly from the field operations, a previously untapped reservoir for process improvement. External customers feel as if they are working with a much improved company, particularly in the level of cooperation and response time.

Introduction

Total Quality Through Team Management: Total quality through team management is an integrated approach to applying quality tools and techniques throughout an organization in a systematic method with the objective of impacting the bottom-line. The structure used to start implementing the process is the natural unit team with the supervisor of that team trained as a team leader. The teams meet regularly to review their "scorecard" that is composed of measures of customer satisfaction and key business indices. The teams identify and analyze their key processes, interview their key customers, problem solve, and make decisions for continuous improvement. Often cross-functional teams emerge to address process improvements that cut across functional lines and disband when their project is finished. In some cases, however, the organization may decide to change their structure so that the cross-functional team becomes permanent if it is more appropriate for managing a key process.

What characterizes this process?

> teams are non-voluntary

> 100% involvement from the organization is required from the most senior managers to the front-line employee

> teams are a permanent structure designed to run their piece of the business or process

> teams make decisions about changes (vs. just recommendations)

> everyone in the organization is trained in the same quality tools and techniques and is expected to practice them routinely

In order to promote a lasting culture change, this process looks for "systems alignment" in the organization. Alignment of systems means that the organization must review not only their work processes but also the "social" systems that drive the behavior of people. These include reward and recognition, compensation, appraisal, structure, information, decision-making, and training to be sure that they are all strengthening and supporting behavior consistent with the vision of the corporation.

Text

The Challenge. In 1990 Texaco Eastern Exploration and Production Region chose to implement the team management system. Along with the problems faced by the entire oil industry in the mid-1980's, Texaco also faced additional adversities including the purchase of Getty Oil, followed by the lawsuit with Pennzoil and a three billion dollar settlement by Texaco. It was during these trying times that Texaco began to build its vision for the future. Jim Kinnear's, (Texaco's CEO), mission was to bring Texaco into the 1990's as, "one of the most admired companies in the world and the competitive leader of the oil industry." It was determined that the vehicle to bring this vision to reality was the implementation of a quality process throughout the organization.

The Implementation Process: In 1989 the region began analyzing its fundamental pro-

cesses and organizational structure. The results of this analysis were a downsizing of approximately twenty percent and a restructuring into five fundamental business units and one region level services group. The senior team (the region's VP & direct reports) surveyed a large sample of the entire employee population to determine the type of culture desired by the organization and to pinpoint the problem areas that most needed addressing. The results suggested that employees wanted more performance feedback and positive recognition for results. They wanted Texaco to be more of a leader in technological areas, and they wanted to see more inspired leadership from their senior management team. Based on this feedback, the senior team developed a mission statement for their quality process that stated

The Eastern E&P Region will enhance quality through leadership and integrity with individual performance as our foundation, teamwork as our strength, and excellence as our goal. This will be accomplished by doing the right things at the right time and at the right cost.

Following this, the region chose The Miller Consulting Group to assist in implementing their quality improvement process through team management. Implementation followed six major steps:

1. Selection of Internal Quality Consultants. The success of a quality process requires dedicated quality professionals (known as internal consultants) to assist in the education and coaching of all the teams in order to change their management practices and create the desired organizational culture. After careful consideration, the senior team selected twenty-three internal consultants to support 2,600 employees in implementing the quality process. These internal consultants provided full-time assistance in training classes, coaching team leaders, and observing team meetings of all employees for a period of twelve to eighteen months.

2. Quality Kick-off and Orientation. The next step was to communicate the plan of action to the rest of the organization. For employees in the regional office, the senior vice president of the region held a "State of the Region Address" to explain the senior team's vision and to introduce both the internal and external consultants who would be assisting in accomplishing this vision. For the employees in the field a senior manager and a consultant made presentations to explain the plan, the roles, and responsibilities of everyone involved and to answer questions or concerns people might have about the process.

3. Forming Teams. For the initial roll-out of the team management process every person from the senior managers to the roustabouts and pumpers was put on a functional team composed of their peers and supervisor, which initially met on a weekly basis. They were required to implement major milestones (see five below). The supervisor was the team leader of his/her own team and team member of the team above him/her. This resulted in approximately 285 "interlocking teams" meeting regularly to discuss their performance, communicate about the needs of the business, and discuss ways to improve customer satisfaction. It was understood that following this initial implementation phase some teams might better serve their customers if they were configured differently or met on a different schedule.

4. Training and Education. Prior to the necessary formal skills training, the senior team attended several seminars such as the Quest for Excellence Forum II (sponsored by the Malcolm Baldrige National Quality Award) and Milliken's Pursuit of Excellence seminar. Every team leader received training in two, two-day seminars on

> ➤ customer focus
> ➤ process mapping
> ➤ performance measurement and tracking
> ➤ problem solving
> ➤ cause analysis
> ➤ group decision-making
> ➤ meeting management

There was additional training in customer interview skills to enable teams to maximize the value of data collected from their internal and external customers. Also team members were trained in many of these same skills in a one-day overview.

5. Coaching Follow-up. Each internal consultant initially had weekly contact with each team. Their task was to have a pre-meeting contact with the team leader to discuss his/her plans and agenda for the team meeting, to sit in the meeting as an observer, and to give feedback to the team leader and the team about their meeting process. Each team was to complete the following milestones over a nine month timeline:

> ➤ Develop a code of conduct for meeting process and behavior
> ➤ Identify team's products, services, and customers
> ➤ Interview customers as to their requirements and satisfaction level
> ➤ Map and analyze the team's work processes that generate the products and services
> ➤ Develop a scorecard for the team: both customer satisfaction and business performance measures are included
> ➤ Graph and track the team's performance and determine team goals
> ➤ Develop recognition systems for improvement and goal attainment
> ➤ Use problem-solving process to analyze and improve team performance
> ➤ Develop action plans for implementing improvement ideas

6. Evaluation and Follow-up. There was continuous re-analysis of the teams, their structure, makeup, and impact. There were additional cross-functional teams developed to address many of the critical processes that crossed department and division boundaries, as well as to address specific issues such as recognition and rewards, innovations, key processes, and cycle time reductions. Employees continued to seek additional training, to attend conferences on quality and to learn from other companies and other divisions of Texaco. Research was done to benchmark key processes, and industry specialists were brought in to teach employees how to analyze Texaco's performance against other oil companies. Quality was incorporated into the region's strategic plan. It became increasingly evident to everyone that this was to be a lifetime commitment, not just a "phase" or "another program" that would end in a year's time.

The Results and Progress: Approximately twenty million have been saved to date as a result of the successes from Texaco's Team Management Process. A significant portion of these financial gains resulted from the development of a cross-company team to evaluate oil and gas properties, generating a potential nine million in new revenues.

However financial successes are not the only result:

➤ Groups of employees who have historically never communicated with one another, petroleum engineers and geologists, are now communicating and sharing information.
➤ Management is making contact with employees; one of their team measures is a "visibility index".
➤ People are sharing ideas openly without fear of being categorized as negative.
➤ Frontline employees, previously left out of the mainstream, now feel as though they're a part of the team and are being listened to; on a recent trip to offshore platforms 100% of pumpers, mechanics, and operators noted that they felt empowered and that they had a voice in the business.
➤ One particular field team decided that the supervisor's position and two direct-report positions were redundant. The team eliminated the positions and handled redeployment of manpower.
➤ A gas plant team interviewed a refinery customer and found that although the plant's product met specifications, it didn't meet the customer's expectations. The team solved the problem, modified the process, and delivered a higher quality product to the customer. This led to increased sales and the capture of a by-product for fuel resulting in approximately half a million dollars a year in revenue gains.

Not all ideas are successes. A growing number of ideas are given a chance and sometimes turn into "learning experiences"... all without shooting the ideal generators! These "bold trys" were identified at all levels of the organization: secretaries, clerks, field operators, geologists, engineers, and managers. In some ways these "bold trys" are successes. Teams use these instances for continuous improvement.

Conclusion

Every change is difficult, and this one hasn't been any different. The region's organized approach to bringing about a systematic and integrated change is sharpening customer focus, improving the morale of employees, spurring innovation and creativity, eliminating bureaucracy, increasing speed of doing business, increasing productivity, generating important bottom line results, and most importantly providing opportunities for employees not only to do their best but to be their best!

The Honda Way
A Visit To Marysville

by Lawrence M. Miller
Miller Howard Consulting Group

It became a practice at Honda America Manufacturing in Marysville, Ohio, to use my book American Spirit as a management development text. This resulted in an invitation to visit and present to the Honda management group. I spent two days touring the plant, speaking with managers, and production associates, sitting in on meetings and asking questions. Why is Honda so good? The answer is both simple and complex. There is little that Honda does that is completely unique. There is nothing that stands out as their secret to quality. The secret is they do everything, and they do it as a team!

I find that in every healthy corporate culture there is a common understanding of philosophy, the values and visions upon which decisions and practices are based. The management practices, the structure, systems, skills, style, and symbols are consistent with the philosophy. At Honda there is clearly a "team" culture.

Even before entering the building, I found that the philosophy became evident. As we drove toward the plant, I noticed lines of newly-planted trees. I was told that they were planted by newly-hired associates. Each new associate plants a tree, "so he can grow with the company." All associates (the term used for all employees) know the company philosophy. They see it everyday in one hundred ways. They hear it consistently from their leaders. There are no contradictions.

The president of Honda of America is Shoichiro Irimajiri, known as Mr. Iri by the associates. Earlier in his career, Mr. Iri was responsible for managing Honda's successful racing efforts, designing engines, and managing production facilities in Japan. He frequently speaks of the "racing spirit." The racing spirit includes five principles: 1) Seek the challenge; 2) Be ready on time; 3) Have Teamwork; 4) Have Quick Response; 5) Winner Takes All! Perhaps more instructive of the Honda philosophy is his story of one of his early racing efforts.

It was in 1965 when Mr. Iri was working on the formula one racing engines. In the British Grand Prix of that year, the engine failed, and it was torn down and examined by Mr. Honda himself.

Examining the failed piston, he turned to Shoichiro Irimajiri and demanded, "Who designed this piston?" "I did," he acknowledged. After examining the engineering drawing, Mr. Honda roared out, "You! Stupid! No wonder the piston gets burned. You have changed the thickness here." After the young Irimajiri attempted to defend his design change with some data from previous engines, Mr. Honda roared again. "I hate college graduates! They use only their heads. Do you really think you can use such obsolete data obtained from old, low-performance engines? I have been making and designing pistons for several years. I am fully aware how critical half a millimeter is here. A company does not need people like you who use only their heads. Before you laid out this design, why didn't you listen to opinions of those experienced people in the shop? If you think academic study in college is everything, you are totally wrong. You will be useless in Honda unless you spend more time on the spot for many years to come.

"You will go to the machining shop," Mr. Honda ordered the young engineer, "and you will apologize to every person there, for you have wasted their efforts." Mr. Honda followed him down the hall to make sure he did as directed. Mr. Iri recalls that he was glad that he had no ambition of becoming president of the company. He was not even sure he would succeed as an engineer. He learned his lesson. He not only succeeded as an engineer, designing several successful racing engines, but he became the president of Honda of America, the first Japanese company to export cars back to Japan. Shoichiro Irimajiri is still listening to those experienced people in the shop, and he is not wasting their time.

The Honda philosophy stresses that you must be on the spot in the plant and see the problem, touch the part, and gain experience in the actual job in order to solve a problem. Engineers and management spend most of their time in the factory in touch with their associates, the product and process.

The Honda philosophy is manifested in all of the management practices. In the *symbols, structure, systems, skills, and style* the philosophy can be seen and experienced every day by every employee every hour.

Symbols: When I arrived, I was given a uniform to wear in the plant. I was told that this wasn't given to all guests, only "honored guests." To cover my tie with the white smock with the Honda name, to look the same as every other associate was an honor. I can assure you that by the time my visit was finished it felt like an honor. To be part of a proud group of people, to share their symbol of equality caused me to feel a part, invested, in their shared goals.

All associates from the president to the newest-hired associate eat in the same cafeteria and park in the same undesignated parking spaces. Managers sit at the same metal desks in open office areas. Most of the desks are arranged in blocks of six, often with paired Japanese and American managers sitting across from one another. All of the managers of the motorcycle plant sit at one block of six identical desks, the Japanese vice president and the American plant manager sitting across from each other.

As I walked through the plant, the cleanest nonfood manufacturing plant out of several hundred I have been in, I observed a vice president stop and pick up a misplaced object on the floor. There is nothing on the floor. There are also NO maintenance people to clean up! Everyone, every associate and manager, cleans his own area.

To many, these symbols will seem trivial. They would be if they stood alone, at odds with the behavior and attitudes of the people, or if the structure and systems stood in contradiction. However they are one part of a total system like a well-engineered engine with all components balanced and moving in unison.

Structure: Everyone is a member of a team. The team is the first level of organization. At 6:30 a.m. each morning every associate meets with his team and team leader. The day's work is discussed, and feedback on the previous day's quality is given. Any problems, changes, or concerns are shared during this meeting.

A team is comprised of fifteen to twenty associates who work in a common area. As I toured both the auto and motorcycle plant, I stood and watched the assembly line in operation. I asked which person was the team leader and which was the production coordinator, the second-level manager. It was very hard to find them or distinguish them. I watched as there was an apparent problem on the motorcycle line. One employee was having difficulty getting a frame over an engine assembly. He had stopped the line. He and another associate worked frantically to get the frame in place. It took about twenty seconds, and the line was moving again. I asked where the team leader was. The other associate, helping to free the frame, was the team leader. The production coordinator was at the next station on the assembly line helping another associate catch-up on the placement of electrical wire assemblies. I watched for about fifteen minutes as the team leader and production coordinator (equivalent of first-line supervisor and department manager) worked on the line, smiling, joking, and working hard and fast with their associates.

Nowhere is there a private office for team leaders or production coordinators. They do not remove themselves from the work. They are on the spot, seeing and touching the product, gaining experience, and solving problems. They are part of the working team.

All managers are organized into teams and solve problems together. The structure of the organization as well as the physical arrangement of desks and offices makes group problem solving a natural and constant occurrence.

Participation in the constant improvement process is also structured through quality circles. NH Circles (NH stands for "now Honda, new Honda, next Honda") are similar to circles in many other companies. However at Honda they are one component of a total involvement process which they call VIP (Voluntary Involvement Program).

VIP includes a suggestion system, quality awards, and safety awards. Twenty percent of all associates participate in circles. The rate of suggestions adoption is 59.4%, and 60% participate in some component of the VIP process. In speaking with several NH Circle members, I was impressed that they felt the responsibility to see that accepted recommendations for improvement were implemented. They also felt that their circles were different from those in other companies in that they are constantly looking for any improvement in the production process, large or small, and even small improvements are highly valued. They said that the success of Honda was the result of constantly finding small improvements, not just looking for major ones.

Systems: I expected to find systems of employee involvement at Marysville. However I was somewhat surprised to see the amount of thought that has been put into the positive reinforcement systems. Honda of America practices performance management. They have found ways to provide constant feedback, recognition, and tangible positive reinforcement for almost every form of desirable performance.

The NH Circle program, suggestion system, quality awards, and safety awards are all tied together with a point system. Every associate can earn points by participating in any of these improvement processes. Awards include award certificates, gift certificates, department

manager's award, plant manager's sward, and president's award. These also result in points accumulating over your career, and these points can earn a Honda Civic (2500 points), and an Accord (5000 points) plus two weeks off with pay and airplane tickets plus spending money to anywhere in the world.

In addition to hourly or salaried compensation, all associates participate in profit sharing. This profit sharing is an innovation of Honda of America and is not part of the system in Japan. Ten percent of the gross profit generated by Honda Motor Company is shared with associates based on their relative compensation. Good attendance results in another bonus. The average bonus check for attendance in 1986 was $832. The average profit sharing check was $2,688.

Performance analysis and feedback is an important part of any total performance management system. In each of the open office areas and in each of the many conference rooms, all of the walls are literally covered with charts and graphs representing different quality and productivity performance variables. The graphs are of every possible variety, some employing statistical process control methods and some simply reflecting historical data with means, trends, and goal lines. Frequently along with the charts on the wall are lists of causes or solutions to problems. Diagrams of auto parts or production machinery with arrows pointing to sources of problems are also frequent. It is obvious that all of the managers at Honda are in touch with plant performance data.

Another system worthy of mention is the discipline system. There are some fairly traditional and sound procedures for gradual counseling and discipline. However the unique part of the discipline process is the peer review provided for associates who are dismissed for poor conduct. If an associate wishes to appeal a termination, a peer review panel is formed by randomly selecting six or eight production associates. One senior manager also serves on the panel with equal vote. The panel hears both sides of the case and then decides to overturn or accept the management decision. Nine out of ten times the decisions are upheld by the associates.

Skills: The measure of skills is found in the product of work. There can be no question that Honda has highly-skilled engineering and quality personnel. The majority of the engineers are Japanese. Hiring and training more Americans is a goal for the coming years. Honda is an engineering company. Most of the Japanese senior managers have served as design engineers for engines, including racing engines, or other components.

Having worked at other auto companies, I found it obvious that at Honda the most valued personnel are those with engineering and technical competence. At many other companies it is the financial managers and management professionals who are most valued. Honda is in the business of making excellent cars. Many other companies are in the business of making money and only secondarily making cars. Honda makes money and does not need layers of bureaucratic managers because they are passionately dedicated to their technology and products.

On the assembly line there is a process of continual skill development. Associates are rotated from one position to another to broaden their skills and increase their flexibility. Even when applicants are interviewed for employment at Honda, they are asked questions to determine their flexibility. Flexibility and the development of broad-based skills are central principles.

At Honda it is assumed that the production associates are intelligent, skilled, and dedicated. They can, therefore, be trusted to manage the quality process. Every associate is a quality control inspector. The assembly process at Honda is based on just-in-time (JIT) inventory and the assumption of 100% quality parts. Each associate understands that it is his or her job to inspect each part to assure conformance to requirements. Any associate can reject a part. If a manager wants the part used after the associate has re-

jected it, the burden is on the manager to explain to the associate why it should be used. There is a quality assurance department with a team of associates who will call the supplier regarding any and every bad part. Every vendor is assigned to one associate, and that associate knows exactly who to call, including home telephones, to provide immediate feedback on any deviation from quality requirements.

Style: All of the methods described above are held together by people with a sense of humor and a high level of people-to-people skills.

As I interviewed managers, I repeatedly asked them how they felt working for or with Japanese managers. I wanted to know if there were any resentment toward the Japanese. I could find absolutely none. I could find only the most sincere respect and friendship. There was no feeling of "us Americans" working for "them." The reason for this mutual respect became more clear the next morning.

Every morning the ten or twelve managers of the motorcycle plant meet to review performance, solve problems, and make plans for the day. The Japanese vice president responsible for the motorcycle operations sat at the end of the table. The meeting was led by a manager who was two levels down. There was a lively discussion about the handling of an "almost-in-time" inventory situation that had almost halted production the previous day. There were three or four Japanese managers and about eight Americans in the meeting. One of the Japanese managers was very vocal about how confusing the situation was and how it should have been handled better. Several others discussed what happened and how it was being resolved today. The vice president sat quietly through a half hour of discussion, never saying anything until the meeting was coming to a conclusion. Only then did he speak out. He had two points. First he wanted to thank everyone for his efforts yesterday, rising to meet the challenge presented by the problem. Second he wanted to stress how important it was to meet another challenge that was coming up within the next week. His tone was calm and reassuring.

These incidents and dozens of others like them proved to me that the integration of cultures is working in Marysville. The Americans have adopted the Japanese patience and view things from a long-term perspective. The Japanese have adopted or at least accepted the American fun-loving familiarity and creativity.

The style at Honda is different than other Japanese companies, and this may be central to their success and initiative in manufacturing in the United States. The traditional Japanese company places a high value on age and seniority. Honda does not. Mr. Irimajiri is a young man excited by winning races and building racing engines. Mr. Honda has retired because he believes the company should be run by young men. The first principle of the Honda management policy is, "Proceed always with ambition and youthfulness." The second is, "Respect sound theory; develop fresh ideas and make the most effective use of time." The third is, "Enjoy your work, and always brighten your working atmosphere."

Honda now employs nearly 6,000 youthful-minded and creative Buckeye associates in Marysville. That number will be raised to over 8,000 as they build their second auto assembly plant nearby. The U.S.-manufactured content of the Honda Accord is now about sixty percent and will be increased to seventy-five percent. The Accord is more American than some GM, Ford or Chrysler nameplates with higher-imported content.

As I left Marysville, I didn't leave with the feeling that I had visited a "foreign" manufacturer. Rather I had the feeling that I had visited something new. I had visited a world-embracing company with a world-embracing philosophy, as much American as Japanese, perhaps the best of both worlds. I could also think of nothing that Honda was doing, no secret in either principle or practice, that could not be adopted by any company if its senior managers were knowledgeable and committed and would "proceed always with youthfulness."

Chapter Twelve

A Personal Note

You can apply the principles and skills of quality and teams to your personal life.

Beyond Work - A Personal Affair

Your personal life beyond the workplace is not the business of your company. The corporation has no legitimate right to invade the privacy of your home or personal life. Some corporate-sponsored change efforts in recent years have with very unfortunate results strayed over the line that separates corporate and private affairs. We wish to make very clear that we strongly believe in the right of each individual to maintain that separation as he chooses.

On the other hand most of the principles you have learned during the previous chapters do have useful application to your home and personal life. Many of the skills and techniques associated with teams such as listening skills and group dynamics have been applied to personal and family relations for many years. Therefore as the authors speaking directly to you, we would like to share a few thoughts on the application of these principles and skills outside of the workplace.

Benjamin Franklin provides an excellent example of self-management. Ben Franklin is credited with possessing one of the most versatile and brilliant minds this country has ever produced. In addition to his statesmanship, hundreds of inventions, and his career as a writer, he is also known for his creative self-management.

"I wish to live without committing any fault at any time...As I knew, or thought I knew, what was right and wrong, I did not see why I might not always do the one and avoid the other." Franklin also understood the need to work at developing the right habits. He said, "The contrary habits must be broken and good ones acquired and established before we can have any dependence on a steady, uniform rectitude of conduct."

To implement his program of acquiring good habits, Franklin identified thirteen virtues and wrote a description of each. Included among his virtues were industry, moderation, sincerity, temperance, order, and silence. He then devised a feedback system that would be admired by many behavioral psychologists. He devised a self-monitoring procedure by which he focused on one of his thirteen virtues for one week, then proceeded to concentrate on a second virtue the second week, the next week the third, and so forth until he completed an entire cycle of his thirteen virtues. He then would begin again.

"I made a little book in which I allotted a page for each of the virtues. I ruled each page with red ink so as to have seven columns, one for each day of the week, marking each column with a letter for the day. I would mark each day I violated a virtue." In other words Franklin used a checksheet.

"I should have (I hoped) the encouraging pleasure of seeing on my pages the progress I made in virtue by clearing successively my lines of their spots." Franklin learned what we all undoubtedly learn when pursuing perfection: "I never arrived at the perfection I had been so ambitious of obtaining but fell far short of it. Yet, I was by the endeavor a better and happier man."

It is encouraging to all of us more ordinary souls that even the greatest minds of time have had to pursue their success with somewhat ordinary efforts. Few would deny Franklin's genius. Yet he resorted to drawing lines on paper and checking off the violations of his virtues each day. He took pleasure in seeing those checks become less numerous, a seemingly childish effort like the youngster earning his allowance by eating his vegetables. Yet this is the kind of disciplined effort that makes the difference between genius hidden and genius in action. We must wonder how many geniuses have lived ordinary lives because they failed to exert the effort to master their own habits to change their own lives.

Guiding Principles

Philosophy or principles are important. They are important in a nation, company, or family.

Just as our nation has a *Constitution* and our company has a statement of values, we each have a personal philosophy. We encourage companies to define their corporate values in a clear manner. Just taking time to meditate on values can be an encouragement to positive change. Similarly you have a personal philosophy, and it is time well spent to meditate on that philosophy and its implications for your daily life.

The team process is built on a philosophy. This philosophy includes the idea of customer service, teamwork, and continual learning. Principles guide behavior and lead to constancy of purpose and trustworthy, satisfying relationships. Similarly well-functioning individuals know their principles and their beliefs. Individuals who are not successful, who lead less satisfying or troubled lives, often lack a knowledge of their principles.

In today's world many people have lost faith in any firm principles. Their behavior follows their skepticism in a random search for meaning and satisfaction. Principle-centered behavior, behavior directed toward a known purpose, results in constancy and satisfaction.

Know your principles. Principles guide careers and families as they guide teams. Some of the same principles that lead to the success of teams lead to the success of individuals. For example you may decide that one of your own personal principles is to continue your own learning and the learning of family members. This principle has enormous implications for how you spend your time. It leads to the action of reading the newspaper, subscribing to magazines, reading professional journals, and buying books related to your career. It is a simple thing, but this obvious principle is not one that most people act on with any regularity. If you have accepted and acted on this principle, it is likely that your children will also accept and adopt the same principle as their own.

The principle of customer focus as practiced in the quality process has implications that extend well beyond the workplace. The idea of customer focus recognizes that our work exists to be of service to others. It also recognizes that self-satisfaction and personal rewards are likely to follow service to others.

Personal happiness and satisfaction rarely result from the pursuit of personal happiness and satisfaction. Rather the greatest satisfactions in life almost always derive from service to others. However without an understanding of this principle individuals tend to pursue their own satisfaction, not service to others. Rather than finding satisfaction, they find emptiness.

We will not attempt to construct a complete personal philosophy on these pages. Hundreds of authors and theologians have articulated personal philosophies. What is most important is that one develop or accept a guiding set of principles. Just as it is the cornerstone of a nation or corporation, firmness in principles is a cornerstone of a satisfying personal life.

The Family Team

The first team to which we all belong is the family. The family is the first organizational structure. The family is the first business unit. The family is the first source of material, intellectual, emotional, and spiritual well-being.

Perhaps it is more correct to say that teams in the workplace can learn from well-functioning families, than to say that families can learn from well-functioning teams. However now that you have studied the principles and skills of well-functioning teams, you may wish to apply those to the family.

Like team members family members have a common purpose, achieve goals together, solve problems together, learn, and grow together. Like team members it is helpful for families to meet together to discuss problems and goals in an environment of mutual trust and respect.

It is surprising how many families today never sit down together to talk about shared goals or problems. The "macho" idea that you "ought to be able to solve your own problems" has even permeated the intimacy of the family so that husbands and wives, parents and children are inhibited in their ability to share their concerns and hopes. This failure to share is destructive to the human personality, to the family unit, and to personal satisfaction.

Americans live in a world of stimulus saturation: turn on the car radio, turn on the TV during dinner, go out and rent a video so we will not be bored. Our lives are dominated by incoming stimuli. The technology of cars, television, radio, and VCRs assures a continual barrage. In a simpler age family members would sit together in the quiet of the home. They would talk. They would listen. They would sing. Deep, private, and powerful thoughts and feelings were shared. This flow was the bloodstream of personal relationships.

You now understand how harmful it would be if members of a work team failed to share their ideas for improvement, their goals and frustrations. You now understand how harmful it is if team members fail to listen openly and respectfully to each other. You now understand the magic of brainstorming and of how new and creative ideas are born when ideas are shared without fear within the team. You now understand how you can learn from your team members, regardless of their "rank" on the organization ladder. You now understand a great deal about a well-functioning family.

You may wish to discuss these ideas with your family. You may wish to schedule a regular family meeting or a "family day" in which all family members agree to stay home, work around the house together, go out for dinner, and enjoy entertainment together. With teenagers always on the run, active children, and two working parents, it is very easy to find yourself too busy to spend quality time with family members. As with the work team a structured, planned meeting time is a helpful forum for communication.

In the history of mankind, one scene has never been recorded. On his death bed, the old man, successful, famous, and wealthy, utters his last words: "I wish only I could have had more time to spend...in the office."

Family Problem Solving

The skills of working together in a group, objectively examining a process (how do meals get prepared in the home?), gathering and analyzing data (how many times per month are lights left burning in the children's bedroom?), brainstorming causes and solutions (how could we increase sharing of home chores?) are all skills that can make the home a more pleasant and cooperative place to live.

You may wish to teach them the problem-solving model. You might want to take a shared problem (where to spend vacation or how to improve the appearance of the house) and practice the five steps. Children are great at brainstorming. Try reaching consensus on the solution to a family problem, and develop an action plan. It works!

You will find many of the same benefits of team decision-making in the family as at work. You will find that family members have a surprising number of creative ideas. You will also find that their motivation changes when they are asked to help solve a problem. You will find that they are willing, even anxious, to do things to improve the home when asked to share in the responsibility of deciding on the plan.

Team problem solving is an excellent example for children to learn. Most children grow up in a traditional, autocratic organizational structure. Dad and mom make the decisions, and sometimes they might listen to us but probably do not. If they learn to be effective team members within the family, they will have a leadership advantage in school and in their future work life. At work they will be judged by their ability to function well with others, helping others to make decisions.

Unfortunately children are not likely to learn the skills of problem solving in groups at school. Most schools organize their work on the assumption that each person should do "his own work." Each student is expected to sit obediently, do what he is told and answer every question by himself or herself. Do not talk to the child next to you. Do not look at his paper. Do not ask him questions. The ability to work alone is valued and rewarded.

Before industrialization, the jobs on the family farm and in the small craft shop were all shared work, small groups working together. The classroom in the rural community was also a shared work environment. We took the mass production model and applied it to our schools. We gained control and efficiency (fewer teachers to students) but lost intimacy.

Few jobs, now or in the future, will be based solely on doing "your own work." Management work in particular is work done with others. The ability to learn from others, to teach others, and to analyze and solve problems with others is far more important than "doing your own work." Most of our schools are still organized according to the system of mass production where order, control, and individual work are the ruling principles. As a result our children are being handicapped.

You can teach you children how to reach effective decisions and create unified action toward common goals by practicing group decision-making within the family. We are not suggesting that every decision should be made by the entire family. Certainly there will be decisions made by Mom and Dad alone or just one of them. This is also true at work. However it is reasonable to select certain types of problems or decisions to make as a family team. What to do on vacation, who to invite dinner, how to keep the home clean, how to save money on the energy and telephone bill, and what to do together as a family one night a week are all good topics for regular family decision-making.

Drive Out Fear

Just as at work problems result in fear and punishment in many homes. Fear destroys relationships, communication, and trust. The principle of continuous improvement is just as appropriate in the home as at work. Problems are normal. As you know, at work problems are opportunities for continuous improvement. You know that there is no reason to yell, point fingers, or blame others when there is a problem. The team simply analyzes the process, defines the variance, gathers data, and gets on with the problem solving process. Comfort with an agreed-upon approach to solving problems eliminates fear.

Problems at home are often a source of great anxiety, frustration, or anger. "My wife never listens to me! My husband never does his share of the work! He or she obviously does not care about me! My kids are completely ungrateful!" These are all emotional statements that contribute to the problem rather than lead to solutions. One person makes an emotional statement, and the other reacts with an equally emotional and oppositional statement. The crisis escalates and verbal and emotional warfare is declared until one or both parties collapse in emotional exhaustion or angry withdrawal.

Healthy problem solving is based on a philosophy or attitude. Problems are normal. Misunderstandings are normal. Most problems can be easily solved if the facts are discussed without blame or accusation. Problems can best be solved when the emphasis is on "win-win" alternatives based on shared ownership and responsibility. Just as at work there are rarely "good guys" or "bad guys" in the home. There are different interpretations of events and different priorities, all of which are often perceived by the other person as good or bad. Teams and families solve problems effectively when members try to empathize with each other and learn from each other.

You have learned the importance of effective listening. Asking open-ended questions, reflecting back your understanding, and expressing empathy for the other person are the critical skills that facilitate effective communication. These skills are the focus of courses for parents such as parent effectiveness training (P.E.T.). Everyone, and teenagers in particular, needs a great deal of active listening. The good parent like the good team leader knows how to listen in a nonjudgmental way which allows the other person to express himself and gain understanding and judgment by sharing his ideas. We are more likely to accept advice when the other person has listened to our feelings and expressed his own understanding of our viewpoint.

The effective parent asks his children questions, encouraging them to develop their own ideas. Asking questions exercises the mind. The dinner table is an excellent opportunity for developing thinking and learning skills. Each night at the dinner table ask your children questions. Ask them what they feel the President should do about the current international crisis. Ask them what they think Congress should do about taxes, the environment, or crime. You may feel that they will not have any idea! Why ask them these questions? They will not have any idea because you have not asked them! Once you ask them the question, when the nightly news is on television, they will have a reason to listen. They will learn to process the information in a useful manner, anticipating your questions. You will find that your children will then ask you questions and will offer their opinion. In other words their brain will be turned on! But it all begins with simple questions that assume your children are intelligent, thinking human beings.

Responsibilities

On your team you may have decided that some team members will serve as subject matter experts (SME), taking responsibility for specific functions. On the family team you may ask for volunteers to serve as subject matter experts on specific functions or to accept periodic responsibilities. Mom and dad do not have to do everything! Children can take responsibility for planning the details of a vacation. A teenager could take responsibility and be the SME for the front yard and another for the backyard. Another could be the SME for maintaining the audio or video library. Assigning specific responsibility (decision-making) to children is an excellent way to teach responsibility. Children who have not had the opportunity to take responsibility for planning and decision-making are at a disadvantage when they leave home.

Stephen Covey, the author of *Principled Centered Leadership* and *Seven Habits of Highly Successful People*, divides the stages of maturity into 1) dependence (infancy to childhood), 2) independence (adolescence to early adult), and 3) interdependence (maturity and marriage).

Who makes decisions and using which style of decision-making changes through the stages of maturity. It is obvious that three or four year olds will not be very good decision makers when it comes to meal planning (unless you are willing to have ice cream for dinner every night). Young children depend on their parents for responsible decisions. As children mature, they learn to make decisions on their own, becoming increasingly independent.

Teenagers have a strong need to "do-their-own-thing." You will hear them say, "I can handle it myself!" They are simply expressing the healthy and inevitable desire to establish their own identity, to prove their ability to fly solo, and to succeed on their own decisions. The wise parent will not prevent but will facilitate the transition to independence by assisting the child to learn to make his own decisions in a responsible manner. At the beginning of the school year, you may have a meeting with your teenager and ask her what time she feels should be the agreed-upon hour that she should be home on school nights and weekends. You may be surprised to find that her answer will be very reasonable.

You have experienced the power of involvement in decision-making. We all want to be involved in making decisions that affect our lives. Only young children are comfortable with someone else making all of the decisions in their lives. Teenagers and adults feel a need to control their own lives. When given the opportunity, they will almost always act responsibly. When the teenager participates in establishing rules, he is much more likely to comply. When involved in a decision, his attitude and desire to please his parents will also improve.

By reinforcing children for being more responsible for decision-making, the parent teaches responsible behavior. Unfortunately many parents spend far more time blaming, arguing, punishing, and creating anxiety in their teenagers and almost no time encouraging responsible behavior in a positive and participative manner.

Reinforcement: How to Eliminate Punishment

Behavior is a function of its consequences. Behavior which is followed by desirable consequences tends to increase. For every misbehavior (failing to do homework, for example), there is a positive behavior that can take its place (doing homework each night). A happy home is one in which the parents focus their energies on reinforcing the desirable behavior rather then punishing the negative.

It is extremely common for parents to ignore desirable behavior when it occurs. They will say, "He's supposed to clean up his room, why should I praise him for that?" Or: "I expect my children to get good grades! I'm not going to bribe them for that!"

These are just excuses for our failure to show our appreciation for desirable behavior. Parents are teachers, and it is important that they understand the key factor in learning: behavior which is reinforced is learned! In the absence of reinforcement the behavior will not be learned. Habits are developed through the experience of positive consequences following a behavior. If doing homework is followed by reinforcement, the child will develop the habit of doing homework. The child comes to value this behavior because mom and dad demonstrate that they value this behavior.

Every child, including teenagers, works for their parents' approval. Approval by parents is reinforcing. Approval is expressed when you walk into your child's bedroom and ask him how school is going, discuss his history course with him, read his English paper, or help him solve a math problem. Simply taking the time to demonstrate interest is reinforcing.

As children and as parents we work for rewards. Your pay checks or promotions are rewards for good performance. Children learn to earn rewards through their own performance when parents provide rewards for good performance. A few years ago my teenage daughter began to think about getting her driver's license and a car. Was I "supposed to" buy her a car? No one bought me a car! I had to earn my cars! Why shouldn't she?

I negotiated a contract with my daughter. For eighty weeks, each Sunday we bought *The New York Times* newspaper. The agreement was that she would read one international and one domestic article on the front page each week. We discussed the articles each week. After eighty weeks I would buy her a car. We put on her wall a graph that went from zero to eighty weeks so she could visualize her progress toward her car.

She earned the car. But more important she developed an interest in world events. In school she was able to share her understanding about events in Russia, national politics, economics, and other issues. Because she was now interested, she watched television news shows. On her own initiative she applied for and went on a summer trip to what was then the Soviet Union with other high school students. The next year she initiated a trip to Africa. The following year as a freshman in college she applied for and went on a trip to Japan sponsored by Japanese and American corporations on tariff agreements.

The important point here is that behavior which is reinforced by parents takes on a life of its own. This includes both desirable and undesirable behavior. Contrary to what some people believe, children do not become dependent on praise or reinforcement from parents. They internalize the value of behavior, and it becomes self-reinforcing.

Managing Personal Quality

Is there something special, mysterious, or mystical about people who have accomplished great things? Or are they successful because they have done some ordinary things consistently well? Most success is often the result of the disciplined application of fairly common talents and abilities. Most success can be managed.

Personal quality is achieved by the individual who applies the force of his or her own will against the resistance of his or her own habits. This is the test!

One night Neil Simon was a guest on the Johnny Carson show. Neil Simon writes several plays each year and has been one of the most consistent producers of successful shows for many years. Johnny asked him, "Where do you get the inspiration to write a play?"

Neil Simon looked at him somewhat puzzled and thoughtfully said, "I've never had an inspiration to write a play."

Johnny laughed and said, "Come on. That's not possible. You must get an inspiration to write. How else would you know when to sit down and start writing?"

"That's easy," Simon responded, "I start writing at eight o'clock each morning."

Johnny said, "But what if you don't have anything to say? What if there's no inspiration there? You can't just sit down and write?"

"Listen," Simon responded, "If I wrote only when I was inspired, I would not have written my very first play. Writing plays is my job and it begins at eight o'clock in the morning. I sit down, and I write. Then I read what I've written. Often I don't like it, and I throw it away. But sometimes I find it interesting. Then I keep working on it. That's how I write plays!"

Anyone familiar with Neil Simon's work would acknowledge that he has talent and creativity, and he is certainly productive. However to him there is little mystery. The key factor is simply the self-discipline to sit down and get the job done. Neil Simon is an accomplished playwright because he has mastered himself. He has created the habit of doing ordinary things such as starting to work at eight o'clock each morning, and that has led to his success.

The following are seven steps to mastering personal quality. The purpose of this self-improvement method is to give you an easy-to-follow, organized, and proven method of self-improvement.

The Seven Steps to Mastering Personal Quality:

1. Create a personal vision
2. Set goals and pinpoint
3. Establish activators
4. Track performance
5. Take action
6. Reinforce improvement
7. Evaluate change

Action Step # 1
Define Your Personal Vision

Tactics follow strategy. In business there is a long-range strategy. It is where we want to be in future years. Immediate actions make sense and can be coordinated when they are in pursuit of an understood strategy. A personal vision is our personal strategic plan. It is how we view ourselves five years from now.

We tend to focus on our present condition (how we are today) and our current skills, attributes, and problems. When our focus is entirely on present conditions, we tend to lock those conditions in. We believe that we were meant to be in second place, last place, rich or poor, fat or skinny.

There is an entirely different dimension to every human being. It is what distinguishes us from the animal which is programmed to respond to instincts. Beyond the present condition we have our potential condition and the ability to exert our free will, our self-determination. In addition to what we are, we are what we could become.

To change, to grow, and to learn are necessities of a healthy life. The only question is, to become what? What is our image of how we can develop? Do we have an image? This vision of our future is so important. Growth is almost impossible without some vision of our future.

It is important to work at clarifying, specifying, and committing to a vision of your own future. It is helpful to force yourself to write down some ideas about the attributes you would like to develop. This is your vision of your own future.

Action Step # 2
Setting Goals and Pinpointing

You may dream of becoming a great baseball player, setting records, and winning the MVP title. How does that dream become a reality? Goals must be set. The high school youth sets the goal of getting on the team, then the goal of playing first string, and then the goal of hitting above .300. These are all intermediate, necessary goals to move toward the ultimate dream.

However even this is not specific enough. What does the baseball player actually have to do if he is to become an excellent player? He observes the batting stance of other great hitters. He observes their swing at the ball. He gets feedback from the coach on his swing. He may watch films or video tapes of his own swing and take corrective action. He practices deliberately hitting the ball to right or left field. These are all more specific and immediate things he must do in order to reach his intermediate goal of hitting .300. Each of these specific activities is a very pinpointed behavior.

Action Step # 3
Activating Performance

All healthy living things are in a state of motion and growth. When anything is in motion, it needs to be guided, directed by cues, and frequently processing feedback on its progress to maintain its course. To manage your own growth and development, you must establish your own guidance system.

There is a guidance system of personal growth and development. How do you know what attributes, goals, performance, or behavior to develop? How do you know whether you are making progress? How do you gain the satisfaction that comes from knowing that you are on course toward your destination? These are key questions if you are going to continue your movement toward personal quality.

Look around you. Who arc your modcls? Who do you admire? What are the specific behaviors, the things these people do to achieve their success? Successful people study other successful people. Excellent musicians listen to excellent music. Excellent writers read other excellent writers. Your guidance system is based on the input of your observations. If you want to be successful, you must arrange for successful input.

Successful people create successful environments. If you wish to concentrate at work, you know that you must reduce distractions. Similarly at home you can create an environment that can help steer your behavior. You can establish activators, cues that will remind you to accomplish your goals. You can post pictures of goals (the new house, car, or vacation) on the wall. You can establish a quiet study area where you can be free of the distraction of television. You can post graphs on the wall to remind you of your progress. All of these are ways to create an environment that will activate desired performance.

Action Step # 4
Track Performance

What is fun? Do you play golf? Bowl? Run?

What all of these activities have in common and almost everything we enjoy as a "sport" is a precise system of keeping score. Your team will enjoy its work to the degree that it keeps score of its performance. People who have developed the habit of running on a regular schedule have usually devised their own personal scorekeeping system. They track the number of miles they run each week, the average minutes per mile, their pulse rate at the end of one mile, etc. Certainly there is nothing inherent in running that requires scorekeeping. What does require scorekeeping is the motivation, the discipline, to maintain the behavior. Keeping score turns running into a game. Without scorekeeping, running is mcrcly work.

You are the hardest person for you to manage. It is so easy to make excuses for yourself and accept them when you would never accept the same excuses from someone else.

This is one of the reasons that scorekeeping is so important. Data does not lie, or make or accept excuses. If you are tracking and graphing the number of times you contacted customers to ask if their needs were being met and the line on the graph begins to move down, you are presented with hard and cold, objective facts about your own performance. When you step on the scale, if you observe your weight increasing, this is an objective fact that confronts you with your own reality. No one else has to say anything.

Progress does not come from a condition of ease but from a condition of challenge, requiring a creative response. This is the testing that leads to human development whether physical, intellectual, or spiritual. The body at ease degenerates. The mind closed and ignoring challenges loses its sharp edge and becomes dull.

There is always a gap. Quality or excellence is the process of continuous improvement closing that gap. How do we know what the gap is? How do we know whether we are actually closing the gap? How do we know whether or not we are dealing with reality? Developing our own self-tracking system is the answer.

Writers who work alone, who are self-employed, and who work for long periods without experiencing feedback or positive consequences from others either develop effective self-management skills or never succeed. Writers are fond of talking about their struggles with their own self-management.

Ernest Hemingway was well known for his struggle with his own self-management. For example he would never allow himself to go fishing unless he had finished a writing task. A drink or fishing were daily rewards for completing a specific number of written words. Believe it or not, Hemingway, like may other writers, actually counted the number of words he wrote each day.

"I love to write very much and was never happier than doing it. Charlie Scribner's ridiculing of my daily word count was because he did not understand me or writing especially well, nor could he know how happy one felt to have put down properly 422 words as you wanted them to be. And days of 1,200 or 2,700 were something that made you happier than you could believe. I found that 400 to 600 well-done was a pace I could hold much better and was always happy with that number. But if I only had 320 I felt good."

Here you see the great artist, whom we imagine acting on mysterious inspiration and inner talents, working at it with the deliberation of a ditch digger.

Action Step # 5
Take Action

Of course you have to take action! How else could you achieve anything?

Most failures are not the result of anything complicated or mysterious. Failures are most often the result of failing to do the obvious. I have known many people who set out to improve their own performance. They read the right books, prepared grand objectives, goals, targets for improvement, scores, graphs, and everything else you can think of. Somehow they never got around to doing those things they had planned and for which they had set objectives.

Without any question one of the qualities that most distinguishes successful people is their action orientation. Certainly they plan, study, set goals, and set targets. More importantly they act. That action leads to the greatest learning of all.

Think of it this way. You have two people, person "A" and person "B," both of equal intelligence, training, and opportunity. They are starting from the same base of experience and are at the same level of skill and achievement. But, person "A" is one of those people who is always active, moving, and initiating. Person "B" is more cautious and waits until it appears that everything is just right. Person "A" acts twice as often as person "B." As time goes by, who will gain more experience, gain greater skill and insight, perhaps even from his failures? Simply by acting twice as often, person "A" will advance over person "B," despite an equal starting point and equal native capability.

If you are a scientist, each experiment is a learning experience. Each action, evaluated and improved upon, leads to more successful action. Most entrepreneurs who have started their own business have experienced business failure, even bankruptcy. However they got up and did it again. The second time, maybe the third time, they did it better. Even Henry Ford succeeded only with his third start of Ford Motor Company; the first two resulted in failure. Most song writers accomplishing their first hit song have written dozens, even hundreds of songs that went unrecorded. Each new song written was an opportunity to learn, to get a little bit better. Eventually they were good enough to be recognized as a success.

Action Step # 6
Managing Consequences

You will remember the basic model of change we presented before, the A-B-C Model. The most powerful ingredient, the element that serves as the rocket fuel of self-improvement, is consequences.

If we want to manage our own performance toward our goals and vision, it is perfectly reasonable to reinforce ourselves for making progress. When behavior is habitual, the only reinforcement needed is the feeling of self-satisfaction.

Positive Self-Talk:

Many people are in the habit of punishing themselves as well as others. They punish themselves by talking negatively. They tell themselves that, "This will never work; it's just a waste of time. I will never succeed." If you keep telling yourself these things, you will make them the reality. We talk to ourselves about expectations and this self-talk becomes our self-concept and self-concept is the most critical factor in personal quality. If you do not think of yourself as worthy, your behavior is not likely to contradict that self-concept. We must create a quality self-concept through quality self-talk.

People who are high achievers may look like they have had the breaks or have been lucky. I like what Ray Kroc, founder of the McDonald's Corporation, said about luck. He said, "Luck is the dividend of sweat. The more you sweat, the luckier you get." Lucky people tend to make their own luck. Successful people seize opportunities as they appear. They seize opportunities because they have faith, belief in their ability to rise to a challenge. They are people who say to themselves, "I can...I am able..." Their response to opportunities appears to be luck.

The late Norman Vincent Peale and others have made a great deal about having a positive mental attitude. People who succeed are positive. They view their world, their associates and their experiences from the standpoint of how each event is meant to help them along their journey. There are not obstacles, only learning experiences, challenges, and opportunities to strengthen your skills and your character. They talk to themselves and say positive, reinforcing things.

Every time we take action, we mentally evaluate that action. What we say to ourselves about our experiences serves as an activator for future performance. It also serves as a reward or punishment which encourages or discourages future action.

One of the things that individuals who possess the attributes of high quality often speak of is pride. What is pride? Pride is a form of self-talk. Pride is saying to yourself, "Hey, I did a good job. I am capable. I feel good about myself. I can do better than I ever have before." We feel proud of ourselves when we recognize our own achievements. This is very important. Of course it is great to have other people recognize our achievements, to experience their praise and recognition. But high achievers do not rely on other people to notice their efforts. They praise themselves and call it pride or self-satisfaction. If you do not notice and praise yourself for your own efforts, who else is in a better position to notice?

High achievers are sensitive to their own state of motivation. If they are feeling too self-confident or perhaps too relaxed, they will set a higher goal, a new challenge. They keep themselves challenged. They also know when they need self-recognition. The human guidance system constantly needs adjustment, feedback encouraging your behavior to move left or right, higher challenge to increase the rate, and self-recognition to make it all worthwhile and keep up the good work. You must guide your own performance system.

The more you manage your self-talk, the less you are dependent upon the feedback of others. The more you can recognize and gain self-satisfaction from your efforts, the better equipped you are to suffer the slings and arrows of those around you. This is a key to self-improvement.

Creating Contingent Relationships:

Mastering your own success requires changing personal habits. All self-improvement, whether it is a matter of quitting smoking, losing weight, or improving your management skills, is a matter of changing personal habits. Habits are learned.

One way to develop new habits is to define the behavior, track the performance, and then establish a contingent relationship between the behavior and the rewards. A contingent relationship is one in which you say to yourself, "If I do X, then I can do Y." Hemingway also employed this technique of self-mastery. He did not allow himself to go fishing each afternoon

until he had written his prescribed number of pages. Fishing was contingent upon completing his work. I know another author who bought himself a car after he finished a book. I know a salesman who sets specific objectives for each morning and will not eat lunch until those objectives are met. I have a friend who runs and will not eat any desserts until he has run fifteen miles that week. These are simple things. They are games you can play with yourself. They are self-managed, contingent relationships. They are simple but effective.

The Balance of Consequences:

One concept which you may find helpful is the idea of the balance of consequences. At any one time there are a number of different consequences acting on our choices of behavior. For example you have come home from work, and it is 6:30 p.m. You are hungry. It would be rewarding to just sit down and eat. You also have ice cream in the refrigerator, and that would help make dinner even more rewarding. On the other hand you have time to exercise before dinner, and it is rewarding to feel more healthy, to feel fit and trim. Also going out and exercising is somewhat punishing because it is hot outside, and you are going to be in some pain.

Should I work late tonight?

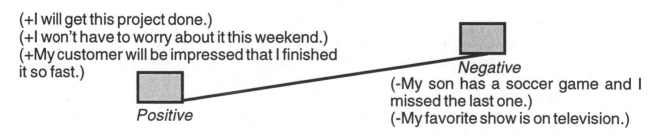

(+I will get this project done.)
(+I won't have to worry about it this weekend.)
(+My customer will be impressed that I finished it so fast.)

Positive

Negative
(-My son has a soccer game and I missed the last one.)
(-My favorite show is on television.)

Here we have a variety of consequences acting on your behavior at the same time. All choices are this way. We could choose to just sit down and eat, throwing on the ice cream afterward, or we could delay that gratification and exercise first. This is where the, "rubber meets the road" of personal development. Think of this choice as a balance with exercising on one end and not exercising on the other. There are some things pushing up and down on both sides.

There are consequences on both sides of every decision. It is only the difference in the balance that matters. If we can just tip the scales slightly, we can make the difference in our choices and habits. For example on this exercise choice you are not going to change or remove all of the consequences affecting this behavior. But just one small thing like moving the graph closer to your goal, thus getting closer to buying yourself something after you have run 100 total miles, can make the difference at the moment of choice. When the right choice is made, you can then praise yourself, feel the inner pride and satisfaction that naturally follows from the disciplined and regular effort.

Shaping Performance:

There is another concept related to habit change that is very important. It is the principle of shaping performance. Learning and growth are gradual processes. No one leaps to his goal in one bounce. Neither do we learn complex skills or new habits in one easy jump. Training others requires patience as does training yourself. I knew someone who wished to develop better communication skills. She went to a seminar that made great claims for how it would change one's life by developing new relationships. She did learn some new skills. The next week she went to two different parties. She was convinced that her new skills would immediately bring her new and more fulfilling relationships. Needless to say she was very disappointed to find that little had really changed.

This does not mean that this woman's efforts were a failure. Her expectations were simply too great. She did not understand shaping. Communications is a complex skill. When you learn new or complex skills, you break them down into their component parts, try out each part separately in small bits and pieces, and praise yourself for learning each piece of the skill. Reinforce progress. Then gradually the pieces will fit together, and the complete skill will be learned and bear fruit. Developing new personal skills is somewhat like gardening. Every good gardener has reasonable expectations as to how fast a tree or shrub will grow in a year. He plans growth over time, gradually shaping the plant in the desired direction.

Our habits are much the same. We must have patience with ourselves. Have grand visions for fulfilling your potential, but have very reasonable, even modest, short-term goals for gradual improvement. In this manner you can experience success, enjoy making progress rather than becoming frustrated and giving up.

You will remember that a basic principle of quality improvement of a product or service is that quality is a process, a journey of continuous improvement. It is not one great leap. The same principle applies to our own development. Achieving personal quality is a process of continuous, gradual improvement.

Action Step # 7
Evaluate and Iterate

People who succeed are constantly seeking to improve. Therefore they are constantly, habitually evaluating their own efforts. They are always focusing on role models and asking themselves how they could develop the quality they find attractive in that role model. They become feedback "junkies," constantly wanting feedback from others. They may not be sure what the next development priority is or how much they have succeeded in their own development, and they want to know. They will make it their own business to gather feedback and opinions that will help them evaluate their own progress.

Self-change is an iterative process. *Iterative* means that the cycle will be repeated over and over again, each turn building on the lessons from the previous. Superstars of quality are constantly evaluating so that they can move their vision forward, set higher goals, and pinpoint new skills to improve. Your program of mastering quality should have numerous stages, each one seeking new ways, new experiments, and new goals for moving toward your vision.

Appendix

Assessment Instruments

To help you evaluate progress and define improvements in your team's performance.

Self-Assessments

Teams develop their skills through gradual training, practice, feedback, more practice, and more feedback.

It is essential that teams evaluate their own process, their functioning as a team. Based on these assessments, they can discuss how to improve.

This appendix includes the following assessment devices:

1. Team Management Self-Assessment: This measures the degree to which the team members perceive that their team is fulfilling the basic functions of a team's managing a quality process.

2. Team Process Inventory: This helps team members assess their own behaviors which contribute to the success of the team.

3. Team Meeting Observation: This form is used by team coaches and may be used by the team itself to identify and provide feedback on some of the important activities in a team meeting.

4. Interaction Diagram: This simple diagram is used to illustrate the pattern of communications between team members. It is a helpful form of feedback to be used by a coach or team observer.

5. Leadership Style Assessment: This is a self-assessment for team leaders.

6. Team Progress Survey: This survey is used to help each individual team track its progress in implementing the team management process.

Note: The spirit in which self-assessments are conducted is critical. It is much like problem solving. There are no problems, only opportunities for continuous improvement. Self-assess-ments should not be conducted to find fault, criticize, or make each other feel bad about how the team is functioning. Every team can improve how it conducts its business. Just as the team will work to improve its services to its customers, it will want to improve continuously how it works together. The purpose is to find opportunities for improvement.

1. Team Management Self-Assessment

When: The self-assessment should take place once every three months during the first year or two and then once a year thereafter. For management teams the self-assessment should take place at the beginning of the quality process.

Who: The assessment should be completed by team members individually. This form applies to both work teams at the first level and management teams. We have used this assessment at the level of the president's team and at every other level.

How: A meeting should be planned for the purpose of conducting this self-assessment. It will require at least one hour. One person acts as the facilitator. Once everyone is finished, the facilitator asks each person to tell his score on the first item in a clockwise or counterclockwise rotation around the room. Then the second item, etc. One person is asked to calculate a mean score. The facilitator uses a flip chart to write down the mean score for each question.

Once all the mean scores are visible to all team members, the facilitator takes a marker and circles the five highest-scored items. He or she then asks the team members whether they agree that these are the items they do best. The facilitator may ask for examples that illustrate their good performance.

The facilitator will then circle with another colored marker the five lowest-scored items. He or she will then ask for a discussion of these items. The facilitator should ask, "What are some of the things that we could do in the future to improve .... (the specific item)?" It is important that the facilitator steer the discussion away from the problems of the past, and toward the positive actions which the team can take to improve their performance.

The facilitator will write down action items on another sheet on the flip chart. He will then ask the team to agree on an action plan.

Team Management
Self-Assessment

How is Our Team Functioning?

On each of the following items, indicate the degree to which you agree with the statement.

	Disagree		Somewhat Agree		Agree
1. My team(s) is defined. I know who my team members are and our common responsibility.	0	2.5	5	7.5	10
2. My team has defined its customers and suppliers.	0	2.5	5	7.5	10
3. My team knows the customer requirements and expectations we are trying to meet or exceed.	0	2.5	5	7.5	10
4. We receive feedback from our customers and track (measure) our performance.	0	2.5	5	7.5	10
5. We are focused on performance. When we meet, we review our performance, study graphs of our performance, and discuss how we will improve that performance.	0	2.5	5	7.5	10
6. There is a "team spirit," a spirit of mutual helpfulness and shared ownership within our team.	0	2.5	5	7.5	10
7. When we discuss problems and performance, the emphasis is on shared responsibility for improvement rather than blaming.	0	2.5	5	7.5	10
8. We have defined our shared work processes. We have reached agreement on how our work gets done, and we all have the same understanding of the process.	0	2.5	5	7.5	10
9. When we try to improve performance, we review our process and continually try to improve it.	0	2.5	5	7.5	10
10. We know the cycle times for our processes, and we are improving speed.	0	2.5	5	7.5	10

	Disagree		Somewhat Agree		Agree
11. We know the key variances from quality that occur in our process, and we are working to improve our quality.	0	2.5	5	7.5	10
12. We have agreed on which decisions are command, consultative or consensus decisions, and we are consistent in our decision-making practice.	0	2.5	5	7.5	10
13. When we meet, we make decisions that are clear and effective.	0	2.5	5	7.5	10
14. There is a regular pattern, time, and schedule to our meetings.	0	2.5	5	7.5	10
15. We use problem-solving skills such as brainstorming, defining the problem, analyzing data, etc.	0	2.5	5	7.5	10
16. When we discuss problems or performance, we develop specific action plans defining **what, when,** and by **whom** action will be taken.	0	2.5	5	7.5	10
17. The team leader and others do an effective job of listening, eliciting the participation of all.	0	2.5	5	7.5	10
18. Our meetings provide an environment free of fear of punishment in which members feel comfortable expressing their opinions in a totally frank and honest manner.	0	2.5	5	7.5	10
19. There is a healthy balance of dealing with problems and recognizing our success.	0	2.5	5	7.5	10
20. All team members are good at acknowledging contributions and expressing appreciation for success and improvement and for efforts on behalf of the team.	0	2.5	5	7.5	10

Scoring instructions: have all members of your team score this survey. As a team share your scores on each item, and compute the average for each item. Look at the five highest average scores, and discuss why you are doing well on those. Then identify the five lowest-scored items, and develop an action plan to improve on those issues. One member of the team should lead a brainstorming session to identify all of the things you could do to improve on an item. Then agree on two or three specific actions, clearly stating the "What," "Who," and by "When" for each action.

2. Team Process Inventory

The purpose of the following inventory is to help each individual assess his participation in the group process. Each of the items is a desirable actions which can help the team move toward true participation.

When: There are several ways this can be used. It can be used on some periodic basis so that team members can be reminded and prompted to evaluate their contribution or at a time when the team feels that they are not functioning as well as they might. Rather than pointing fingers at members for doing too much of something, or not enough of another, they might try having every member assess himself with this inventory.

Who: All members of a team.

How: Have each team member fill in the inventory assessing his perception of his own behavior. Then with a facilitator recording scores, have everyone raise his hand if they scored a three or less on each item. Those items which received the most scores can be prioritized for the team to work on as a group for improvement in their communication practices. An alternative is to let each member assess himself and make personal objectives to improve on two or three behaviors. Following each meeting he can score himself to see if he had improved on those items.

Team Process Inventory

Initiating	**Rarely**		**Occasionally**		**Often**
I suggest new procedures or ideas for solving problems or completing tasks.	1	2	3	4	5
I help define team problems.	1	2	3	4	5
I attempt to redirect the team when we get side-tracked.	1	2	3	4	5

Seeking Information

I ask others to share relevant facts or opinions.	1	2	3	4	5
I ask for the implication of input made by others.	1	2	3	4	5
I ask for the rationale behind the opinion stated by others.	1	2	3	4	5

Giving Information

I share my opinion and the reasons for it.	1	2	3	4	5
I provide relevant information.	1	2	3	4	5
I share concerns I have regarding process/content affecting my commitment.	1	2	3	4	5

Clarifying and Elaborating

I ask for clarification of ideas to ensure I've heard them accurately.	1	2	3	4	5
I help others communicate their ideas effectively.	1	2	3	4	5
I relate my comments to those of others.	1	2	3	4	5

Summarizing

I summarize ideas and the progress of the team.	1	2	3	4	5
I point out similarities of ideas expressed by others.	1	2	3	4	5
I offer conclusions for group consideration.	1	2	3	4	5

Testing for Consensus	*Rarely*	*Occasionally*			*Often*
I check for consensus on decisions.	1	2	3	4	5
I offer trial solutions as the team approaches a decision.	1	2	3	4	5
I ensure everyone is heard when the outcome affects the whole team.	1	2	3	4	5

Harmonizing

I encourage others to discuss their concerns.	1	2	3	4	5
I empathize with others when they become upset.	1	2	3	4	5
I reduce tension by using humor.	1	2	3	4	5

Gatekeeping

I comment on mood changes in the team and help refocus on the task at hand.	1	2	3	4	5
I ask silent members to share their opinion.	1	2	3	4	5
I ask dominant members to allow others to express their views.	1	2	3	4	5

Encouraging

I praise others for their contributions.	1	2	3	4	5
I listen to others when they speak.	1	2	3	4	5
I acknowledge others' remarks verbally and non-verbally.	1	2	3	4	5

Compromising

I encourage others to explore their differences and identify areas of agreement.	1	2	3	4	5
I am open to feedback from others whose opinions differ from mine.	1	2	3	4	5
I recommend compromises where differences of opinion exist.	1	2	3	4	5

3. Team Meeting Observation

This is a coaching tool. It is often helpful to have someone outside of the team, a trainer or coach, a manager, or even a member of another team sit in your team meetings and observe the team process. This form identifies the activities that can be observed which are characteristic of a well-functioning team and team leader. It is unrealistic to expect that any team will be observed doing all of these things in any one meeting. However if some of these activities do not go on regularly, the team may wish to discuss how they could improve in this area.

When: During the early period of development the team might be observed each week (assuming weekly meetings). The frequency would reduce as the team became more proficient at the process and better able to assess themselves. Once a month would be appropriate after six months of experience. After a year perhaps quarterly would be appropriate.

Who: Observation and completion by someone outside of the team - a coach, manager, or member of another team - are necessary. Eventually, the team can fill it out on themselves.

How: The team should discuss the observation and be aware of it beforehand. They should agree to conduct their meeting as they do routinely. They are being evaluated only for their own feedback. The observer should sit in the meeting with the form in front of her and make notes on how each item was performed.

Following the meeting, the coach should ask the team how they felt the meeting went. Then the coach should share with the team the three to five things that they did exceptionally well and the three to five things the team might do better in the future. This feedback should concern those items that apply to the entire team such as following the problem-solving model, or identifying and tracking quality and business measures. Items concerning the team leader or facilitator should be discussed with the person alone, separate from the team meeting. Again the positive as well as the areas for improvement should be discussed.

Team Meeting Observation

Team: _____   Team Leader: _____

Date/Time: _____   Coach: _____

Procedures	Observations
1. Agenda distributed.	
2. Agenda followed.	
3. Meeting date and time are regular.	
4. Meeting location appropriate.	
5. Starts/ends on time.	
6. Meeting interruptions.	
7. Code of conduct posted.	
8. Code of conduct used.	
9. Flip chart used.	
10. Previous action plans reviewed.	
Performance Review	
11. Customers defined.	
12. Customer requirements defined.	
13. Work process defined.	
14. Work process improved.	
15. Quality measures tracked & reviewed.	
Conformance to customer requirements.	
Conformance to specifications.	
Innovations or improvement rate.	
Cycle time.	

	Observations
16. Business measures.	
Profitability.	
Costs of operations.	
Quantity or rate of production.	
17. Measures updated/current.	
18. Causes of variability identified.	
19. Variability under control.	
20. Improvement goals established	
21. Data visually displayed.	
22. Recognition for improvement.	

Problem Solving

23. Problem defined.	
24. Causes brainstormed.	
25. Data gathered and analyzed.	
26. Solutions brainstormed.	
27. Consensus developed.	
28. Action plan developed.	
29. What, who, when identified.	
30. Prior action plans reviewed.	

Facilitation Skills

31. Reinforces contributions of others.	
32. Asks open-ended questions.	
33. Encourages participation.	

	Observations
34. Rephrases when appropriate.	
35. Keeps meeting on topic.	
36. Summarizes discussion.	
37. Summarizes decisions.	
38. Summarizes action items.	
39. Remains objective.	
40. Expresses empathy.	
41. Focuses on problem, not person.	
42. Creates an environment of sharing.	

4. Interaction Diagrams

The purpose of the interaction diagram is to define the pattern of communication among the team members. It is not unusual to find that two or three individuals dominate the communication patterns, sending and receiving messages to each other while other members are not involved in the interaction. This knowledge can help members improve their communication patterns.

When: There should be interaction diagrams after the first four or five meetings and once every two or three months during the first year, then twice a year thereafter.

Who: The diagram can be completed by a coach or by a designated team member.

How: The drawing below represents a table with the team members seated around it. The names of the team members are written as they are seated. The lines represent communications from <u>s</u>ender to a <u>r</u>eceiver. If there is more than one communication from that sender to receiver, the line is crossed for each additional communication. If the sender addresses the entire group, the line goes to the center of the table. You can use one diagram for an entire meeting, or you can use more than one for different segments of a meeting.

You can see in the example below that there are some dominant communication patterns. There are others who are not participating.

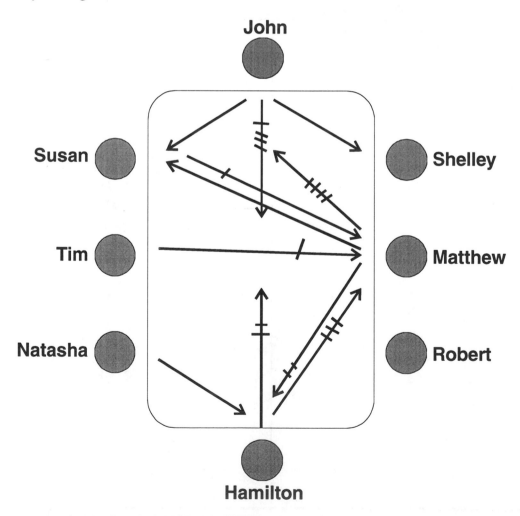

Interaction Diagrams

5. Leadership Style Assessment

This is a self-assessment for team leaders. As the organization embarks on team management, each team leader will be facing the challenge of his or her own personal behavior.

When: This assessment could be useful in the beginning of the process implementation (when scores understandably would be low) to establish a baseline. Then repeat the assessment every six months to track progress and focus on key areas to improve.

Who: This can be completed by the team leader, the team members, or both.

How: The team leader may want to self-evaluate and then have team members separately assess the behavior. Another alternative is to discuss each item together. Your team coach would also be an excellent source of candid feedback on team leader skills.

Leadership Styles Assessment

	Usually	Sometimes	Rarely	Never

1. Developing and Communicating a Vision

	Usually	Sometimes	Rarely	Never
A. You have developed a vision with your team that describes your business plans.	1	2	3	4
B. You have developed an internal vision with your team that describes what type of culture or mini-society you want to create to meet that future business vision.	1	2	3	4
C. There is a written statement of both the external and internal vision that has been shared with all of the employees.	1	2	3	4
D. You speak frequently about these visions and make business decisions consistent with these desired changes.	1	2	3	4
E. Your behavior is consistent with your vision and with how you expect others in the organization to behave.	1	2	3	4

2. Decision-Making Styles

	Usually	Sometimes	Rarely	Never
A. You make it clear to your team what decision style (command, consensus, consultative, or delegation) you are using and what level of involvement you are expecting from them.	1	2	3	4
B. At least eighty percent of your decisions are made in a style other than command (consensus, consultative, or delegation).	1	2	3	4
C. You make one decision per week in a participative manner.	1	2	3	4
D. You can point to at least three major areas of decision-making in which participation has increased. (Example would be establishing budgets, manpower allocation, hiring decisions, work assignments.)	1	2	3	4
E. The frequency of your subordinates coming to you for decisions has decreased, but performance has maintained or improved.	1	2	3	4

	Usually	Sometimes	Rarely	Never
3. Meeting Behavior				
A. You solicit participation in the setting of agendas and in determining the time and place of meetings.	1	2	3	4
B. You listen at least as much as you talk in team meetings.	1	2	3	4
C. You solicit others' opinions before offering your own.	1	2	3	4
D. You use some or all of the steps of the problem-solving model when your group encounters a performance problem.	1	2	3	4
4. Facilitation Skills				
A. You exhibit good reflective listening skills in your meetings to draw out quiet people and control disruptive members.	1	2	3	4
B. You facilitate your team through a consensus decision-making process, leaving everyone with the sense of being committed.	1	2	3	4
C. You effectively use brainstorming techniques when the group is trying to produce creative ideas.	1	2	3	4
D. When conflict surfaces, you are able to use rephrasing and questioning to help produce a satisfactory solution.	1	2	3	4
5. Performance Manager				
A. You influence performance through feedback and positive reinforcement rather than through directives and negative control.	1	2	3	4
B. When you spot poor performance, you give pinpointed feedback in a timely manner so that the individual or team can correct the problem.	1	2	3	4
C. You shape behavior change by giving recognition for steps moving toward the desired goal rather than by waiting for goal attainment to reinforce performance.	1	2	3	4

	Usually	Sometimes	Rarely	Never
D. You reward independence, creativity, and risk-taking as well as good performance from your team.	1	2	3	4
E. You encourage problem-solving and corrective action in team meetings.	1	2	3	4

6. Coach/Mentor

	Usually	Sometimes	Rarely	Never
A. You help others to balance the relative importance and priority of information and work that you pass on to them.	1	2	3	4
B. You help others analyze data and information that are new to them in order to make quality decisions.	1	2	3	4
C. You help your team diagnose and analyze problems versus finding solutions for them.	1	2	3	4
D. You communicate a sense of purpose to your team so that they understand how their work fits into the larger vision.	1	2	3	4

6. Team Progress Survey

This survey is used to help each individual team track its progress in implementing the team management process. It takes the five critical components of team management and breaks them down into individual behaviors or activities to be accomplished.

When: This tool can be used regularly (probably monthly) throughout the first year of implementation.

Who: The team leader, team members, or team coach can use this instrument to track individual milestones.

How: Each month (or bimonthly) observe a team meeting to determine progress of each activity. Set realistic targets for accomplishing the milestones, but don't be driven by the activity; *be driven by the needs of the business.*

(*Note: Our appreciation goes out to Shell E&P team consultants who developed this form and allowed us to adapt it for our manual.)

Team Progress Survey

	Excellent	Competent	Used	Aware
I. Team Tools and Principles				
II. Customer Focus				
III. Process Management				
IV. Scorekeeping				
V. Performance Improvement Results				

Team Progress Survey
Criteria

AWARE = Team understands the tool or concept and knows how to implement.

USED = Team has used this tool or concept at least once.

COMPETENT = Team has repeated experience with this tool or concept and sees value in it.

EXCELLENT = Team is self-directed with this tool or concept.

Team Progress Survey

Team Name _____

Team Tools & Principles

This team utilizes a charter/mission statement to guide its actions. The team has regular meetings and utilizes meeting tools such as ground rules, agendas, action records, etc.

	Charter/mission definition.	Roles and responsibilities definition.	Agenda management.	Ground rules.	Action record.	Problem solving methodology.	Recognition is used.	Idea generation.
Excellent								
Competent								
Used								
Aware								

Team Progress Survey

Team Name _____

	Excellent						
	Competent						
	Used						
	Aware						

Customer Focus

This team has identified its products, services, customers, and suppliers. They have planned and conducted customer interviews, analyzed customer/supplier feedback, and established a continuous feedback system.

Identify team's customers.

Identify products and services.

Identify customer contacts.

Obtain and analyze customer feedback.

Integrate customer requirements into performance measures.

Establish customer-supplier loops.

Use customer feedback in work process improvement efforts.

Team Progress Survey

Team Name _____

Process Management

This team has identified their key processes, analyzed them, mapped them, improved them, and implemented improvement plans.

	Aware	Used	Competent	Excellent
Identifying work processes.				
Work process mapping.				
Analyze variances.				
Develop and implement process improvements.				

Team Progress Survey

Team Name _____

Scorekeeping

This team has identified its key business and customer measures, has graphed and tracked those measures, and has taken improvement steps based on those measures.

	Excellent	Competent	Used	Aware
Goals with measures in place.				
Balanced scorecard in place.				
Scorecard reviewed, analyzed regularly.				
Scorecard used to guide work process management/improvement.				
Scorecard changed as appropriate.				
Scorecard variance vs. variability.				

Team Progress Survey

Team Name _____

	Excellent				
	Competent				
	Used				
	Aware				

Performance Improvement Results

This team has identified and solved problems, implemented improvement actions, incorporated and shared team successes, and realized measurable improvement in their scorecard.

Eliminate waste (time, effort, space, money,....).

Clearly exhibits business improvements.

Plans in place to sustain achieved improvements - plan-do-check-act.

Continuous Improvement is ongoing, routine part of overall work.

Scorekeeping/measurement/benchmarking is active and ongoing.

Assistance

Our Mission

The mission of Miller Howard Consulting Group is to enhance the quality of work and worklife for our clients and our society; to contribute to the material, intellectual and spiritual wealth of our clients; to advance the skills and knowledge of our field; and to contribute to the total well-being of our associates. We are dedicated to the principles of democracy, free expression, and enhancement of self-esteem of all through self-management and teamwork.

Consulting

For over two decades, Miller/Howard Consulting Group has been a leader in organizational change. Our extensive experience has taught us that training works well to initiate change, but lasting improvement requires comprehensive follow-up. The experienced professionals at Miller/Howard Consulting Group are available to assist you toward your pursuit of becoming a high performance organization.

We work at every level of the organization, from the chief executive to the entry level, and have implemented our methodologies in a variety of industries, ranging from Fortune 1000 companies to small businesses.

Our clients have included the following companies:

Air Canada
Alabama Power Company
Alcan Cable
Allina Health Systems
Amoco Production Company
Augusta Newsprint Company
Avery Dennison
Bell Canada
The Bradford Exchange
Chick-fil-A
Clark-Schwebel
Collins & Aikman Products Company
Corning
Dad's Products Company
Delmarva Power & Light Company
Dial Corporation
Dun's Marketing Services
Eastman Kodak
Engelhard Corporation
Exxon U.S.A.
Georgetown Steel Corporation
Harris Corporation
Landmark Communications
McDonald's Corporation
Merck
Metropolitan Life Insurance Company
Moody's Investor Services

Murray Ohio Manufacturing
NationsBank
Northern States Power
Olin Ordnance
Petroleum Development Oman
Pharmacia & Upjohn
Plymouth Tube Company
Printpack
QuikTrip
Sara Lee Corporation
Scott Paper Company
Shell Canada
Shell Chemical Company
Shell Oil Company
Southwestern Bell
Springs Industries
Star Paper Tube
Star Tribune
SunTrust Banks
Tennessee Eastman Company
Texaco Refining & Marketing
Texaco U.S.A.
United Technologies
Varig Airlines
Wellman
Xerox Corporation

Internal Consultant Development

An essential part of any change management program is the selection and development of internal resources. Miller/Howard Consulting Group has long been a leader in developing internal consultants who assist in organizational change. From the selection and basic skills training of internal consultants to advanced skills development and certification, we have created a systemic process that ensures your internal consultants are prepared to support your organization during its change efforts. There are two "tracks" available in our Internal Consultant Development process, the Organizational Design Consultant Track and the Team Consultant Track. Both begin with an introduction to change management, *Consultant Training School: Introduction to Change Management.* Following is a description of these tracks and the accompanying workbooks. Workbooks can also be purchased separately.

All seminars are offered as public courses as well as customized, on-site programs. Some programs and products are available in Spanish and French.

For additional information call (404) 255-6523
http://www.millerhoward.com

Team Consultant Track

Seminars:
Consultant Training School
Introduction to Change Management
This seminar teaches the fundamentals of good consulting, including how to: help your client articulate a positive vision of your organization's future; develop an implementation plan to accomplish this vision; manage the dynamics of individual and organizational change; and determine organizational readiness. You will also learn the interpersonal skills critical to becoming an effective consultant, including active listening, assertiveness, persuasion, negotiating, and behavioral contracting. Different models for organizational interventions will be discussed, including strategy planning, whole system architecture, and team-based organizations.

Creating a Team-based Organization
This seminar introduces participants to the essential skills needed for establishing a dynamic organization. As a participant, you will learn how to develop an organizational culture based on the principles and characteristics of a high performance organization; implement natural work teams for continuous improvements in quality, productivity, cycle times, and costs; design an implementation plan for organization change; plan and manage team meetings and group interaction to have a significant impact on business results; and establish measurement criteria and feedback systems for continuous improvement.

Team Consultant Training School
During this course participants will focus on two avenues of interventions: coaching team meetings and teaching team effectiveness skills. Participants will learn how to develop an implementation plan for creating a team-based organization, including how to identify and successfully complete critical milestones and measures. Participants will also receive instruction in how to

---

train the Team Management modules and use the Trainer's Toolkit. Through role plays, class presentations, and group feedback participants will sharpen the skills essential to effective team consulting.

Advanced Team Consultant Training School

This course is structured for internal consultants who have experience implementing a team-based organization. We will delve into the specific challenges of implementing teams throughout your organization and cover topics such as team assessments, project management, new roles for managers and leaders, aligning teams with business strategy, and group dynamics and group process.

Customized Advanced Team Training

Most of the topics featured in The Advanced Team Guide can be delivered as customized training programs for your organization.

Workbooks:
The Internal Consultant's Guide
Tools and Techniques to Create and Sustain a High Performance Organization

This 185+ page workbook provides coaches, facilitators, and internal consultants with essential coaching skills to guide them through managing change and implementation. Topics covered include how to manage change and an organizational change model; creating, monitoring, and managing the implementation process; the role of the internal consultant; interpersonal skills critical to effective internal consultants; and internal consultant tips.

Team Management
Creating Systems and Skills for a Team-based Organization

The 330+ page Team Management workbook provides both team leaders and members with the necessary skills to create and sustain a high-performance organization. Topics include establishing teams, the changing role of leadership, the organizational systems required to support teams, defining customer requirements, developing scorecards, having effective meetings, decision-making, assessments, and problem-solving.

Team Management
A Guide for Trainers

The easy-to-follow 130+ page Team Management trainer's guide provides the team trainer with invaluable training tips for each step in the Team Management process. Playful illustrations highlight key training topics, while exercises, action items, troubleshooting, and helpful hints offer you practical advice and guidance on creating, implementing, and maintaining teams as a part of your day-to-day business operations.

Team Management
Team Trainer's Toolkit

The Team Management Team Trainer's Toolkit accompanies Miller/Howard Consulting Group's *Team Management* workbook and seminar series. The toolkit consists of nearly 100 full-color overheads and *Team Management: A Guide for Trainers*. Each overhead illustrates a key learning point in the Team Management workbook, covering all of the skills needed by teams to define their customers and requirements, create a scorecard, participate in problem solving, and continuously improve their processes.

The Advanced Team Guide
Tools, Techniques, and Tips for Experienced Teams
Finally, a guidebook that addresses key issues teams face as they mature. The 400+ page book provides useful, practical suggestions for team leaders, members, and coaches as they internalize the principles of a team-based organization. With over a hundred years of combined experience, the authors share their knowledge, expertise, and experience about how to make teams successful in your organization. Chapters in the book include exercises, case studies, and examples about issues every team faces in its development, such as technology and teams; alternate compensation and teams; aligning teams with business strategy; team structure; team and individual feedback; new roles for managers and leaders; advanced performance analysis; advanced problem solving and decision-making; managing diversity and differences; group process and group dynamics; and frequently occurring problems and how to solve them.

Organizational Design Consultant Track

Seminars:
Consultant Training School
Introduction to Change Management
This seminar teaches the fundamentals of good consulting, including how to: help your client articulate a positive vision of your organization's future; develop an implementation plan to accomplish this vision; manage the dynamics of individual and organizational change; and determine organizational readiness. You will also learn the interpersonal skills critical to becoming an effective consultant, including active listening, assertiveness, persuasion, negotiating, and behavioral contracting. Different models for organizational interventions will be discussed, including strategy planning, whole system architecture, and team-based organizations.

Leading Change Management
This one-day overview will provide you with an understanding of whole system methodology to create the future capabilities, organization, systems, and processes that will lead to your competitive success. Also available as a customized, on-site program is a three-day seminar that will facilitate a greater understanding of how to design and implement change in your organization.

Organization Design School
A Whole System Approach
This four-day seminar offers an in-depth look at how to effectively create and implement organizational change from a whole systems viewpoint. As organizations move through various stages of improvement, internal consultants need increased knowledge and understanding of whole systems design to create a well-aligned organization. This course is designed to provide training, skills, practice, and a strong foundation for those who need advanced knowledge and skills regarding the whole systems method, redesign, reengineering, and large-scale change. This is a great opportunity to learn from others who are creating dynamic organizations.

Workbooks:
Change Management
Creating the Dynamic Organization Through Whole System Architecture

Whole system design and implementation is clearly explained in the 400+ page Change Management workbook. The change management process described in the book is based on the authors' years of experience and knowledge on how best to transform an organization and its culture to a high performance system. Specific chapter topics that will guide you through this transformation include an overview of the organization as a dynamic system, principles of Whole System Architecture, how to prepare for change, the roles and responsibilities of leading a change effort, understanding and creating the business system strategy and scorecard, writing the design charter, designing the work and human systems, aligning and implementing the new architecture, and how to use conference methodology for high involvement design. Insightful case studies are located throughout the book along with exercises, action steps, and assessment tools.

The Leader's Guide to Change Management
Creating and Sustaining the Dynamic Organization

There are two sections to this leader's guide. The first section provides a capsulated overview of the whole system change methodology, including a brief history of change, principles of Whole System Architecture, defining the business system and scorecard, and designing the work and human systems.

The second section focuses on the leadership of change management. Chapters include the competencies of change leaders, how to lead strategic change, different leadership styles and their responses to challenges, team management, and corporate center strategy.

Certification

One of the most critical components to sustained behavior change is continuous feedback. While our internal consultant seminars spend a large portion of time role playing, it is difficult to achieve real behavior change over a period of a few days. To that end, we provide an on-site coaching and certification process for internal consultants to help them lead your organization through a variety of change efforts.

Books

AMERICAN SPIRIT: Visions of a New Corporate Culture
By Lawrence M. Miller

This remarkable book plots a course for the future of American management as Mr. Miller redefines corporate culture and the relationship between managers and workers. He explains by means of eight revolutionary principles the most important elements of competitive advantage. This book provides a specific plan of action for every executive and for every company on the way to the top. Available in hardback and paperback.

BARBARIANS TO BUREAUCRATS: Corporate Life Cycle Strategies
By Lawrence M. Miller

This book presents a brilliant new solution to an old business problem: how to halt a company's descent into stifling bureaucracy. Mr. Miller argues that corporations, like civilizations, have a natural life cycle and that by identifying the stage your company is in, and the leaders associated with it, you can avert decline and continue to thrive. Available in hardback or paperback.

BEYOND CORPORATE TRANSFORMATION: A Whole Systems Approach to Creating and Sustaining High Performance
By Christopher W. Head

Unlike most books written by a consultant that express only one perspective, Beyond Corporate Transformation incorporates the views, insights, and change methodologies from several of the finest management consulting firms and a number of leading-edge companies. The author's research for Beyond Corporate Transformation indicated that the companies most successful in their change efforts take a holistic approach to change as opposed to jumping from one change program to another. The book provides a methodology for educating, preparing, and leading employees through the many stages necessary to transform the organization into one that is capable of creating and sustaining a lasting competitive advantage.

Index

Index

This is not intended to be a detailed and complete index but a source to help you locate the most commonly used concepts in the Team Management workbook. Please feel free to make additions to this index.

F

G

H

I

L

M

N

O

P

Q

R

S

T

V

W